Introduction to Comparative Politics

Second Edition

EW HORIZONS IN
/IPARATIVE POLITICS

Introduction to Comparative Politics

Concepts and Processes

Second Edition

Howard J. Wiarda
The Leonard J. Horwitz Professor of Comparative Politics
University of Massachusetts–Amherst
and
Senior Associate
Center for Strategic and International Studies (CSIS)
Washington, D.C.

Harcourt College Publishers
Fort Worth Philadelphia San Diego Orlando San Antonio
Toronto Montreal London Sydney Tokyo

Publisher Earl McPeek
Executive Editor David Tatom
Market Strategist Steve Drummond
Developmental Editor Stacey Sims
Project Editor Katherine Dennis
Art Director Chris Morrow
Production Manager Diane Gray

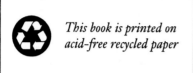

*This book is printed on
acid-free recycled paper*

ISBN: 0-15-507869-0

Library of Congress Catalog Card Number: 99-63621

Address for Domestic Orders
Harcourt Brace College Publishers
6277 Sea Harbor Drive
Orlando, FL 32887-6777
800-782-4479

Address for International Orders
International Customer Service
Harcourt Brace & Company
6277 Sea Harbor Drive
Orlando, FL 32887-6777
407-345-3800
(fax) 407-345-4060
(e-mail) hbintl@harcourtbrace.com

Address for Editorial Correspondence
Harcourt Brace College Publishers
301 Commerce Street, Suite 3700
Fort Worth, TX 76102

Web Site Address
http://www.harcourtcollege.com

Printed in the United States of America

9 0 1 2 3 4 5 6 7 8 066 9 8 7 6 5 4 3 2 1

Harcourt Brace College Publishers

New Horizons in Comparative Politics Series

Boilard

Russia at the Twenty-First Century

Grayson

Mexico: From Corporatism to Pluralism?

McCormick

Comparative Politics in Transition
Second Edition

Moody

Tradition and Modernization in China and Japan

Rasmussen

The British Political Process

Tiersky

France in the New Europe:
Changing Yet Steadfast

Wiarda

Introduction to Comparative Politics
Second Edition

Wiarda

Latin American Politics

Wiarda

Non-Western Theories of Development:
Regional Norms versus Global Trends

Preface

The field of comparative politics, one of the main fields in political science, has gone through some ups, downs—and then ups again—in recent decades. During the 1960s and the early 1970s, comparative politics was the most exciting and innovative field in the political science discipline; but in the later 1970s, much like the rest of the country, comparative politics entered the doldrums. It was afflicted with a variety of discontents—"malaise," to use President Jimmy Carter's term for those times—just as were many of our social, political, and economic institutions.

But since then the field has recovered. Comparative politics has again taken its place as one of the most interesting and exciting fields in political science. There are new and exciting research terrains in Africa, Asia, Europe, Latin America, the Middle East, and the territories of the former Soviet Union; innovative approaches and methodologies such as dependency theory, corporatism, and rational choice theory; and fascinating new themes and subject areas such as globalization, transition to democracy, and economic and political integration. The field no longer has one dominant methodology and approach as it had in the 1960s, but rather a variety of approaches and modes of analysis that need to be woven together.

Most of us who work in comparative politics find these new developments in the field healthy, intoxicating, and useful, even while the greater diversity, pluralism, and global scope of the field make our research, teaching, and writing more complicated. This book was designed to make that job easier. An integrated volume, it introduces students to the field, tracing the history and development of comparative politics, assessing the newer approaches to the field in sequential and systematic fashion, while taking account of such recent events as the unraveling of various Marxist-Leninist regimes, the transition to democracy in many developing nations, and the political impact of economic integration and globalization. These trends cry out for an updated, readable, and challenging volume that analyzes the past and present of comparative politics, while also surveying the field as a coherent whole. That's exactly what this book does.

The second edition has been revised to reflect recent changes and to make the book even more stimulating and attractive. It now includes two new chapters. Chapter 4, "Political Culture and Comparative Politics," introduces the history, arguments, and perspectives of this sometimes controversial topic now enjoying a renaissance in response to the recent emphasis on multiculturalism as well as to developments in the former Soviet Union and other regions around the world. Chapter 10, "Frontiers of Research in Comparative Politics," is an innovative new chapter designed to stimulate student interest in the field. It examines a number of exciting new areas of comparative research, including women in politics, comparative environmental or "green" politics, issues of decentralization and comparative regionalism, the comparative treatment of gays, and the relations overall of larger global issues to domestic politics—for example, drugs, pollution, the environment, and immigration. Other new coverage includes the introduction of rational choice theory in Chapter 5 and a discussion of China's future in Chapter 8. As a matter of course, every chapter in the book has been updated and rewritten to reflect the most recent developments in world politics.

My experience as a teacher has been that, while students are often very interested in the diverse countries, regions, and global issues that comparative politics studies, they often lack the means to get a good grip on the subject, to decide where to begin, or how to develop a good idea for a term paper or thesis and carry it through. This book tries to provide clear and levelheaded answers to the questions students raise. They frequently need some guidance on how to proceed, how to think comparatively, how to bring the main concepts and approaches in the field to bear on their reading and research on individual countries, the hot topics, or their particular region of specialization (Africa, Asia, Europe, Latin America, the Middle East).

Those are some of the insights this book provides. It is specifically designed for an introductory course in comparative politics, to be used before or in conjunction with a student's plunge into country-by-country, regional, or cross-country analysis. However, it is also intended for upper-division courses that focus on the regions listed above, but that need a good, solid introduction to the field before delving into regional specialization. Graduate students taking their first seminars in comparative politics or studying for comprehensive exams will find the book's integrating concepts useful as well.

This book hopes to get students at all levels interested in comparative politics. It is not a dry, technical, or methodological treatise—the main methodological disputes in the field are presented in a provocative way. Nor is it arcane and highly philosophical—although all the main theories in comparative politics are set forth. Instead, the book explores in a clear and challenging way what comparative politics is all about. It is practical, down-to-earth, and focused on the nuts and bolts of how to study and do comparative politics. It aims at explaining comparative politics, its global as well as country, or region-specific topics of inquiry, and why the field is so stimulating and interesting. It addresses all the important topics in the field, contains numerous useful suggestions for research studies, and assesses where the field has been, where it is now, and where it is going. These issues are discussed in a straightforward narrative style that avoids jargon, tells the story of comparative politics, raises numerous important questions to contemplate about our changing world, and examines not just how but what to compare and why.

Some of the more interesting developments of recent years include the collapse of the Soviet Union and the transition of formerly Marxist-Leninist states toward democracy and free markets, the transitions to democracy in many previously authoritarian regimes of the developing world, the crisis of the welfare state in the advanced industrial societies and the new pressures to streamline and privatize, and recent trends toward both economic integration and globalization. All of these are world-shaking, even epochal events, and all of them have major implications for comparative politics. Indeed, comparative politics can help us better understand these changes, see the patterns emerging, and thus contribute strongly to a better understanding of worldwide changes.

This volume stands on its own as an introductory text in a variety of comparative politics courses, but it also serves as the first and flagship volume in a new series in comparative politics published by Harcourt Brace, and for which the author of this book also serves as General Series Editor. Our plan from the beginning was to publish a variety of comparative politics books but also to maintain an integrated series. We have published or are in the process of publishing single-country studies, comparative studies, regional and area studies, thematic studies, and broad overviews—books on Africa, Asia, Latin America, Western Europe, Great Britain, France, Russia, the developing nations, global politics, and such important themes as comparative democratization and comparative environmental policy (for the details, see the Series list). These books are lively, interesting, and highly readable; all are designed for classroom use, but the books are all so challenging and innovative that scholars at all levels will find them useful.

In the preparation and development of the first and, now, second edition of this book, numerous editors, fellow scholars of comparative politics, and institutions played a major role. Cindy Stormer and David Tatom have been particularly innovative and supportive as editors; it has been a pleasure to work with them over the years. Colleagues and fellow scholars, Iêda Siqueira Wiarda, Robert H. Cox, Rodolfo de la Garza, Michael Kryzanek, Stephen Pelletier, and Larman C. Wilson have offered extremely useful comments on earlier versions of the book. My able research assistant Emily Hardt, holder of the Leonard J. Horowitz assistantship in Iberian and Latin American politics, read the entire first edition twice and gave me the benefit of her critique from a graduate student point of view. Doris Holden assisted in numerous ways with the preparation of the manuscript. My students in Amherst, Cambridge, and Washington, D.C., raised many interesting questions about the text and challenged their professor in numerous ways. Finally, I wish to thank the institutions I called "home" during the writing of this book: the University of Massachusetts–Amherst, the Center for Strategic and International Studies (CSIS) in Washington, D.C., and the National War College also in Washington. None of these individuals or organizations is responsible for this book, however; that responsibility rests solely with the author.

Howard J. Wiarda
Washington, D.C.

About the Author

Howard J. Wiarda is Professor of Political Science and the Leonard J. Horwitz Professor of Iberian and Latin American Politics at the University of Massachusetts–Amherst, and a Senior Associate at the Center for Strategic and International Studies (CSIS) in Washington, D.C. A longtime associate of the Center for International Affairs at Harvard University, Professor Wiarda was also editor of the political science journal *Polity* and director of Latin American studies programs in Amherst and Washington. Professor Wiarda has been a visiting professor at MIT and George Washington University; has directed foreign affairs programs in several Washington think tanks; and has lectured extensively at universities in Europe, Asia, the United States, Russia, Japan, Israel, and Latin America. He was lead consultant to the National Bipartisan (Kissinger) Commission on Central America, served by nomination of the president of the United States on several White House task forces and advisory panels, and has been a consultant to various foreign policy–making agencies of the U.S. government. Professor Wiarda is best known for his writings and edited volumes on Latin America, Europe, and comparative and foreign policy studies, including *New Directions in Comparative Politics, American Foreign Policy, U.S. Foreign and Strategic Policy in the Post–Cold War Era, Corporatism and Comparative Politics, Politics in Iberia: The Political Systems of Spain and Portugal, Latin American Politics and Development,* and *Foreign Policy without Illusion: How Foreign Policy Works and Doesn't Work in the United States.*

Contents

Preface   vii

About the Author   xi

CHAPTER 1
....

What Is Comparative Politics   1

Comparative Politics Defined   7

Why Study Comparative Politics?   11

The Comparative Method   12

Models and Paradigms in Comparative Politics   15

Approaching the Subject   17

Aspects of Change   21

The Plan of the Book   23

CHAPTER 2
....

The History of Comparative Politics   25

The Ancients   25

The Old Testament and the "People of God"   26

The Spartans: Lycurgus   26

The Greeks: Plato and Aristotle   27

The Romans: Cicero   29

The Middle Ages: Christianity   30

The Moderns   30

Comparative Politics in American Universities   36

CHAPTER 3
• • • • • • • •

Political Development   42

Origins of the Developmentalist Approach   43

The Early Development Literature   47

The Economists   47

The Sociologists   48

The Political Scientists   50

The Proliferation of Development Studies   52

Criticisms of the Developmentalist Approach   56

A Reassessment of the Developmentalist Approach   60

CHAPTER 4
• • • • • • • •

Political Culture and Comparative Politics   62

History of Political Culture Approaches   63

The Civic Culture   66

Criticisms of the Political Culture Approach   70

The Renaissance of Political Culture   73

A Summing Up   78

CHAPTER 5
• • • • • • • •

Challenges and Alternatives to Development   79

**Bureaucratic Authoritarianism, Dependency Theory and
World Systems, Corporatism, Political Economy, State–Society
Relations, Indigenous Theories of Change, Rational Choice Theory,
and the New Institutionalism**

Dependency Theory and the World Systems Approach   80

Corporatism   84

Bureaucratic-Authoritarianism   87

Political Economy   89

State–Society Relations   91

Indigenous Theories of Change   93

Rational Choice Theory   95

The New Institutionalism   97

Implications for the Future   98

CHAPTER 6
·········

Democracy and Democratization: Transitions from Authoritarianism   100

The Rise and Fall of Authoritarianism   102

Returns to Democracy   104

Causes of the Democratic Shift   107

Domestic Forces   108

International Forces   109

Issues of Democratic Transition 110

Strengths and Weaknesses of Democracy 112

A Global Overview   112

Strengths   113

Weaknesses   115

Prospects and Implications 117

CHAPTER 7
·········

The Future of Communist Regimes   120

Authoritarianism, Totalitarianism, and Marxism:
  How Our Intellectual Models Led Us Astray   121

Change, Vulnerability, and the Collapse of the
  Communist Systems 124

Crisis of Ideology   124

Social Change   125

Economic Crisis   126

Crisis of Culture   126

Political Institutions   127

International Pressures   127

Patterns of Postcommunist Change   128
Policy Reforms   132
Social Policy   132
Economic Policy   134
Political Change   137
Toward the Future   138

CHAPTER 8
· · · · · · · · ·

The Developing Nations: What Works in Development—and What Doesn't   141

The Theory of Development   142
The Practice of Development   145
Case and Patterns of Development   148
East Asia: The NICs   148
Oil-Exporting States   150
Latin America   151
India   154
China   155
The Middle East   156
Depressed Areas   157
Eastern Europe   158
New Trading Blocs   159
What Works in Development   160
Implications for U.S. Policy   162
The Transformation of the World   164

CHAPTER 9
· · · · · · · · ·

The Future of the Developed Nations   167

Patterns of Success   168
New Trends   170
The End of Ideology   171
The Decline of Political Parties   172

The Decline of Farm and Union Groups; the Dominance of Business   173
Postmodernity   176
Postmodern Issues   176
Corporatism and Corporatist Structures   177
Bureaucratization/State Downsizing   180
Changing Public Policy   183
Ungovernability?   186
Global Political Economy   188
International Politics: The Post–Cold War Era   191

CHAPTER 10
· · · · · · · · ·

Frontiers of Research in Comparative Politics   194

Women in Politics   194
Comparative Drug Policy   199
Immigration   201
Regionalism/Decentralization   204
Legal Rights for Gays   206
Environmental Issues and Pollution   208

CHAPTER 11
· · · · · · · · ·

Conclusion   212

Comparative Politics Methodology   213
Comparative Politics: Particularistic or Universalistic?   215
Theory and Comparative Politics   216
Tasks for Comparative Politics   217

Suggested Readings   221

Index   227

1

What Is Comparative Politics?

Comparative politics is a very rich and dynamic field. It is especially rich because its range of inquiry, its laboratory—really a living, ever-changing laboratory—is all the world's political systems. As of this writing, this includes some 180 independent countries plus assorted territories, colonies, and other entities.

The majority of these countries are listed in the accompanying Table 1.1, "Basic Indicators for the World's Countries." This table provides basic information on the population of each country, its geographic size, its average per capita (per person) income in a given year (1997), as well as its *rate* of growth per year over the preceding ten years. The table is fascinating to study because it enables one to place one's own country in comparative context, to locate other favorite countries or those in which one is particularly interested, and to see the broad patterns of similarities and differences that exist between countries. (Table 1.2 shows the basic indicators for countries that do not report their basic data or have populations of less than one million.)

Note that the table is arranged starting with the poorest or least developed countries and ranging up to the richest or most developed countries. The table is derived from figures

Table 1.1   Basic Indicators for the World's Countries

Economy	Population 1997 (millions)	Land area 1995 (thousands of sq. km)	Population density 1997 (people per sq. km)	Gross national product (GNP) Billions of dollars 1997[a]	Avg. annual growth rate 1996–1997 (%)	GNP per capita Dollars 1997[a]	Avg. annual growth rate 1996–1997 (%)
Low income	2,048	30,178	66	721.7	8.0	360	2.8
1 Mozambique	10	784	22	1.7	8.6	90	5.7
2 Congo, Dem. Republic	47	2,257	18	5.1	——	110	——
3 Ethiopia	60	1,000	56	8.5	5.3	110	2.0
4 Burundi	7	28	244	1.2	3.7	180	1.1
5 Niger	10	1,287	7	2.0	3.6	200	0.1
6 Sierra Leone	5	72	83	0.9	——	200	——
7 Nepal	23	143	150	4.6	2.7	210	0.0
8 Rwanda	8	25	259	1.7	15.1	210	−2.0
9 Tanzania	31	884	34	6.6	——	210	——
10 Malawi	10	84	104	2.3	3.1	220	0.5
11 Burkina Faso	11	274	38	2.6	6.8	240	4.0
12 Chad	7	1,259	5	1.6	6.8	240	4.2
13 Guinea-Bissau	1	28	38	0.3	7.4	240	5.0
14 Madagascar	14	582	23	3.6	4.7	250	1.6
15 Mali	10	1,220	6	2.7	6.6	260	3.5
16 Nigeria	118	911	122	30.7	4.2	260	1.2
17 Bangladesh	124	130	920	33.2	5.4	270	3.7
18 Yemen, Rep.	16	526	29	4.3	——	270	——
19 Cambodia	11	177	57	3.2	——	300	——
20 Central African Rep.	3	823	5	1.1	5.8	320	3.4
21 Uganda	20	200	96	6.8	8.3	320	2.3
22 Vietnam	77	325	227	24.5	——	320	——
23 Haiti	7	28	260	2.5	1.1	330	−0.8
24 Kenya	28	568	47	9.3	2.3	330	−0.1
25 Tajikistan	6	141	42	2.0	2.2	330	0.7
26 Togo	4	54	76	1.4	5.0	330	2.1
27 Angola	11	1,247	9	3.8	15.4	340	12.1
28 Ghana	18	228	75	6.8	3.1	370	0.6
29 Benin	8	111	49	2.2	5.3	380	2.3
30 Zambia	9	743	12	3.6	7.8	380	5.3
31 India	961	2,973	313	373.9	5.0	390	3.2
32 Mongolia	3	1,587	2	1.0	——	390	——
33 Laos PDR	5	231	20	1.9	6.5	400	3.8
34 Nicaragua	5	121	36	1.9	13.5	410	10.4
35 Kyrgyzstan Republic	5	192	24	2.0	5.1	440	4.0
36 Mauritania	2	1,025	2	1.1	5.9	450	3.2
37 Pakistan	137	771	169	67.2	2.8	490	0.0
38 Azerbaijan	8	87	87	3.9	3.1	510	2.8
39 Armenia	4	28	133	2.0	5.6	530	5.4
40 Moldova	4	33	132	2.3	——	540	——
41 Senegal	9	183	43	4.9	4.4	550	1.6
42 Guinea	7	246	27	3.9	7.2	570	4.6
43 Turkmenistan	5	470	10	2.9	——	630	——
44 Cameroon	14	465	29	9.1	8.4	650	5.3
45 Congo, Republic	3	342	8	1.6	0.5	660	2.2
46 Lesotho	2	30	65	1.4	5.2	670	2.9
47 Côte d'Ivoire	15	318	44	10.2	6.9	690	4.2
48 Honduras	6	112	53	4.4	7.6	700	4.6
49 Albania	3	27	118	2.5	——	750	——
50 Zimbabwe	11	287	28	8.6	2.1	750	0.0

continued

Table 1.1 *continued*

Economy	Population 1997 (millions)	Land area 1995 (thousands of sq. km)	Population density 1997 (people per sq. km)	Gross national product (GNP) Billions of dollars 1997[a]	Avg. annual growth rate 1996–1997 (%)	GNP per capita Dollars 1997[a]	Avg. annual growth rate 1996–1997 (%)
Middle income	**2,555**	**66,963**	**40**	**6,401.8**	**4.9**	**1,880**	**3.6**
Lower middle income	**2,286**	**45,188**	**48**	**2,817.9**	————	**1,230**	————
51 Sri Lanka	18	65	280	14.6	8.9	800	5.8
52 Georgia	5	70	78	4.6	————	840	————
53 China	1,227	9,326	129	1,055.4	8.9	880	7.8
54 Hong Kong, China[b]	7	1	6,218	164.4	5.2	25,280	2.1
55 Papua New Guinea	8	453	8	4.2	14.0	940	18.9
56 Bolivia	8	1,084	7	7.4	————	950	————
57 Uzbekistan	24	414	55	23.9	2.2	1,010	0.3
58 Ukraine	50	579	89	52.4	3.0	1,040	2.3
59 Macedonia, FYR	2	25	77	2.2	————	1,090	————
60 Indonesia	200	1,182	107	221.8	4.4	1,110	2.8
61 Bulgaria	8	111	78	9.4	8.8	1,140	6.1
62 Syrian Arab Republic	15	154	77	17.1	2.0	1,150	0.6
63 Egypt, Arab Republic	60	995	58	71.2	4.9	1,180	3.0
64 Philippines	73	288	238	89.3	5.8	1,220	3.6
65 Morocco	28	446	59	34.4	2.7	1,250	4.4
66 Kazakhstan	16	2,671	6	21.8	1.3	1,340	2.2
67 Romania	23	230	98	32.1	5.5	1,420	6.3
68 Algeria	28	2,382	12	43.8	2.0	1,490	0.1
69 Guatemala	11	108	98	16.6	3.6	1,500	0.9
70 Jamaica	3	11	233	4.0	1.8	1,560	1.0
71 Jordan	4	89	47	7.0	4.4	1,570	1.5
72 Ecuador	12	277	41	19.0	4.4	1,680	2.3
73 Dominican Republic	8	48	162	13.5	11.7	1,870	0.8
74 El Salvador	6	21	273	10.7	3.5	1,810	0.9
75 Paraguay	5	397	12	10.2	14.5	2,010	11.8
76 Tunisia	9	155	58	18.4	11.5	2,090	8.7
77 Belarus	10	207	50	22.1	11.1	2,150	11.5
78 Namibia	2	823	2	3.6	3.8	2,220	1.3
79 Lithuania	4	65	57	8.3	2.7	2,230	2.9
80 Colombia	38	1,039	35	96.8	————	2,280	————
81 Latvia	2	62	41	6.0	————	2,430	————
82 Peru	25	1,280	19	60.6	1.7	2,480	0.1
83 Costa Rica	4	61	66	9.3	2.6	2,640	.07
84 Russian Federation	147	16,869	9	403.6	————	2,740	————
85 Thailand	61	511	116	159.6	0.4	2,800	1.3
86 Panama	3	74	35	8.4	4.3	3,080	2.6
Upper middle income	**571**	**22,826**	**24**	**2,664.0**	**4.7**	**4,620**	**3.2**
87 Turkey	64	770	80	199.5	8.1	3,130	6.4
88 Estonia	1	42	35	4.8	6.4	3,330	7.7
89 Lebanon	4	10	391	13.9	————	3,350	————
90 South Africa	38	1,221	30	130.2	1.3	3,400	0.5
91 Venezuela	23	882	25	78.7	7.4	3,450	5.3
92 Poland	39	304	127	138.8	6.8	3,690	6.7
93 Mexico	85	1,809	48	348.6	6.0	3,660	6.2
94 Slovak Republic	6	48	111	19.8	6.1	3,700	5.9
95 Mauritius	1	2	553	4.3	5.2	3,800	4.2

continued

Table 1.1 *continued*

Economy	Population 1997 (millions)	Land area 1995 (thousands of sq. km)	Population density 1997 (people per sq. km)	Gross national product (GNP) Billions of dollars 1997[a]	Avg. annual growth rate 1996–1997 (%)	GNP per capita Dollars 1997[a]	Avg. annual growth rate 1996–1997 (%)
96 Gabon	1	258	4	4.8	6.4	4,230	3.8
97 Trinidad and Tobago	1	5	251	5.5	6.4	4,230	5.5
98 Hungary	10	92	111	45.0	3.9	4,430	4.3
99 Croatia	4	56	85	20.7	——	4,610	——
100 Malaysia	21	329	81	98.2	7.6	4,650	5.2
101 Brazil	164	6,457	19	773.4	2.4	4,720	1.1
102 Oman	2	212	10	10.6	——	4,850	——
103 Chile	15	749	19	73.3	7.6	5,020	6.1
104 Czech Republic	10	77	134	53.5	0.7	5,200	0.8
105 Uruguay	3	175	18	19.4	3.4	6,020	2.8
106 Saudi Arabia	20	2,150	9	128.9	——	6,790	——
107 Argentina	36	2,737	13	306.7	6.1	8,570	4.7
Low & middle income	**4,903**	**99,199**	**48**	**6,123.6**	**4.8**	**1,250**	**3.0**
East Asia & Pacific	**1,752**	**15,569**	**108**	**1,707.3**	**6.8**	**870**	**6.6**
Europe & Central Asia	**471**	**23,344**	**20**	**1,105.3**	——	**2,320**	——
Latin America & Carib.	**494**	**20,054**	**24**	**1,918.8**	**4.4**	**3,880**	**2.7**
Middle East & N. Africa	**283**	**10,972**	**28**	**682.7**	——	**2,060**	——
South Asia	**1,289**	**4,781**	**260**	**601.9**	**4.8**	**390**	**2.9**
Sub-Saharan Africa	**914**	**23,628**	**28**	**308.1**	**4.2**	**500**	**1.2**
High Income	**926**	**30,971**	**30**	**23,602.1**	**2.8**	**28,700**	**2.2**
108 Slovenia	2	20	99	19.3	——	9,680	——
109 Portugal	10	92	108	103.9	3.4	10,450	3.3
110 Korea, Republic	48	99	456	485.2	4.8	10,550	3.6
111 Greece	11	129	81	126.2	3.4	12,010	3.1
112 Spain	39	498	78	570.1	3.2	14,510	3.1
113 Israel	6	21	268	87.6	——	15,510	——
114 New Zealand	4	268	13	60.6	1.9	16,480	1.0
115 United Arab Emirates	3	84	29	42.7	——	17,360	——
116 Ireland	4	69	52	66.4	7.5	18,280	7.3
117 Canada	30	9,221	3	883.9	3.6	19,290	2.6
118 Italy	57	284	195	1,155.4	1.3	20,120	1.2
119 Australia	19	7,682	2	380.0	2.8	20,540	1.8
120 United Kingdom	59	242	243	1,220.2	3.4	20,710	3.2
121 Finland	5	305	17	123.8	4.6	24,080	4.3
122 Netherlands	16	34	458	402.7	3.2	25,820	2.7
123 France	59	550	106	1,526.0	2.3	26,060	1.8
124 Sweden	9	412	21	232.0	1.8	26,220	1.7
125 Belgium	10	33	310	268.4	——	26,420	——
126 Austria	8	83	97	225.50	2.1	27,880	1.8
127 Germany	82	349	234	2,310.51	——	28,260	——
128 United States	268	9,159	29	7,890.1	3.8	28,740	2.9
129 Denmark	5	42	123	171.4	3.4	32,500	3.1
130 Singapore	3	1	4,896	101.8	8.8	32,500	7.2
131 Norway	4	307	14	188.8	4.0	32,940	3.5
132 Japan	126	377	333	4,772.3	0.5	36,850	0.2
133 Switzerland	7	40	178	313.5	——	37,850	——
World	**6,529 t**	**130,129 t**	**44 w**	**29,926 t**	**3.2 w**	**8,130 w**	**7.8 w**

Source: World Bank, *World Development Report, 1997/98.*
[a]Preliminary World Bank estimates calculated using the World Bank *Atlas* method. [b]Included in High Income totals.

Table 1.2 Basic Indicators for Other Countries

Economy	Population 1997 (thousands)	Land area 1995 (thousands of sq. km)	Population density 1997 (people per sq. km)	Gross national product (GNP) Millions of dollars 1997[a]	Gross national product (GNP) Avg. annual growth rate 1996–1997 (%)	GNP per capita Dollars 1997[a]	GNP per capita Avg. annual growth rate 1996–1997 (%)
Afghanistan	24,844	652.1	38	——	——	——[b]	——
American Samoa	60	0.2	298	——	——	——[c]	——
Andorra	71	0.2	160	——	——	——[d]	——
Antigua and Barbuda	66	0.4	151	489	1.9	7,380	1.0
Aruba	80	0.2	421	1,181	——	16,640	——
Bahamas, The	289	10.0	29	3,288	——	11,830	——
Bahrain	619	0.7	897	4,514	——	7,820	——
Barbados	265	0.4	616	1,741	——	6,590	——
Belize	228	22.8	10	625	1.6	2,740	−1.0
Bermuda	62	0.1	1,242	2,128	——	34,950	——
Bhutan	736	47.0	16	296	5.7	400	2.8
Bosnia and Herzegovina	——	51.0	——	——	——	——[b]	——
Botswana	1,510	566.7	3	4,922	7.8	3,260	5.7
Brunei	295	5.3	56	7,151	——	25,090	——
Cape Verde	399	4.0	99	436	23.0	1,090	19.9
Cayman Islands	35	0.3	130	——	——	——[d]	——
Channel Islands	148	——	——	——	——	——[d]	——
Comoros	518	2.2	232	208	−0.4	400	−2.9
Cuba	11,091	109.8	101	——	——	——[e]	——
Cyprus	747	9.2	81	10,839	——	14,930	——
Djibouti	636	23.2	27	——	——	——[e]	——
Dominica	74	0.8	99	232	3.1	3,120	——
Equatorial Guinea	421	28.1	15	444	106.6	1,050	101.4
Eritrea	3,827	101.0	38	801	——	210	——
Faeroe Islands	47	1.4	30	——	——	——[d]	——
Fiji	815	18.3	45	2,009	1.0	2,470	−0.5
French Guiana	153	88.2	2	——	——	——[d]	——
French Polynesia	225	3.7	61	——	——	——[d]	——
Gambia, The	1,180	10.0	118	409	5.2	350	2.2
Greenland	58	341.7	0	——	——	——[d]	——
Grenada	99	0.3	290	296	2.7	3,000	2.9
Guadeloupe	426	1.7	252	——	——	——[c]	——
Guam	155	0.6	282	——	——	——[d]	——
Guyana	848	196.9	4	677	4.9	800	3.8
Iceland	272	100.3	3	7,513	4.9	27,580	——
Iran, Islamic Republic	60,973	1,622.0	38	113,506	3.2	1,780	1.2
Iraq	21,970	437.4	50	——	——	——[e]	——
Isle of Man	72	0.6	120	——	——	——[c]	——
Kiribati	83	0.7	114	76	1.7	910	−0.5
Korea, Dem. Republic	22,773	120.4	189	——	——	——[e]	——
Kuwait	1,637	17.8	92	35,152	——	22,110	——
Liberia	2,894	96.3	30	——	——	——[b]	——
Libya	5,292	1,759.5	3	——	——	——[c]	——
Liechtenstein	31	0.2	190	——	——	——[d]	——
Luxembourg	422	2.6	160	18,837	——	45,330	——
Macao	471	0.0	23,555	——	——	——[d]	——
Maldives	262	0.3	874	301	6.0	1,150	3.3
Malta	376	0.3	1,174	3,203	——	8,630	——
Marshall Islands	57	0.2	290	108	——	1,770	——
Martinique	388	1.1	366	——	——	——[d]	——

continued

Table 1.2 *continued*

Economy	Population 1997 (thousands)	Land area 1995 (thousands of sq. km)	Population density 1997 (people per sq. km)	Gross national product (GNP) millions of dollars 1997[a]	Gross national product (GNP) Avg. annual growth rate 1996–1997 (%)	GNP per capita Dollars 1997[a]	GNP per capita Avg. annual growth rate 1996–1997 (%)
Mayotte	108	0.3	340	——	——	——[c]	——
Micronesia, Fed. Sts.	111	0.7	160	220	——	1,980	——
Monaco	32	0.0	16,840	——	——	——[d]	——
Myanmar	46,680	657.6	71	——	——	——[b]	——
Netherlands Antilles	204	0.8	250	——	——	——[d]	——
New Caledonia	202	18.6	10	——	——	——[d]	——
Northern Mariana Islands	63	0.5	110	——	——	——[d]	——
Palau	17	0.5	40	——	——	——[c]	——
Puerto Rico	3,792	8.9	428	25,380	——	7,010	——
Qatar	675	11.0	61	7,429	——	11,570	——
Reunion	673	2.5	269	——	——	——[b]	——
Samoa	173	2.8	61	199	4.0	1,150	3.1
São Tomé and Principe	138	1.0	144	38	-2.8	270	-5.1
Seychelles	78	0.5	173	537	2.4	6,880	0.6
Solomon Islands	401	28.0	14	362	1.5	900	-1.5
Somalia	10,130	627.3	16	——	——	——[b]	——
St. Kitts and Nevis	41	0.4	113	252	6.0	6,160	6.1
St. Lucia	159	0.6	261	576	3.5	3,620	2.7
St. Vincent/Grenadines	112	0.4	288	281	5.0	2,500	4.3
Sudan	27,861	2,376.0	12	7,801	6.4	280	4.2
Suriname	437	156.0	3	544	5.6	1,240	4.3
Swaziland	952	17.2	55	1,369	2.6	1,440	-0.2
Tonga	98	0.7	136	179	0.0	1,830	-0.4
Vanuatu	177	12.2	15	233	3.0	1,310	0.4
Virgin Islands (U.S.)	97	0.3	286	——	——	——[b]	——
West Bank and Gaza	——	——	——	——	——	——[e]	——
Yugoslavia, FR (Serb./Mont.)	10,614	102.0	104	——	——	——[e]	——

Source: World Bank, *World Development Report, 1997/98.*
[a]Calulated using the World Bank *Atlas* method. [b]Estimated to be low income ($785 or less). [c]Estimated to be upper middle income ($3,126 to $9,655). [d]Estimated to be high income ($9,656 or more). [e]Estimated to be lower middle income ($786 to $3,125).

compiled by the World Bank, which means their accuracy is probably as good as any; roughly comparable figures are also available from the United Nations and other reliable sources. We have used the World Bank figures here because they go beyond just a straightforward listing to also place countries in various developmental categories.

The first category is *low-income* countries. This category includes fifty countries (plus some others for which no data are available), located mostly in Africa, Asia, Central Asia, and Latin America, which are among the poorest in the world. These are countries that are not only mired in poverty but whose social and political institutions are often underdeveloped and unstable as well. A very high percentage of them are dictatorships.

The second category is *middle-income* countries, a group of fifty-six countries, which are further subdivided into lower-middle-income and upper-middle-income. The lower-middle-income category includes a number of countries from Latin America and the somewhat better-off countries of the Middle East, Africa, Eastern Europe, and Southeast Asia. These are, generally, countries that are developing and becoming better off but are doing so slowly. The upper-middle-income countries include the more prosperous countries of Latin America, the Middle East, and East Asia—formerly underdeveloped countries that are now "making it" and becoming developed and modern nations. Note that this category also includes some of the poorest of the European countries, particularly those in Eastern Europe.

The next category is what the World Bank calls *high-income countries* and what we would call *developed countries*. The category includes Slovenia, South Korea, Portugal, Greece, and Spain (for which it was a great day—the equivalent of a national holiday—when it finally made it over the hump into this category) at the poorer end, and Japan and Switzerland at the richer end. Note that the countries in this category are mainly from Western Europe, North America, or the British Commonwealth (Australia and New Zealand). Japan, South Korea, Singapore, and the United Arab Emirates are, so far, the only non-Western countries to have made it into this category. Note also that almost all of the countries located in this category are functioning democracies.

Now, if one thinks about these tables for a time and ponders their various categories and entries, then one is well on the way to being a student of comparative politics. Why are some countries poor and others wealthier? What enables some countries to "make it" in the modern world while others remain locked in poverty? Why are the poorer countries more inclined to be governed autocratically while the richer countries are democratic? What accounts for the regional, cultural, and geographic differences that exist? What are the politics of the transition from underdeveloped to developed, and what helps stimulate and sustain that process? What are the internal social and political conditions as well as the international situations of these various countries that explain the similarities as well as the differences? What are the patterns that help account for the emergence of democratic as distinct from Marxist-Leninist or authoritarian political systems? These are precisely the kinds of questions that lie at the heart of the field of comparative politics.

Comparative Politics Defined

Comparative politics involves the systematic study and comparison of the world's political systems. It seeks to explain differences between as well as similarities among countries. In contrast to journalistic reporting on a single country, comparative politics is particularly interested in exploring patterns, processes, and regularities among political systems. It looks for trends, for changes in patterns; and it tries to develop general propositions or hypotheses that describe and explain these trends. It seeks to do such comparisons rigorously and systematically, without personal, partisan, or ideological axes to grind. It involves hard work, clear thinking, careful and thorough scholar-ship, and (hopefully) clear, consistent, and balanced writing.

Since the world is our laboratory, the types of studies that can be encom-passed in comparative politics are (as would be expected) varied. Different scholars will have different preferences in these regards, but that should not worry us overly or cause concern that the field has no one single focus. Rather, it includes several different kinds of studies—and legitimately so, in my view. Among the types of studies that students of comparative politics ac-tually do are the following:

1. *Studies of one country*—or a particular institution (political parties, mili-taries, parliaments, interest groups), political process (decision making), or public policy (for instance, labor or welfare policy) in that country. Such single-country studies are probably the easiest for young students in the field to do. But in focusing on only one country or institution, it will be necessary in an introductory statement or paragraph to put that study into a larger comparative framework. That means we should tell why the subject is important and where it fits in a larger context. For instance, if we're interested in military intervention in the politics of a country, then we should explore the general literature on interventions as well as study the politics of that particular country. We should also offer a set of com-ments, usually called a "model" or "conceptual framework," that explains the broader implications of the study and its possible relevance to the same or similar issues in other countries or to global trends. In other words, even though our study may concentrate on a single country, we are still interested in the "bigger picture" and in *comparison*. Such broader concerns, the effort to analyze patterns and general behavior, are what distinguish comparative politics from newspaper reporting or a historical survey of a single country.

2. *Studies of two or more countries.* Such genuinely comparative studies are harder to carry out, and they are usually more expensive in terms of travel and research costs. It is often difficult for the beginning student to understand and master one foreign country; two or more are even harder. Hence, often the student of comparative politics does a case study of one country first in the form of a paper, thesis, or doctoral dissertation; later he or she may move on to study a second (or third, fourth, and so on) country and to elaborate the comparisons between them. Such a step is very important intellectually because it is in knowing and writing about two or more counties that students can begin to make genuine comparisons.

3. *Regional or area studies.* These may include studies of Africa, Latin Amer-ica, the Middle East, East Asia, Southeast Asia, South Asia, Europe, or other subregions (Southern Europe or North Africa, for example). Such studies are useful because they involve *groups* of countries that may have

several things in common—for example, similar histories, cultures, languages, geographic locations, legal systems, religions, colonial backgrounds, and so on. Such regional or area studies are often particularly interesting because they are almost like a science laboratory. That is, if a group of countries have many common features—let us say the colonial background or Catholicism in Latin America—the investigator can hold such factors constant while examining or "testing" for certain other features (for instance, the level or degree of authoritarianism in the society), almost as if he or she were carrying out a chemistry experiment. The investigator can then make statements about the area as a whole or make comparisons between countries within a given area. The danger lies in overgeneralizing, in making comments about the area as a whole without sufficient attention to the specific differences of individual countries even within a particular region.

Among some scholars, area studies are controversial. The student may become so enamored of his or her own area that he or she loses objectivity. Or the student may become so engrossed in one particular culture that he or she forgets the larger goal of *comparison*. In addition, many issues today—human rights, democracy, the environment, drugs—are global; they are not limited to one country or area. Even with these potential problems, however, area studies have a very important role in comparative politics: they enable a student to study and immerse him- or herself in one particular area; they facilitate comparison among often similar or at least *comparable* countries, and it is out of such area studies, as we see later in the book, that some of the most exciting new approaches in the field—dependency theory, corporatism, bureaucratic-statism—have emerged.

4. *Studies across regions*. Such studies are becoming more prevalent, but at more advanced levels they are often expensive and difficult to carry out. One must know, master, and travel to not just one region but two or more. Such studies might involve comparisons of the role of the military in Africa and the Middle East or of the quite different paths to development of the East Asian countries and Latin America. (My own research, for example, has involved comparisons among Latin America, Southern Europe, and East Asia.) Such studies can be very interesting, although one must recognize that it is very difficult for a single scholar to stay well informed on so many countries and areas.

5. *Global comparisons*. With the improved statistical data collected by the World Bank, the UN, and other agencies, it is now possible to do comparisons on a global basis. For example, using the same kind of data presented in Table 1.1 over, let us say, a thirty-year period might enable us to trace the relationship in *all* countries between economic development and the growth of democratization, or between the size of the middle class

and democratization, or between greater affluence and the decline of authoritarianism and Marxism-Leninism. Such studies can best be done through the use of statistical correlations. But such correlations cannot be said to prove *causation*—that is, that economic growth causes democratization. There is a relationship between economic growth and democracy, but the first does not necessarily *cause* the second. In addition, students of such global comparisons often lack expertise in the specific areas or countries studied and thus may make egregious mistakes. For example, Nicaragua under the dictator Anastasio Somoza was sometimes listed as "overdemocratized" for its level of economic development because one of the indices used to measure democratization—the presence of opposition members in the congress—was consistently high in that country. What the global comparativists didn't know, what only an area or country specialist would know, was that in Somoza's emphatically nondemocratic regime the constitution *required* one-third of the legislature to come from opposition parties so that the dictator could portray his regime as more democratic than it really was.

Other problems involved in global comparisons include the frequent unreliability of the statistical data used and the problems of developing meaningful comparisons between countries and regions that are so different in their cultures and histories—such as Africa and Latin America or Asia and Europe—so that it's like trying to add apples and oranges. I think of such global comparisons as provocative, suggestive, and interesting even though treating them with a good dose of healthy skepticism, especially if one tries to draw too strong a conclusion out of them.

6. *Thematic studies.* Comparative politics focuses on themes as well as countries and regions. For example, some scholars may be interested in the changing role of the state in comparative perspective, in the process of military professionalization as seen comparatively, in the structure of class relations as analyzed comparatively, or in the process of political socialization (how we learn about politics, where our political ideas come from) from a comparative perspective. Others may be interested in such themes as dependency theory (the dependence of some countries on others), the processes by which emerging countries achieve national development, or the newer systems of interest group representation called "corporatism" (all of these terms and themes are examined in greater detail later in the book) viewed from a comparative viewpoint. Such studies are often complex, difficult, at the theoretical level, and usually carried out by more senior scholars in the field because they presume a great deal of knowledge about various areas and require the ability to see the "big picture" at a highly conceptual level.

Several interesting lessons emerge from this survey of the types of research that students of comparative politics do. First is the variety of approaches and perspectives used. Most of us find such diversity in the field healthy and stimulating. The important thing at this stage is not so much the *type* of study that one chooses to follow but to begin to *think comparatively*, in terms of the patterns and comparisons that exist between countries and regions.

A second admonition is to look at what students of comparative politics actually *do* in their studies rather than getting bogged down in the stale, often disruptive and inconclusive debates over approaches and methods that mar the field. There are rich country, area, global, and thematic studies "out there" that students should peruse in order to get a feel for the field; some suggestions along these lines are contained in the Suggested Readings at the end of the book.

Third, one should recognize degrees of difficulty. For the beginning student a single-country study or a two-country comparison may be appropriate, or an area study, or perhaps a topical study that cuts across regions; but remember that even these require an introduction and conclusion that places the topic in a broader comparative perspective.

Why Study Comparative Politics?

There are a number of reasons for studying comparative politics. First, it's fun and interesting, and one learns a lot about other countries, regions, and the world.

Second, studying comparative politics will help a person overcome ethnocentrism, defined as the inability to understand other countries except through one's own rose-colored lenses. All peoples and countries are ethnocentric, but Americans seem to be particularly afflicted. Instead of studying and trying to understand other countries through *their own* eyes, in their own cultural and social context, and in their own language(s), Americans tend to look at the rest of the world from the perspective that our ways and institutions are best and these other countries should therefore learn from the United States. Americans seldom perceive that they could also learn from other nations' experiences or that they should study American as well as other countries' institutions *comparatively*, neutrally, without bias, from the pragmatic point of view of what works best rather than from a perspective of superiority and condescension.

Third, we study comparative politics to understand how nations change and the patterns that exist. What accounts for the fact that some nations have forged ahead while others remain poor and backward? What can we learn from the recent, very heartening transitions from authoritarianism to democracy in so many parts of the world? And how does one explain the unraveling of so many Marxist-Leninist regimes and their transactions to more open politics and economies? Comparative politics may not have all the answers to such questions, but it does offer some, and it has an approach and methodology that enable us to get at quite a few others.

A fourth reason for studying comparative politics is that it is intellectually stimulating. Consider these questions: Why do some countries modernize and others not? Why are some countries democratic and others not? Why are interest groups and political parties structured one way in some countries and other ways in others? Why do some countries and their political systems fail while others succeed? These are among the most challenging questions that one can grapple with in today's world. Comparative politics helps us get at the answers by showing the change process in all its dimensions and wrestling with the problems posed by the complexity and multiple causes of these processes.

Fifth, comparative politics has a rigorous and effective methodology. The comparative method, really a way of thinking comparatively about the world and its individual political systems, is both a sophisticated tool of analysis and one that is always open to new approaches. (We have more to say about the comparative methodology in the next section.)

Finally, comparative politics is necessary for a proper understanding of both international relations and foreign policy. Without knowing thoroughly, from the inside, empathetically (the opposite of ethnocentrically) the other countries with whom we conduct our foreign relations, we cannot have an informed, successful foreign policy. Hence, there is an intimate connection among international relations, foreign policy, and comparative politics; in my view, these are distinct fields of study, but in the real world they are also inseparable, complementary, and mutually necessary for an understanding of today's world.

The Comparative Method

Comparative politics provides a means by which we can learn about other societies, how they work and how they change. Through comparison, we can learn that what works in one society may not work in another, and why. Comparative politics also provides an antidote to ethnocentrism—a method by which to understand other societies on their own terms and in their own context.

The comparative method is usually thought of as involving two distinct levels of comparison. One is the snapshot approach: it is the easiest to comprehend and operationalize since it involves a comparison, a snapshot, of two or more countries or specific institutions within them *at a certain, given point in time*—usually the present. The second approach, trickier and more complex, involves a comparison of the same aspect or issue in two or more countries but *at different points in historical time*. For example, if we are interested in the comparative development of democracy or of political parties, can we perhaps compare Europe and the United States in the nineteenth century when parties and democracy first emerged, with late-twentieth-century development of democracy and political parties in many developing countries? In other words, to what extent do the already developed or industrialized nations of today present a picture of what the developing nations will be like in the future? Do the developed nations at every stage of their development provide us with a picture, a mirror, of what all nations must go through eventually on their road to development? Comparison, in other words, can be across nations at a single point in time, or it can involve comparisons across time periods to test whether the same processes (economic development and greater social change, for example, giving rise to greater demands for democracy) are operating at different historical periods.

The comparative method has often been compared, somewhat pretentiously, to the scientific method in physics or biology. Like the natural sciences, comparative politics has its "laboratory": the world's political systems. And with this image of a laboratory in mind, it sometimes appears that we can carry out scientific measurements involving those systems. For example, in comparative politics we can sometimes hold one or more variables constant—religion or culture or social structure or a particular political institution—while we look comparatively at policy outcomes. In other words, if we're interested in studying comparative welfare policy, we can pretty much control for some variables while we test for others. In this case welfare policy outcomes are viewed as the *dependent* variable, while religion, culture, socioeconomic factors, and so on, are the *independent* variables.

One can see why this method is sometimes compared to the laboratory methodology of the hard sciences. In this case the globe is our comparative politics experiment station, and we have 180 nations (plus other kinds of units) to consider. We also know how to test for certain variables and to control for others. In comparative politics, as in the laboratory sciences, we use hypotheses, tests, and "proofs." One can understand why it would be tempting to equate comparative politics' methodology with that of natural sciences.

Although the analogy with the hard sciences is attractive, it should not be taken literally: Comparative politics is *not*, in most respects, a hard science. The field and its concepts—political culture, political socialization, interest group activity, decision making, policy implementation—are often vague and imprecise, not amenable to empirical scientific experimentation. In addition, the exact meaning and measure of these concepts may vary from country to country. There are, furthermore, too many variables in human affairs that may intervene in unlikely or unanticipated ways, so that it is very difficult to be quantitatively precise about our findings. Nor, in the social sciences, can one readily isolate these variables and thus replicate the test and get the same results as in a science laboratory. Because the concepts often carry diverse meanings to different researchers and the tests are difficult to replicate, one cannot speak of comparative politics as a precise, empirical science as one would of physics or biology.

A mistake often made by beginning students in comparative politics, however, involves the confusion of "science" with the experimental method. Not all sciences need to use the experimental method of the physics or chemistry laboratory. Those are more precise, to be sure, but other methods may also be used. For example, if science is defined as an "orderly body of knowledge," then surely comparative politics qualifies. It *may* use the experimental method, but it may use other, more interpretive methods as well—such as library research, interviewing, or participant observation in the country studied—that carry their own specific rules of data collection, logical argumentation, and interpretation. Here we emphasize comparison as a mode of inquiry or way of knowledge. To achieve the desired results, the experimental method *may* be employed, but the traditional approaches are also valid methods of research.

For some students, the fact that comparative politics is not a strict science in the sense that the natural sciences are is a cause for despair and even the abandonment of the field. That feeling is shared by some scholars in comparative politics, who have embarked on a sometimes frustrating quest to quantify and mathematicize, or to find universal rules for, the entire field. But the conclusions of most scholars of comparative politics lie in between these two extremes. That is, just because comparative politics is not always as quantifiable as, say, chemistry is not a reason for us to throw up our arms in despair and abandon the field. At the same time, while recognizing that comparative politics is not and probably never will be a strict or hard science, that does not absolve us from trying to be as precise and careful in our research as we can possibly be.

Where, then, does that leave us—or the field of comparative politics? The following injunctions may be helpful:

1. Let us recognize realistically that for most questions comparative politics is not a science in the same sense that, say, physics or biology is. It has its "orderly body of knowledge" as other sciences do, but it cannot often replicate the experimental method of laboratory science.

2. Nevertheless, we need to be as careful and as rigorous as possible in setting forth our hypotheses and research plans, in testing our hypotheses, and in carrying out and reporting on our research.

3. Some of the methods used in comparative politics, such as interviewing and library research, are often not as exact as we would like them to be; they are useful methods but by their very nature may be open to different interpretations.

4. Nevertheless, the goal must remain a study that is as systematic and precise as possible.

5. We must also recognize that some of the new approaches in the field, employing statistics, mathematical modeling, regression analysis, and computers, enable us to use sophisticated and quantifiable measures that

were previously unheard of. Every student of comparative politics now must master these techniques. Furthermore, while the field is unlikely to achieve the precision of an exact science in answering the most important questions that we are interested in, its scientific measures are expanding, and in the future it is likely that such mathematical and computer-based measures will be used even more frequently.

6. At this stage what comparative politics can mainly do is produce tendency statements rather than scientific proofs. For example, we can say that countries with high income levels *tend* to be more likely to have democratic political systems than do very poor countries; Table 1.1 clearly illustrates that relationship. Note that this is not an absolute statement, nor is it a scientific law of behavior, because there are numerous variations and exceptions; for instance, Costa Rica is a relatively poor country but is also a well-established democracy; in contrast, Saudi Arabia is a rich country but is not a democracy. There is, however, undoubtedly a relationship, and a rather close one, between economic development and democracy, a relationship that is best described by what we here call "tendency statements" rather than absolute laws. In most areas of comparative politics, such tendency statements are at present about as much as we can hope for—although more rigorous "proofs" of hypotheses such as the one provided earlier are what one should strive for.

7. Above all, we need to avoid bias and special pleading in the field. Some people use the "soft science" underpinnings of comparative politics as an excuse to advance their own biases or ideologies or to grind their own pet political axes. Because the field is inherently biased, they say, our bias is as good as any, and bias itself should be advanced and celebrated. Most scholars in the field deplore that approach. There may be biases in the field or in some parts of it, but that should not lead to an equally biased view on the other side. The goal should be not the celebration of one bias or another but rather a comparative politics approach that is as unbiased, unprejudiced, fair, and balanced as possible.

Models and Paradigms in Comparative Politics

Frequently, the field of comparative politics employs various models, frameworks, or paradigms as a way of simplifying and thus explaining various political phenomena more easily. In fact, the tracing, history, and analysis of these several approaches in the field lie at the heart of the presentation later in Chapters 3 to 5. Although each of them is defined and explained in subsequent chapters, examples of such models include the developmentalist approach, corporatism, and dependency theory. A model of this sort is a simplification of reality and should not be confused with the real thing.

For example, if we say that the developmentalist approach helps us explain the modernization processes of various Third World countries or that corporatism helps us understand the relations between interest groups and the state or government, then we are using developmentalism or corporatism as models or paradigms that signify some aspects of the political process. A model is a shorthand way of referring to a larger and more complex phenomenon or process. Again, such models as corporatism, developmentalism, or dependency represent simplifications of reality, not reality itself—they are metaphors for or abstractions of reality, not the genuine product. But such models are very useful in political analysis—indeed they are used all the time—enabling us to simplify for discussion purposes what are often very complex processes.

A model is a heuristic device—a kind of teaching aid—used to sort out, organize, and simplify more complex processes. An effective model simplifies reality by breaking it up into clear and manageable components to enable us better to understand it. But reality is always more complex than any single model or even several models can capture. A model is a very helpful tool in social science and comparative politics analysis, but it should not be confused with the even more complicated kaleidoscope that is reality itself. A model helps us understand and come to grips with events and processes that otherwise would be so disorganized, complex, and random that they would not make sense. At the same time, we should understand that the term *model* is a neutral one; when we use that word, we are not making a value judgment. A model is simply an intellectual device; in contrast to the term's popular usage, it implies neither approval nor disapproval.

What, then, is the utility of our employing such models in our analysis of comparative political systems? To recap:

1. Models help us organize, highlight, and give coherence to otherwise diverse events, processes, and institutions.

2. Models help put many seemingly unrelated events in a larger context, enabling us to see the "big picture," to provide perspective.

3. Models enable us to think more clearly about complicated events.

4. Models are heuristic devices; that is, they *teach* us things and enable us to see patterns.

5. Models help simplify complex events, enabling us to understand them more clearly.

Models should also be seen as pragmatic instruments. To the extent they are useful and helpful in terms of the purposes outlined here, we can use them to help order our thinking. But such models as used in comparative politics should not be worshiped or reified. They are not forever. They are not sacrosanct. New events or facts—the unraveling of the communist world, for example, or the emergence of democracy as a nearly universal political system—often force us to alter our interpretations, obliging us to change or revise our models, or to scrap them altogether. Often students of comparative politics become so attached to their particular model (as happened with developmentalism in the 1960s) that they fail to recognize that it must be reformulated or that it has outlived its usefulness. Models are devices to be used as long as they are useful and help us shed light on events, but we should not hesitate to rethink or replace them when they have outlived their utility. In either case, the overall usefulness—and limits—of such models should be recognized.

Approaching the Subject

Studies of *all* the world's political systems using a global model and statistical correlations are useful in some respects in suggesting relationships and patterns that otherwise we might not be aware of. However, such studies ignore regional and cultural differences and, as noted, too frequently involve the inappropriate mixing of apples and oranges. In any case, they are not for the beginning student. Beginning students should probably start off studying a single country, perhaps a pair of countries, or perhaps a group of countries in a single region or with other comparable features.

How, then, should we proceed? I have found it useful in my own studies to use the following outline, which can also be thought of as a potential table of contents for a book or thesis. The outline also suggests numerous topics for a smaller, narrower term paper or thesis and shows where they might fit in the broader scheme of things. Someone doing a complete country study should probably have chapters on each of the following subject areas; someone writing a research paper would probably be advised to narrow the focus and try to cover only one aspect within this larger outline.

I. *Introduction.* The introduction should try to interest, stimulate, or "grab" the reader, tell him or her why the particular country or subject matter is important and why someone should spend time researching or reading about it. The introduction should also "introduce" the subject and the author's preliminary ideas or hypotheses about it, explore the previous literature on the subject, and tell precisely what it is the author intends to do in his or her study. A good introduction should also explain the methodology of the study and present a plan of it so readers have a "road map" of where they are going.

II. *Political history.* History is so important in so many countries, where the shadow of the past still lingers, that it is useful to have a chapter on the historical background. One need not necessarily do original research for this information, but one ought to review all the secondary literature in order to trace the historical pattern of the country's formative development, to place the study in historical context, to bring the history right up to the present, and thus to provide a setting for the author's own study. One can also, if one wishes, do a comparative political history of two or several countries.

III. *Political culture.* Political culture refers to the values, ideas, norms, belief systems, and patterns of behavior of a particular people or country. History obviously helps shape the political culture, but other factors are also involved. An assessment of the political culture can derive from the art, literature, religious beliefs, modes of expression, and ways of behaving of the society—particularly as these affect politics and give it a certain style. To be more accurate and quantitative, however, assessments of political culture should be based on public opinion surveys. In studying political culture, in addition, one should avoid national stereotyping (Germans are this, Italians are that), but by careful research one can get a picture of what political-cultural patterns exist and how they influence countries.

IV. *Socioeconomic background.* This chapter or section should present information on the country's level of economic development and how it compares with other countries, as in Table 1.1. What is the nature of its economy? What does it produce? What is its relationship to outside markets and economic forces? This chapter or section should also contain data on the country's level of social modernization, its class structure and social relations, and how these are changing. Is it an agricultural or an industrial country? Does it have two traditional social classes (elites and masses), or is it more pluralist? What are its ethnic, caste, tribal, and other divisions? In short, the writer needs to outline the social and economic basis of politics. And here, most often, political scientists will have to do their own research because economists and sociologists frequently do it badly, not at all, or in a form that political scientists cannot use.

V. *Interest groups.* It is often a short step from socioeconomic data and class structure to interest groups. Many interest groups—businesses, farmers, middle-class associations, labor, peasants—are economic. However, others that are important—the armed forces, religious bodies, ethnic associations, student groups, professional associations—are not. In addition, many countries have other outside actors—the U.S. embassy, multinational corporations, the International Monetary Fund, the Vatican, the German, Japanese, or Russian embassies—that are so powerful that they function like domestic interest groups. One can study any one of these interest groups in a particular country or group of countries, or one can try to gauge the overall structure of interest group power in a particular country. One should also try to determine whether the interest group system is based on an authoritarian, democratic, corporatist, or totalitarian pattern.

VI. *Political parties*. Almost all countries now have political parties, or, if not, they frequently have socioeconomic, class, clan, caste, or tribal groups that function like political parties. That is, they educate their people in a certain belief or interest system (called *political socialization*), and they bring people together as an effective political movement (called *interest aggregation*). One can study a particular political party, a group of similar parties (Socialist, conservative, Communist, Christian-Democrat) in different political systems, various functions (leadership recruitment, electioneering) of the parties, or the entire political party spectrum, left to right, or structure (one-party, two-party, multiparty) of a particular country.

VII. *Political communications*. This topic involves how ideas and interests are communicated to government officials. In a less developed country, political communication may take place mainly via interpersonal communications, family networks, or gossip; in more developed countries, the mass media (radios, newspapers, television, the Internet) tends to be more important. Political communication is thus related to levels of literacy, newspaper circulation, and per capita radio or television ownership. It is also important to know who owns the media, what are its biases, and how the media both manipulates and is manipulated by political leaders. Another important issue is the new trend toward globalization of news and culture, what some have called, as distinct from purely national values and ideas, the "world culture" of rock music, blue jeans, television (*Friends, Ally McBeal*), Coca-Cola, and—not least, demands for democracy and freedom.

VIII. *Institutions of government*. We now move from what are called the "inputs" of politics, or what goes "into" the political system (history, political culture, socioeconomic data, interest groups, political parties, political communications), to the actual institutions and decision-making processes of government. This topic may either be subdivided into three separate chapters or sections or be combined in a more abbreviated form into a single unit. The first of these subdivisions looks at the institutions of government: the legal system, the constitutional structure, president/prime minister, congress/parliament, justice and the court system, local government, and so on. There are many topics to study in this category (comparative federalism, presidentialism versus parliamentarism, executive-legislative relations, decentralization, and so on), which, since it focuses on the institutions of government, is what many beginning students think of as the proper realm of political science or governmental research.

IX. *Bureaucracy and the state.* Because the state system and bureaucracy in the United States are comparatively small, most Americans do not spend much time thinking about these subject areas. In some other countries, however, the state plays a far larger role than in the United States, either in directing the economy or in providing a fuller range of social programs. Thus, in this second subdivision of government institutions, one would want to show how the state system and the bureaucracy are organized, who controls them, what their role in social welfare and directing the economy is, and so on. Or, in this new era, how does the state handle downsizing, privatization, and reform campaigns?

X. *Decision making.* This is the third subdivision in our analysis of government institutions. It focuses on who makes decisions, how they are arrived at. What influences are felt? For example, I once had the president of a Latin American country tell me that when he made important decisions, he checked first with his armed forces chiefs, then with his country's economic elites, and third with the American embassy—but not necessarily in that order! If he had time, he might check with other groups, but such was rarely the case. That rank-ordering certainly tells us a lot about the structure of power and decision making in his country. Comparable information on decision making in other countries would likely reveal parallel or divergent, but perhaps equally striking, patterns.

XI. *Public policy.* Moving now from governmental structures and decision making to the actual decisions that come out of the political system, we arrive at the subject area of public policy. Comparative public policy is one of the fastest-growing subjects in the field. There are a great variety of public policies that can be studied comparatively: housing policy, economic policy, industrial policy, social policy, agrarian reform, education, population policy, environmental policy, and so on. One can also compare the foreign policies of different countries. In some country and comparative studies, domestic policy and foreign policy will be combined within a single chapter or section; in others the two subjects will be divided into two discussions.

XII. *Conclusion.* In this chapter or section we will want to sum up our findings, examine the patterns that emerge, look back at our original hypotheses to see whether they can be confirmed or denied, and draw out the assessments of our research. What makes this country or political system unique? In what ways is it comparable to others? What lessons can be learned from this? Does the system work? Is it functional? How do its parts fit together? What are its weak or missing links? A good conclusion should not only sum things up in this fashion but might also indicate what gaps still exist, and thus point in the direction of another, future research project.

A number of things should be reemphasized about this chapter or paper outline and organizational scheme. First, and most obviously, it offers a practical guide to both the range of subject areas encompassed within comparative politics and a plan for organizing them in book or thesis form. Second, it is quite appropriate for students to focus on only one or a few aspects within this outline, not on the "big picture" as one would do in a complete, sophisticated comparative country study. Third, this outline can easily be expanded or contracted like an accordion; depending on our time frame, motives, or particular research focus, chapters or sections can be either combined or further subdivided.

In addition, as perceptive students will note, there is a logic, coherence, and sequence to the way these materials are presented. We proceed from the most general (history, political culture, socioeconomic background) to the more specific (interest groups, parties, political communications, government institutions, decision making, public policy). Finally, the outline follows a systems or process model of the polity (see Figure 1.1): That is, it has "inputs" that go into the political system in the form of values, history, interests, and so on; it has a government or decision-making system that processes these demands; it has "outputs" in the form of government decisions and policies; and it has "feedback," by which those decisions and policies in turn have an effect on values, interests, and behavior, as well as what again goes "into" the political system.

I hasten to add, however, that I think of such a systems plan as purely a heuristic device, a teaching aid, a picture that helps us envisage the interrelated parts of the system, an outline that seems to make some logical sense but that can be modified to fit new facts and particular circumstances. For example, this schema, with its focus on interest groups and political parties, may be more appropriate for a liberal-pluralist polity than it would be for an authoritarian or totalitarian regime, where some modifications in the outline might have to be introduced. None of us should be married now or forever to the organizational plan presented here: Where it is useful and helpful, let us use it; where it is not, let us feel free to modify it.

Aspects of Change

Change within the system presented in Figure 1.1 can take a variety of forms and stem from a variety of sources. Change may take peaceful evolutionary or violent revolutionary directions, or it may stem from the use of limited structured violence to achieve limited goals. Change may come under authoritarian, totalitarian, or democratic auspices, and it may come gradually or rapidly. Change is ubiquitous, but it takes many forms, and the processes of change have themselves often been the subject of comparative study.

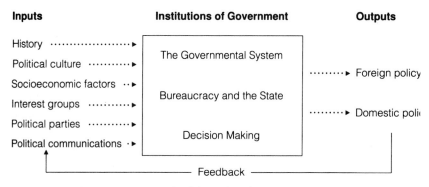

Figure 1.1   A Systems Framework of the Political Process

What are the causes of change? Over the past thirty years students of comparative politics have gotten into some terrible arguments over this question. Is it historical, political-cultural, value-based, or ideological forces that drive change? Or is it socioeconomic forces, foreign investment, the class system, the ownership of the means of production and of distribution (mainly a Marxist interpretation) that initiate change? Or is it political-structural factors: the organization of the state system, the strength of political parties, the coordination of business and labor to achieve national development? Or could it be biological and genetic forces—what is now called sociobiology—that are involved?

My answer is that probably all of these factors are involved—and at the same time it is often a silly debate, like asking which came first, the chicken or the egg? No one knows the answer to that, either—the question can never be answered—and it doesn't get us anywhere to even ask the question.

Clearly, in studying the change process in comparative politics, cultural, socioeconomic, and political-structural factors are always involved. If one does not know or understand the role of religion and cultural factors in Asia or Latin America, for example, then that is an admission that one knows little about the area. Similarly, one must understand the power of the great motor forces of economic development and industrialization in giving rise to class changes (the rise of an entrepreneurial class, a middle class, and an organized working class), which, in turn, affect politics and political institutions at all levels. At the same time, political institutions are themselves often "independent variables," filtering the process of cultural and political change and shaping the form, direction, and speed of economic development.

Hence, if we ask, as in our chicken-egg dilemma, whether it is culture change that sets the conditions in which economic growth can begin or economic change that changes the culture and the political system, the answer is *both*. That is, culture helps determine the form of the economy and, at the same time, is itself changed by economic growth. Meanwhile, political factors affect both culture and the economy and are, in turn, changed by them. Change is, therefore, not one-way or monocausal but multifaceted; the image we should draw on is that of a lattice with multiple routes to development and various crossing members that mutually influence one another.

Having said that, we should also recognize that the relative influence of these three main factors—cultural, socioeconomic, political-structural—as well as doubtless other factors (accidents, biology, chance, and so on) may vary over time and from country to country. Culture may be the most important factor at some points in history; at other times it will be socioeconomic factors; at still others the main forces will be political and institutional. Moreover, in some countries and areas the cultural influences will be stronger, in others the economic forces will be strongest, and so on. It will be up to students of comparative politics to wrestle with these issues, to sort them out, and to try to draw conclusions from them. The issues are complex; those who simply assert the predominance of one factor over another or jump to hasty conclusions about them are probably making an ideological statement rather than engaging in serious scholarship. For *serious* students of comparative politics, these issues, and our minds, must remain open; there is no simple or pat formula. Rather, it is one of the joys and enthusiasms of the field that we must remain open-minded, pragmatic, and always willing to explore new relationships.

The Plan of the Book

Having set forth some of the main themes and issues in comparative politics, we next trace in Chapter 2 the history of the field—its origins, development, and controversies. Chapter 3 focuses on the political development approach, which, with the sudden emergence of scores of new nations onto the world's stage, became the dominant approach of the 1960s. Closely related to the study of political development was the study of political culture (values, beliefs, religion, history, ideas), as described in Chapter 4. With the mounting criticisms of that approach, however, along with the Vietnam War and the national malaise of the 1970s, a host of new and alternative approaches came to the fore, including dependency theory, corporatism, bureaucratic-authoritarianism, political economy, and state–society relations. These newer approaches are analyzed and assessed in Chapter 5.

In Chapters 6 to 9 we move from the major approaches in the field to a consideration of the main contemporary events and issues in today's world of nations. Chapter 6 deals with the issue of the transition to democracy in so many nations: How solid and stable is democracy? How long will it last? Has democracy now emerged as triumphant? What are the differences between former authoritarian and right-wing regimes and former Marxist-Leninist regimes in the transition to democracy? Chapter 7 returns to the Third

World and examines the issue, after some thirty years of experience, of what works in development and what doesn't. Chapter 8 looks at the already developed world: Are we in a new postindustrial world? What are the implications of our new global interdependence? Who is ascendant and who is in decline? What does the future hold? Chapter 9 focuses on new issues in comparative politics, including women and women's movements, comparative environmental policy, the comparative treatment of gays and lesbians, and the comparative policy response to drugs, immigration, and pollution.

Chapter 10, "The Conclusion," returns to many of the themes of this introductory chapter. Having by that point completed our survey of the main approaches in the comparative politics field as well as of the main groups of countries, we look at the common features among nations, their differences, and set forth an argument for theory and comparison at middle-range and other levels.

Comparative politics is a very exciting and innovative field. We hope some of that excitement is contagious.

2

The History of Comparative Politics

Comparative politics has a long and distinguished history dating back to the very origins of systematic political studies in ancient Greece and Rome. Comparative politics is about 2,500 years old—and maybe older. In this chapter we trace the history of the comparative politics field. Our purpose is both to provide a picture of the past and to link the past to the present so as to provide background for today's comparative politics: its origins, its evolution, its assumptions and biases, as well as its accomplishments. Our history begins with the ancient Greeks and carries right up through the 1950s, with the decline of what was called the "traditionalist" school and the triumph of developmentalism. The developmentalist school as well as other contemporary approaches are then treated in subsequent chapters.[1]

The Ancients

One could say that the study of comparative politics goes all the way back to humankind's

---

[1]For more extensive treatment of some of these themes, see Howard J. Wiarda (ed.), *New Directions in Comparative Politics*, rev. ed. (Boulder, CO: Center for International Affairs, Harvard University/ Westview, 1991).

first recorded history—even to prehistory. Even the most ancient of peoples, organized as clans, tribes, or extended families, compared their situations with those of other peoples with whom they came in contact. They also learned from other peoples.

Domesticated agriculture spread through Europe because of travelers and the increasing contact of the peoples in one region with another; and forms of political organization followed the same routes. War, conquest, commerce, and the immigration of peoples in what are now the Middle East, Europe, Asia, Africa, and the Americas provided a means by which people moved, were uprooted, compared, and learned from the experience of others. In this sense we can say that virtually all learning is by comparison and uses the comparative method.

The Old Testament and the "People of God"

The Bible is perhaps one of the first written statements of comparative politics. Particularly in the Old Testament the prophets are constantly comparing the people of Israel with other peoples: Egyptians, Babylonians, Persians, Canaanites, and so on. Their purpose, of course, was to emphasize the contrasts between the people of God and those who were not of God. The form of government in these ancient times was usually kingship, but the king of Israel was expected to be God fearing. The people of God had to follow Jehovah's way in their political and family life as well as their religious life, the three being inseparable. Their leaders were required to obey God's will if they wished his favors to accrue to them, to abide by God's commandments, and to lead a holy life. The ways of the peoples of God and the benefits showering upon them are compared throughout the Bible with other peoples and religions, who are called "heathen." Comparison therefore had a preeminently religious purpose.

The Spartans: Lycurgus

The earliest *systematic* comparisons of a more modern, secular sort—with virtually all the ingredients of today's comparative politics—were carried out by the ancient Greeks. Plutarch tells the story in his *Lives of the Noble Grecians and Romans*[2] of one Lycurgus, a heroic figure from the Greek city-state (about the size of an American county, with a central city and a surrounding countryside) of Sparta. Lycurgus traveled widely around Greece and the

---

[2]Plutarch, *Lives of the Noble Grecians and Romans* (New York: AMS Press, 1967); see also Thomas Magstadt, *Nations and Governments: Comparative Politics in Regional Perspective* (New York: St. Martin's, 1991), Chapter 1.

eastern Mediterranean studying the workings—the weaknesses as well as the strengths—of various political regimes. We would say that he was engaged in the study of comparative politics. Lycurgus was not just a scholar, however; he had a political purpose in mind. In part because in Sparta slaves outnumbered citizens and there was always fear of a mass uprising, and in part to frighten off potential foes, Lycurgus wanted to create in Sparta a strong, austere, and battle-ready regime. We would call Sparta a "national security state"; it might also be called "lean and mean."

Sparta isolated itself and tried to adapt all aspects of life—economics, marriage, politics, education—to the needs of national security. Sparta became the strongest city-state in ancient Greece, and even today we use the word *spartan* to imply strict discipline, a militaristic spirit, and austere living standards. For just these reasons, Michigan State University's athletic teams are known as "the Spartans." Sparta became for a time an invincible military force, but its entrenched and unchanging conservatism, authoritarianism, and unwillingness to evolve eventually helped undermine its institutions. Lycurgus, whom we can call a political scientist with a comparative politics specialization, was the main intellectual architect of the Spartan system. He was, in a sense, like the biblical prophets: his purpose was not just to study comparative political systems objectively but to apply the knowledge gained to fashion a particular kind of political regime.

The Greeks: Plato and Aristotle

The two foremost political scientists in almost a modern sense in ancient Greece were Plato and Aristotle. Their books, *The Republic of Plato*[3] and Aristotle's *Politics*,[4] are really the beginning of political science as we know it today and among the great books of all time. In these two books the authors cover almost all the key issues of politics: the nature of power and leadership, the different forms of government, the sociological bases of politics, public policy, and so on. Almost all the major controversies about how properly to organize the political system were first presented in these books.

Although Aristotle and Plato shared many ideas and beliefs, their approaches were quite different. These differences also have contemporary relevance, helping to account for the differences we still see among students in the field. Aristotle was more a "scientist," a collector of facts (including constitutions), an empirical academic, a chronicler, a serious scholar. By con-

---

[3] *The Republic of Plato*, trans. Francis M. Cornford (London: Oxford University Press, 1945); various editions.
[4] *The Politics of Aristotle*, ed. and trans. Ernest Barker (New York: Oxford University Press, 1958); various editions.

trast, Plato, although also a serious scholar, had a political agenda. He believed that society should be governed by a political elite, which he called "philosopher-kings"—persons who were well educated, who knew what was best for society, who were guided and instructed by the best minds around (presumably, himself).

For our purposes, what is especially important about Aristotle and Plato is their analysis of comparative political systems. Aristotle, ever the scientist, had collected approximately 150 of the constitutions of his time, mainly from the Greek city-states but from other areas as well. Aristotle's universe or "laboratory" of cases, therefore, was nearly as large as the 180-odd nation-states that students of comparative politics study today. He studied these constitutions extensively, as well as their social, cultural, and economic underpinnings. He wanted to know (his hypothesis) which form of government was best and most stable, so he began looking at the causes of instability. Both he and Plato (although with variations between them) arrived at a system or scheme for classifying the then-known world's political systems. There could be rule by the one (monarchy), the few (aristocracy), or the many (polity). In turn, these three systems also had their degenerative forms: Monarchy could degenerate into tyranny, aristocracy could become an oppressive oligarchy, and polity could degenerate into anarchic democracy, by which was meant mob rule. These six types of regimes are represented in Table 2.1.

This is a six-part classificatory scheme: three "ideal types" based on the number of persons in command, and then three more degenerative forms. This is a pretty good system of classification; with refinement, it is still sometimes used today. Note the use of "models" or "ideal types" to designate these regimes; the classificatory scheme employed by Aristotle and Plato is thus a model of the kind described in Chapter 1. Note, too, that this is purely a secular political science model: It has no specific religious or teleological significance, although the Greeks were concerned with discovering the "good life." One could do far worse than follow the Greeks in their analysis of comparative political systems.

Table 2.1   The Greek System of Classifying Regimes

Rule by	Called	Degenerative Form
The one	Monarchy	Tyranny
Few	Aristocracy	Oligarchy
Many	Polity	Anarchic democracy (mob rule)

But Aristotle, Plato, and the ancient Greeks were not through yet. They had compared the then-known city-states in terms of the number of rulers and analyzed both their pure and their degenerative forms. They also analyzed their cases in terms of their modes of operations—whether they were run by popular rule at the grass roots level or from above by an elite. They further examined the class structure and socioeconomic bases of power in the different city-states. Aristotle then related the results of his classificatory scheme to the issue of stability/instability (his original hypothesis) to see which kind of political system—judged by number of rulers, mode of operation, and class structure—was least or most stable. He found that pure democracies or pure oligarchies were the most unstable while systems that combined aspects of polity and aristocracy and that also had a strong middle class were the most stable. In his analysis, in keeping with his scientific orientation, Aristotle reached some conclusions or generalizations that followed from his evidence and that also explained what causes stability or instability. Hence, almost all the ingredients of systematic comparative politics— hypotheses, testing, analysis, generalization—are evident in Aristotle's work; and the basic logic of comparative politics as an enterprise and method of inquiry is present.

The Romans: Cicero

The Greek city-state, however, was already in decline at the time that Aristotle wrote. It was replaced by the system of *empire*, first the Macedonian empire under Alexander the Great and then the great Roman empire encompassing the entire Mediterranean region and much of what is now Western Europe. As these great empires conquered and absorbed the city-states, there were fewer and fewer cases to compare; the focus of political analysis thus became politics *within* the empire rather than comparisons between discrete political systems. The peoples living on the edges of these empires were subject to conquest and absorption within the larger entity, as distinct from the more scientific and value-free *observations* of other peoples and their institutions made by Aristotle. Hence, during the Macedonian and Roman empires, and then during the Middle Ages, comparative politics, as Plato and Aristotle had conceived it, would all but disappear for the next 1,500 years.

Cicero was the foremost Roman political theorist; he initially employed basically the same six-part classificatory scheme as had Aristotle and Plato. But Cicero was not so much interested in classification as he was in analyzing the best possible form for the Roman republic. Cicero's contribution to comparative politics was his arguments, initially found in Aristotle, for a mixed form of constitution, employing both aristocratic and civic features, and his theory of the historical cycle and evolution of constitutions. But Cicero's main contribution to general political theory was his emphasis on natural law (law that is inherent in nature or in the ordering of the universe) as the basis of political life, a concept that would remain dominant in Western political philosophy at least until the nineteenth century. In Cicero this took the form of an admiration for republicanism, which he felt had its basis in "nature," but in subsequent centuries natural law would form the basis of the Christian covenant of the Middle Ages.

The Middle Ages: Christianity

The rise of Christianity led to a greater emphasis on the spiritual life and a lesser emphasis on the secular or political. The "city of God" took precedence over the "city of man." Hence, there was very little study of other political systems for their own sake, nor was the emphasis on the classification of political systems. Rather, the Christian fathers of the Middle Ages—Augustine, Thomas Aquinas, and others—already "knew" the answers. Their goal was to establish a Christian, God-centered kingdom, not to study a variety of political regimes and compare them scientifically for their best and worst features. Augustine, for example, put forth the conception of a Christian commonwealth as the best and *only* appropriate form of political organization. He coupled this with a philosophy of history that presented the Christian commonwealth as the culmination of history, God's plan for the universe, and man's spiritual development. Saint Thomas further systematized these arguments, gave them the weight of history and Greek logic, and provided a powerful foundation for the establishment of a universal Christian state. Because of Augustine's and Thomas's authority and that of the other Church fathers, this conception became an integral part of Christian thought, not only during the Middle Ages but even into modern times. Protestant as well as Catholic thinkers were powerfully influenced by Augustine's and Aquinas's writings on this subject. The Augustinian-Thomistic conception served to advance the cause of a universal *Christian* community; it was not very much interested in the value-free study of comparative politics.

The Moderns

The field of comparative anthropological studies was very much stimulated in modern times by Columbus's discovery of, and encounter with, America and the increasing contact of Western Europeans with native peoples. Some of the earliest and best anthropological field studies were carried out by the friars who accompanied the explorers to the New World.

At about the same time, comparative *political* studies were again stimulated by the rise of the European nation-state and the breakup of monolithic medieval Catholicism during the Protestant Reformation of the sixteenth century. Portugal, Spain, France, England, Holland, Belgium, eventually Italy, Germany, Sweden, and others began to emerge as separate political entities with their own cultures and political institutions. The Protestant Reformation accelerated this process by identifying these emerging nation-states with distinct religious beliefs (generally Protestantism in the north of Europe, Catholicism in the south) as well as distinct cultural and institutional forms.

These developments, naturally, gave rise to comparisons: between the Prot-estant and the Catholic countries; between the north and south of Europe; between Portugal and Spain, Spain and Italy, Spain and France, France and England, England and Holland, Holland and the several German provinces, and so on. Particularly during the Renaissance and the scientific revolution ushered in by Galileo and Newton, political analysis began again to take a scientific and secular orientation unencumbered by religious preconceptions or constraints.

Machiavelli, who wrote in the early sixteenth century, is usually considered the first modern political scientist.[5] Machiavelli is thought of as "modern" precisely because his writing is so secular; he analyzes power in a dispassionate, cool, calculating manner largely devoid of moral, ethical, or religious presuppositions—unless those, too, could be used as tools of political manipulation. Machiavelli is usually thought of as a great political theorist, which he was; but he was also—maybe preeminently—a student of comparative politics.

Machiavelli's main goal was the unification of his native Italy and the restoration of Italy to its ancient Roman glory. To that end Machiavelli not only shrewdly analyzed political power—how to get it, wield it, and maintain it—but also analyzed the successful princes (hence the title of his classic work, *The Prince*) who achieved national unification. His favorite case (and model) was Ferdinand of Aragon who, along with his wife Isabella of Castile, had succeeded in unifying Spain—indeed, had helped make Spain the foremost power of the sixteenth century. Ferdinand and Isabella had shrewdly manipulated the Catholic Church, the nobility, and the military orders in their drive to unify Spain, and Machiavelli admired and analyzed Ferdinand's and Isabella's political skills and accomplishments in these regards. Interesting for us is Machiavelli's conscious use of the comparative method to study what other princes had done and what could be applied to Italy.

Not everyone agreed with Machiavelli's purely secular analysis, of course, or of his separation of politics and morality. In Spain, Portugal, and their

---

[5]Machiavelli, *"The Prince" and Other Works*, trans. Allan H. Gilbert (New York: Hendricks House, 1946); various editions.

colonies in Latin America, and in other countries as well, Catholicism continued to be the foundation of political beliefs. Their systems continued to be based on the writings of Augustine, Thomas Aquinas, and the Church fathers. The political system had to be grounded on "right reason," on Christian morality, on the Thomistic hierarchy of laws and persons. This was the ideology of neoscholasticism, of the counter-Reformation; its chief sixteenth-century spokesman was Francisco Suárez. So while Machiavelli and other secular political philosophers held sway in some countries, Aquinas's and Suárez's ideas continued to dominate in others, providing a religious, ideological, and political split between the north and south of Europe, and between North and Latin America, that continued into the twentieth century. This tradition of thought and the political systems based on it remains woefully understudied in comparative politics.

Thomas Hobbes was a seventeenth-century English political philosopher.[6] In contrast to Machiavelli, Hobbes was a conservative; in contrast to Suárez, he was a secular writer. For him the best political system could not be conceived apart from order and authority. Hobbes lived during a time of tremendous disorder: the Protestant Revolution in England of the 1640s and 1650s, the beheading of King Charles I, and the civil war of 1642–1648. For Hobbes, anarchy such as this was the great enemy of progress and civilization. He was appalled at the sweeping away of the ancient customs and ways of doing things during this turbulent period, and his classic book *Leviathan* of 1651 is a powerful defense of security and authority. In contrast to some of his contemporaries, Hobbes believed that in a "state of nature" such as that ushered in with the English civil war, "life would be solitary, poor, nasty, brutish, and short." Only a powerful state could prevent anarchy and keep in check humans' unruly nature.

Hobbes was not a comparativist in the same way that Machiavelli was. He was trained in the classics, he drew on examples from other societies, and his book aspired to universal norms; but his case study material was largely drawn from his native England. He did not, like Aristotle, endeavor systematically to study other nations and to draw from them laws of political behavior governing all nations. Rather, he presented a model of the political system that he presumed would have universal applicability. Hobbes's methodology was more deductive, abstracting from logical analysis of a single case to a more general and presumably global set of laws of political behavior, as contrasted with Machiavelli's more empirical inductive method.

John Locke followed Hobbes, in terms of both chronology (about forty years later) and methodology.[7] By Locke's time the English civil war of the

---

[6]Thomas Hobbes, *The Leviathan* (London: Everyman, 1964); various editions.
[7]John Locke, *Two Treatises of Government*, ed. William Carpenter (New York: Dutton, Everyman, 1924); various editions.

mid–seventeenth century had been contained, and things had settled down. In contrast to Hobbes, whose purpose was to defend the order and authority of the old regime, Locke sought to channel the new regime in the direction of representative government. Although both Hobbes and Locke still had numerous religious references in their arguments, both were thoroughly modern political scientists: The case that each made was based on logic, natural law, and secular arguments rather than religious ones.

Locke is considered the apostle of American liberalism—not liberalism in its present partisan form but in the sense of standing for limited government, a system of checks and balances, and representative rule. Like Hobbes, he was not, strictly speaking, a comparativist. However, the arguments and logic he set forth, based largely on the English experience, were presumed to have universal applicability. Thus, when the U.S. Department of State or the U.S. Agency for International Development (AID) attempt to spread U.S. ideas and institutions of democracy abroad, they still rely largely on Locke's ideas. Many comparativists believe that the Lockean ideas are appropriate for Great Britain and the United States, but, as we see in more detail in Chapter 3, they may be less appropriate for the rest of the world, where the culture, history, and institutions are often quite different.

The eighteenth-century French *philosophe* Montesquieu is the next great comparativist.[8] Unlike Hobbes or Locke, who focused on one country but assumed it had universal validity, Montesquieu, a product of the Enlightenment, was a true comparativist. In his book *The Spirit of the Laws*, Montesquieu attempted to move beyond the constitutional procedures of a country to examine its inderlying culture and "spirit." His greatest contribution to the field was his model for the separation of powers that influenced the U.S. system. Part of Montesquieu's focus was on climate as well as culture; he sought to link these to political outcomes. He argued, for example, that despotism was more likely in tropical climates than in cold ones and that liberty was more natural in temperate latitudes. Hot regions, he believed, promoted indolence as well as authoritarianism. He suggested that if the climate induces people to shun hard labor, then the religion of the country ought to energize them to it; and so he criticized Indian Hinduism because it taught passivity, thus reinforcing the indolence brought on by hot temperatures.

Undoubtedly, climate affects food production; geographic location can cause droughts, floods, and other natural disasters; and hot climates produce more intestinal diseases and debilitating maladies. However, no one believes anymore that climate per se produces laziness or that democracy cannot flourish in tropical locations. Historically, when agriculture was the only economic base of society, Montesquieu's arguments might have had greater

---

[8]Montesquieu, *The Spirit of the Laws*, trans. Thomas Nugent (New York: Hafner, 1949).

validity; but not today. That is, in effect, to assert that Brazilians, Indians, Costa Ricans, Venezuelans, and so on, cannot have democracy because of their climate, when in fact all of these countries today are functioning democracies. Montesquieu is probably on the right track in suggesting that geography and culture *influence* politics, but they do not determine it.

Jean-Jacques Rousseau was both a comparativist and a philosopher of natural law.[9] In contrast to Hobbes, he believed that at birth human beings are good; it is only through education and experience that they come to be greedy, acquisitive, and power-hungry. Hence, he imagined a "state of nature" in which people would live together harmoniously and in accord with their true natures. Private property, according to Rousseau, was one of those institutions that taught people to be greedy and thus should be abolished; people should also learn to respect nature rather than exploit it for short-term gain. In Rousseau's political system, however, power was invested in a small elite who would *know* the general will (unlike Locke's system, in which this was periodically tested through elections) and would rule *for* (not "of" and "by") the rest of the population. Hence, Rousseau's plan is often thought of as a forerunner of modern totalitarianism in which the leadership also presumes to know what the people want without bothering to "ask them" by holding elections.

With Karl Marx in the nineteenth century we come to a quite new tradition in political thought that also had important implications for comparative politics.[10] Like Rousseau, Marx was convinced of the evils of private property, but he went beyond Rousseau in claiming to have discovered scientific *laws* of societal development. In Marx's scheme history was driven by economic forces, the class structure, and those who controlled the means of production and distribution. Moreover, history proceeded dialectically (thesis → antithesis → synthesis) through the stages of slavery, feudalism, capitalism, and eventually to socialism, which represented the end product of the dialectic. According to Marx, it was the economic substructure that determined the political superstructure. For our purposes, that means in slave societies politics would be controlled by the slave owners, in feudalism by the landowners, under capitalism by the industrialists or the bourgeoisie, and under socialism by the people (the masses). In short, for Marx politics became a dependent variable, while economics was the independent variable.

Very few serious scholars accept the complete Marxian analysis uncritically anymore. Marxian economics has proved to be a disaster for all who have tried it, the dialectic has not followed the inevitable route that Marx

---

[9]Jean-Jacques Rousseau, *The First and Second Discourses*, ed. Roger D. Masters and Judith Masters (New York: St. Martin's, 1964).

[10]Karl Marx and Friedrich Engels, *Basic Writings in Politics and Philosophy*, ed. Lewis Feuer (Garden City, NY: Doubleday, 1959).

predicted, and economic determinism is far too simple an explanation of how societies do in fact change. Most social scientists, while acknowledging the value of the emphasis on economic factors stressed by Marxism, hold a more complex, multicausal view of history than the monocausal view of Marx. Moreover, political scientists, naturally enough, tend to emphasize the autonomy and independence of political factors and institutions rather than their complete subordination to economic forces. Most political scientists acknowledge the contribution to the field made by Marx, as by the other writers surveyed here, but few of them accept his whole scheme.

The main answers to Marx came from the German Max Weber, on the one hand, and the English utilitarians and liberals, on the other. Thoroughly modern in his approach, Weber wrestled with contemporary industrial and bureaucratic life, emphasizing the complex multicausality of historical change.[11] Weber's own writings tended to focus on the influence of cultural and religious factors on political and economic life, but he also acknowledged the immense driving powers of capitalism and industrialization. He explored the Protestant Reformation and its contribution to the rationalization of European society, which led to the Industrial Revolution; he also studied Hinduism, Confucianism, Islam, and Buddhism to provide comparative contrasts.

Like Marx, Weber also set forth a developmentalist view of history, but his emphasis was on political and bureaucratic rather than economic forces: traditional forms of authority sanctioned usually by religious precepts in the early stages of a nation's development, populist or charismatic leadership during the transitional phase, and rational-legal or bureaucratic authority at a more developed state. Note that this latter three-part classification is often used by social scientists in studying the development of today's emerging nations; Weber's stress on the complex multicausality of most historical events is also appealing to contemporary students of comparative politics.

The English utilitarians stressed "the greatest good for the greatest number" as their test of public policy and were thoroughly pragmatic in their approach to politics.[12] The utilitarians believed that the value of anything, including political institutions, is to be judged by its ability to bring pleasure or happiness to people. They saw the institutions of democracy and representative rule as the best way to achieve these goals. Meanwhile, modern English and American liberalism itself, now considerably updated from the writings of Locke or, in the American tradition, Jefferson and Madison, came to stress social welfare, more participatory democracy, and societal as well as

---

[11]Max Weber, *The Theory of Social and Economic Organization*, ed. Talcott Parsons (New York: Macmillan, 1964).

[12]John Plamenetz, *The English Utilitarians* (London: Oxford University Press, 1949).

political pluralism. Along with Weber's developmentalist scheme and his multicausality, these latter institutions of modern liberalism had a major impact on comparative politics, especially on its efforts, beginning in the 1960s, both to analyze and to aid development in the Third World.

One other strain of thought commands our attention here: the attempt of some early European writers to understand *America* in a comparative perspective. The two most prominent were Alexis d' Tocqueville, a Frenchman, and Lord James Bryce, an Englishman. Tocqueville had previously written books about France and the French Revolution of 1789; but in the 1830s (the time of Andrew Jackson), he spent several years in the United States and then published a masterful book entitled *Democracy in America*, which analyzed the assumptions and workings of the American system.[13] Bryce's *Modern Democracies*, published in 1891, is a comparative study that has also achieved the level of a classic.[14] It can be said that in these and other works the study of the American political system is most enriched when a comparative perspective is used to analyze it.

The prior discussion has surveyed some of the classic writings, the pioneers, in comparative politics. It provides setting and context for the analysis of comparative politics themes in the rest of the book. We now move from the general to the specific by focusing on the development of comparative politics as a separate field of study in the political science departments of most American colleges and universities.

Comparative Politics in American Universities

Courses on "Foreign Governments" were offered in a few American universities as early as the 1890s. Or else, as in Woodrow Wilson's *The State* (1889), the European experience was used to shed light on the traditions of American democracy.[15] The courses on foreign governments in these early days concentrated almost exclusively on the European countries, primarily Britain and France. Great Britain was, of course, a fellow English-speaking country, the source of many of our political and constitutional ideas, and the destination of most Americans when they traveled abroad—if they traveled abroad at all. France was the most accessible continental country and a font of culture and civilization; its unstable parliamentarism was usually contrasted with the more stable British version as well as with American presidentialism.

---

[13]Alexis d' Tocqueville, *Democracy in America* (New York: Knopf, 1960).
[14]James Bryce, *Modern Democracies* (New York: Macmillan, 1924).
[15]Woodrow Wilson, *The State*, rev. ed. (Boston, NY: Heath, 1918). Woodrow Wilson was the first political scientist to become president of the United States.

However, it was not until the aftermath of World War I, which thrust America onto the world stage and made it a world power, that comparative politics emerged as a separate field within the political science discipline and that the range of camparisons began to grow. There now began to be separate panels at the Annual Meeting of the American Political Science Association on comparative politics; some political scientists began describing themselves as students of comparative politics—at that time, actually, called "comparative government." At the same time, the number of countries covered began to grow as well: Germany, now that it was unified and a major power; sometimes Italy, now also unified and under Mussolini's fascism; and the Soviet Union following the Communist revolution of 1917.

The focus of comparative government in the period between World Wars I and II was (as the title implies) on the formal-legal aspects of government. Political scientists in the comparative field mainly studied the laws and constitutions of the countries with which they were concerned. They looked at how the *government* system operated: the powers of the House of Parliament, of the House of Lords, of the French parliament; executive-legislative relations; local government; the judiciary; electoral laws; and so on. Some attention was devoted to political parties, especially in England and France. But little attention was paid to political dynamics such as public opinion, interest group activity, the processes of change, decision making, political behavior, or public policy. In part, this reflected the lack of research and literature on these topics more generally in the political science discipline; in part, it reflected the difficulties of carrying out research in foreign countries in this pre–jet travel era.[16]

World War II had a profound effect on comparative politics in a number of ways:

1. It introduced the phenomenon of totalitarianism as practiced in Nazi Germany and fascist Italy.[17] Some scholars extended the analysis to include Stalin's Soviet Union also, so that the totalitarianism phenomenon encompassed both right- and left-wing regimes.[18]

2. It considerably expanded our interest in and knowledge of other countries. Some comparative politics courses now began to be offered for the first time on China and Japan, Latin America, Scandinavia, and the British Commonwealth (Canada, New Zealand, Australia, India, and others).

---

[16]A good example of the formal-legal approach is S. E. Finer, *Comparative Government* (Baltimore: Penguin, 1970).

[17]Hannah Arendt, *The Origins of Totalitarianism* (New York: Harcourt, Brace, 1971).

[18]Carl J. Friedrich and Zbigniew Brzezinski, *Totalitarian Dictatorship and Autocracy* (New York: Praeger, 1962).

3. It brought to the United States many European refugees from fascism. Many of these were highly educated or acquired advanced degrees in American universities. Many of them also brought detailed knowledge of the European legal and political systems from which they had come.

The period after World War II witnessed several major developments in comparative politics. First, the number of countries covered continued to expand—albeit slowly. In addition to new courses on Asia, Latin America, or Scandinavia, in some universities courses were developed on Eastern Europe (the Soviet bloc), Southern Europe (Portugal, Spain, Italy, Greece, Turkey), or comparative communism (the Soviet Union, China, Eastern Europe). Second, the field began—again, slowly—to be influenced by the shift in American political science toward the study of political behavior (as distinct from the formal-legal approach) and informal political processes such as interest group lobbying or decision making, and the use of more rigorous research designs and methodologies.[19] Third, now influenced by the cold war as well as the Nazi experience, the totalitarianism phenomenon remained a major focus. And fourth, the field continued to be enriched by the work and insights of European immigrants, whose main interest, naturally enough, was often the countries from which they had come.

During most of the 1950s, the field retained its European and its formal-legal focus. Most of the European scholars who came to the United States, after all, had been trained in law; political science as a separate discipline was at that time still not taught in the European universities. So, not surprisingly, much of the writing in the field continued to concentrate on comparative constitutions, comparative legal systems (common law versus civil law),[20] various institutions of government (parliament, executive, judiciary), and the structure (as distinct from the *processes*) of government. Within this focus there were important innovations: comparative studies of legislatures, of federalism in different countries, of legal restraints on interest group or political party activities, of the impact of distinct types of electoral systems, of bureaucracies and their role.[21] Nevertheless, the main emphasis was still the formal-legal institutions of government.

Some scholars sought to bridge the gap between formal-legalism and the new emphasis on informal processes that was beginning to bubble up in American political science. For example, Karl Loewenstein, a brilliant

---

[19]Heinz Eulau, *The Behavioral Persuasion in Politics* (New York: Random House, 1963).
[20]John Henry Merryman, *The Civil Law Tradition* (Stanford, CA: Stanford University Press, 1969).
[21]Maurice Duverger, *Political Parties* (New York: Wiley, 1954); Ivo D. Duchacek, *Comparative Federalism* (New York: Holt, Rinehart & Winston, 1970); K. C. Wheare, *Legislatures* (New York: Oxford University Press, 1963).

scholar at Amherst College (and in the 1920s the last student of the great sociologist Max Weber in Germany), was originally trained in law in Germany. But because of Weber's influence, Loewenstein's early writings in Germany contained many sociological themes—for which he was severely criticized by his German legal colleagues as violating what was called the "pure theory of law." Later on, Loewenstein emigrated to the United States, but in this country his writings were criticized within the political science profession as "too legalistic."[22] "Too sociological" for the Germans and "too legalistic" for the Americans, Loewenstein was in a sense caught between two academic cultures. But his story is also significant in light of the fresh winds that were beginning to blow through the field.

The early to mid-1950s witnessed increasing discontent in the comparative politics field over its continued emphasis on the formal-legal and constitutional aspects of government. The discontent came from a new generation of scholars, trained after World War II, who were also influenced by the focus in American political science on the more informal aspects of politics and by what was called the "behavioral revolution" (an emphasis on political behavior rather than institutions) in political science. A number of these "young Turks" met at Northwestern University in 1952 to vent their frustrations with the field; the next year they published a calm, reasoned report on their views in the *American Political Science Review*.[23] Over the next few years other expressions of discontent were heard as well.

Not until 1955, however, with the publication of a little book by Roy Macridis of Brandeis University, did the field begin to turn around.[24] Macridis's critique was sharp and stinging; it was in the nature of a polemic. He argued that the field of comparative politics was tired and old-fashioned, that it had not kept pace with the newer currents in political science. Specifically, he charged that comparative politics was:

1. parochial—it focused on Europe far too much, to the exclusion of other areas;

2. descriptive rather than genuinely analytical;

3. formalistic and legalistic, instead of concentrating on the more informal and dynamic processes of politics;

[22]Karl Loewenstein, *Political Power and the Governmental Process* (Chicago: University of Chicago Press, 1957).

[23]Social Science Research Council, Interuniversity Research Seminar on Comparative Politics, "Research in Comparative Politics," *American Political Science Review* 47 (September 1953): 641–65.

[24]Roy Macridis, *The Study of Comparative Government* (New York: Random House, 1955).

4. not really comparative at all but dominated mostly by case studies; and

5. too often anecdotal rather than systematic.

The Macridis criticism of the field was strongly worded and somewhat overstated (for the sake of more dramatically making the case), posed the issues in stark, either-or terms, and had an enormous influence on the field. Put out in paperback form, his little monograph was probably read by every teacher and aspiring graduate student in comparative politics. Henceforth, the view that comparative politics should be nonparochial or inclusive of more countries, genuinely analytical, focused on more informal political processes, genuinely comparative, and systematic became the dominant view in the field.

In the aftermath of Macridis's book, comparative politics underwent a major shift in emphasis. Symbolizing that change was how the field came to be known: no longer comparative *government* but now comparative *politics*, a term with more dynamic, informal, and process connotations. Of course, some of the older, senior scholars in the field, ignoring the Macridis critique, continued to write as they always had, emphasizing formal-legal aspects or focusing on their own narrow research interests. Among the younger generation of rising scholars, however, the Macridis criticism—which was no longer limited to one man but was now widespread within the discipline—was enormously influential. Comparative politics would never be the same again.

Meanwhile, other developments in the field would have important implications later on. First, in the mid-1950s David Easton began publishing an influential series of works tying the various aspects of political life together as a *system*.[25] His analysis, which included "inputs" (culture, history, interest groups, political parties, and the like), decision making, and outputs (government decisions or policies), was very similar to the organizational scheme presented in Chapter 1 and served as a useful way to see the different parts of the political system as an integrated whole. Second, Gabriel Almond, utilizing Easton's scheme, began focusing on the common *functions* that all political systems performed and thus laid the basis for a truly global comparative politics.[26] Third, there was new research and emphasis on comparative interest groups and other more informal aspects of politics.[27]

The Macridis critique and the accompanying revolution in comparative politics happened to occur at the same time—the late 1950s and early 1960s—

---

[25]David Easton, "An Approach to the Study of Political Systems," *World Politics* 9 (April 1957): 383–400.

[26]Gabriel Almond, "Comparative Political Systems," *Journal of Politics* 18 (August 1956): 391–409.

[27]Henry W. Ehrmann (ed.), *Interest Groups on Four Continents* (Pittsburgh, PA: University of Pittsburgh Press, 1958).

that a host of new nations in Africa, Asia, Latin America, and the Middle East were emerging as independent states. Throwing off the yoke of colonialism, these former dependencies emerged as newly independent countries precisely when the study of comparative politics was being revolutionized. The emergence of these new nations doubled almost literally overnight the number of cases in the comparative politics universe or laboratory. In addition, the themes of new nationhood posed numerous intriguing questions for students of comparative politics, the most important being how to create a strong, viable, prosperous, democratic, and socially just country out of the ruins of colonialism. When this interest was combined in 1960 with the shift in the United States from the rather tired Eisenhower administration to the new and vigorous presidency of John F. Kennedy (which featured the Peace Corps, the Alliance for Progress, and a "pay any costs, conquer every mountain" mentality), it was truly an exciting time for comparative politics. All these themes—the revolution in comparative politics, the host of new nations on the world's stage, and Kennedy's New Frontier—came together in the study of development and the developing nations, the subject of Chapter 3.

3
—

Political Development

We saw in the last chapter that comparative politics has had a long and distinguished history. As it emerged as a separate field in political science in American universities between World Wars I and II, comparative politics was dominated by a formal-legal approach that emphasized constitutions, laws, and the formal procedures of government. That approach continued into the 1950s when it faced a challenge by a younger group of scholars who sought to emphasize the informal processes of politics: public opinion, interest groups, decision making, and the like.

By the late 1950s, there were already several "schools" within the field of comparative politics. Some scholars, whose background often included legal training, continued to do research—often very interesting and valuable research— on what was now considered rather old-fashioned topics by younger scholars: constitutional and governmental institutions. Most of these senior scholars concentrated on European affairs and continued to do the noncomparative, case study projects that Macridis and others had strongly criticized. Other scholars, though not so numerous as those in the first group, were area specialists whose concentrations included "newer" areas such as China,

Japan, the Soviet Union, or Latin America. But there was also a third and younger group beginning to form that was intrigued by the politics of the newly independent and gradually emerging nations in Asia, Africa, and the Middle East. Over the course of the next decade, the 1960s, not only did this group become the most numerous, but its theory and approach—called "political development" and focused on the politics of the developing nations—became the dominant one in the field.

Origins of the Developmentalist Approach

At least seven major influences help explain the new focus in comparative politics on the politics of the developing nations.

The first, already discussed in the previous chapter, was the new emphasis in political science more generally on political behavior and the more informal aspects of politics: political socialization, interest group activity, and decision making. This focus, as we have seen, came at the expense of attention to the more legal-formal aspects of government. But in the developing nations, it was reasoned, the formal rules and constitutions did not work very well anyway. Moreover, with the strong influence in the developing nations of tribal associations, caste associations, and family, clan, and patronage networks, it was appropriate to focus on these informal aspects of politics. In short, political science was already moving toward a focus on informal actors, and in the developing areas, given the weaknesses of laws and constitutions, that focus seemed particularly appropriate.

A second reason for the new interest in the developing nations was the sudden entrance in the late 1950s to early 1960s of a host of new nations onto the world's stage. Several of the Middle Eastern countries had become independent with the breakup of the Ottoman (Turkish) empire in World War I; after World War II India, Pakistan, and several others became independent; the People's Republic of China emerged from the fallout of the Chinese Revolution; Indonesia became independent from Dutch colonial rule in the early 1950s; and Indochina became independent from France. By the late 1950s and on into the early 1960s, a large number of newly independent African and Caribbean, and more Asian and Middle Eastern, nations had emerged onto the scene. The independence of all these new nations more than doubled the number of political entities available for comparative politics to study; it enormously expanded our universe of countries and provided whole new laboratories for the study of political change.[1]

---

[1] Karl Deutsch and William Foltz (eds.), *Nation Building* (New York: Aldine, 1963).

Some distinctions need to be introduced at this point. Most of the Latin American countries had become independent from Spain and Portugal as early as the 1820s, so it was hardly appropriate to lump them together with the new nations. In addition, Latin America was at that time considerably more developed economically and institutionally than was most of Asia and Africa, occupying intermediary or middle-level positions in most of our indices, so it was not useful either to consider all these nations together with the poorer, less institutionalized developing nations. Because Latin America didn't fit very well in the "new nation" category, it was either left out of or treated peripherally in most of the books dealing with development produced during this period. The same was often true for such nations as Iran, India, and Egypt: These were old cultures and civilizations dating back thousands of years, with proud and sometimes glorious histories. They often resented being included with the other "new nations" that lacked their long histories, and they were sometimes especially resentful of the United States and its scholarship for using the "developing nations" designation. After all, U.S. history spanned only two hundred to three hundred years as compared with their thousands, so who were the Americans or U.S. professors to treat them disparagingly and lump them with nations that lacked similar backgrounds or histories?

A third reason for the focus on the developing nations had to do with the former colonial powers themselves. As Belgium, France, Great Britain, the Netherlands, and eventually (the mid-1970s) Portugal withdrew from their colonial possessions, they often sought to keep in place both a political system and a framework for change that would protect their long-term interests. Developmentalism seemed to serve that purpose since it provided for cooperation with rather than hatred toward the former colonial masters and since it seemed a reasonable, centrist, nonradical formula for growth. Already we see that developmentalism had political purposes as well as strictly academic ones.

A fourth reason for comparative politics' focus on the "new" or "developing" nations was the growing influence of new academic hybrids in the social sciences that seemed particularly appropriate for studying the developing nations. Here we have in mind the emerging fields of cultural anthropology, political anthropology, political sociology, and political economy. In the developing nations, less institutionalized, less specialized, and generally less egalitarian and democratic than the nations of the West, it was almost impossible to separate social position based on family, clan, or patronage headship from political power, or to separate economic wealth from political influence. Hence, the fields of political anthropology, political sociology, and political economy, then coming into their own in any case and *combining* the insights of anthropology, sociology, economics, and politics, offered particularly useful categories and ideas for the study of the developing nations.

A fifth important reason was U.S. government policy. With the Chinese (Communist) Revolution in the late 1940s, North Korea's invasion of South Korea in 1950, and the attraction of socialism as an ideology and Marxism-Leninism as a formula for seizing and holding power in many developing nations, the United States became worried. It feared that unless the West offered an attractive alternative, much of the developing world would be tempted to socialist solutions and would provide the Soviet Union with important allies and access to immense natural resources in the cold war. Hence, as early as 1952, the U.S. government began meeting with economists and students of comparative politics to try to devise a foreign policy strategy for dealing with the new or developing nations and to fashion a model or ideology of development that would serve as an alternative to Marxism. This effort received added impetus after the Bandung (Indonesia) conference of 1956, which gave rise to the nonaligned movement (what we would today call the *South* of poor, developing nations) and which was strongly sympathetic to socialism and strongly critical of the United States. Hence, the U.S. government (often using CIA money) began during this time to fund various centers for the study of international affairs that focused on the developing nations, asked scholars to provide an alternative, noncommunist model of development, and, with Castro's revolution in Cuba in 1959, provided fellowship programs for a whole generation of young graduate students to study the developing nations.[2]

Once again, some further explanation and distinctions are necessary. Nothing is wrong with the U.S. government getting involved in these issues of the future of the developing nations. It is in our interest to know as much as we can about these nations and the development processes involved. However, it was probably not appropriate to covertly use CIA money for these purposes, and, as we see later on, the U.S. government's involvement probably skewed the research results in various ways. Moreover, it must be emphasized that the scholars of development who worked on these matters were not of one mind on the issues. Some were idealistically committed to the developing nations and wanted only to help them out, while others were cynically intent on using the focus on development as a way of manipulating the emerging nations for purely cold war and ideological purposes. But the vast majority of scholars who got involved in these programs wanted to serve both purposes at once and saw no contradiction or incompatibility between them. That is, they wanted both to assist the developing nations in advancing

---

[2]Max F. Millikan and W. W. Rostow, *A Proposal: Key to an Effective Foreign Policy* (New York: Harper, 1957); also Irene I. Gendzier, *Managing Political Change: Social Scientists and the Third World* (Boulder, CO: Westview, 1985).

their economies and building democratic institutions *and* at the same time to assist U.S. foreign policy by putting forward a noncommunist model of development. They believed their idealistic goal of advancing development would also assist U.S. foreign policy goals, which they identified with the same purpose.

Note that this position stands in marked contrast to, and is less simplistic than, the inaccurate charges of some radical critics, who argue that the United States and the scholars of development wanted to keep the new nations poor and "in chains."[3] In fact, nothing could be further from the truth: Both the U.S. government and the scholars it supported wanted the developing nations to advance and develop, and they saw such development as the best way to guard against Marxian advances. Thus, they put forward a positive model of development, an alternative to Marxism to be sure, but one based on the notion that the developing nations and U.S. policy interests would *both* be best served by a strategy that advanced development rather than holding it back.

A sixth reason for the new interest in the developing areas was the sheer excitement of it. Here were fifty to sixty new nations that no one had ever studied before. There were neither theories nor models to work with, nor much factual knowledge about them. Here was a chance to do truly pioneering work in unexplored research terrains. To a scholar, this is heady, exciting stuff. This was a chance to advance and test new concepts, to acquire new knowledge of countries few people had studied or written about before—a chance to be an innovator. Few scholars could resist those attractions.

The final factor, stimulating research on the developing nations, was modern jet travel. In the late 1950s to early 1960s, when all these new nations were emerging, commercial jet travel was becoming widespread for the first time. A few years earlier, for example, it would have taken three or four days to travel by propeller plane from the United States to Jakarta, Indonesia. Now all these research sites in Africa, Latin America, the Middle East, and Asia were only one day away or less. Plus, there was new research money for scholars to undertake the travel. Whereas before a scholar of comparative politics had been able to spend a year or even a few months in a new country maybe once or twice in a lifetime, now, with jet travel and adequate research funds, he or she could go abroad for extended periods virtually every year—often several times per year. Thus, not only could the researcher keep current on a favorite research country, but it also became possible to study several countries and areas at the same time. The revolution in modern travel enormously facilitated the ability to do comparative politics.

---

[3] Noam Chomsky and Edward Hermann, *After the Cataclysm: Postwar Indochina and the Construction of Implied Ideology* (Boston: South End Press, 1979).

The Early Development Literature

The Economists

The earliest literature on development was written by economists. The main contributors were Karl Polanyi, who wrote a classic book around the time of World War II on European industrialization[4]; Everett von Hagen and Bruce Morris, who wrote in the 1950s on economic development[5]; and Robert Heilbroner and W. W. Rostow, who similarly wrote on global economic development but were also concerned with the emerging nations.[6]

All of these books used Europe or the United States as their models of how economic development occurs. That was quite natural given that there were abundant data about Europe and the United States, scholars knew and understood their historical patterns of development, and these were considered the most developed regions at that time. It was simply assumed (and the terms used reinforced those assumptions) that the "less developed countries" (they were no longer called "backward" or "primitive") would follow the same general path as the already developed ones. Europe and the United States would provide the examples, and the emerging nations, it was assumed, would follow the same trajectory and thus be able to "catch up." The model employed, of course, was one of liberal capitalism or perhaps a mixed form of capitalism combined with some elements of socialism and central planning. But the question of whether the new, emerging nations would, inevitably, follow the European or U.S. model—or whether that model was even appropriate given these countries' vast cultural and other differences in relation to the West—should have remained an open one.

Another problem, common to economists, was their inattention to political factors and the assumption—a large one, as it turned out—that social and political development would *inevitably* follow from economic growth. The economists who formulated the first plans for development in the emerging nations thought, again using the European and U.S. models, that the motor forces of economic growth and industrialization would inevitably give rise to a new entrepreneurial class, a moderate middle class, and organized labor and farmer groups that would in turn produce stable, responsive, pluralist,

---

[4]Karl Polanyi, *The Great Transformation: The Political and Economic Origins of Our Time* (Boston: Rinehart, 1944).

[5]Everett von Hagen, *On the Theory of Social Change: How Economic Growth Begins* (Homewood, IL: Dorsey, 1962); Bruce Morris, *Economic Growth and Development* (New York: Pitman, 1967).

[6]Robert Heilbroner, *The Great Ascent* (New York: Harper & Row, 1963); W. W. Rostow, *The Stages of Economic Growth: A Non-Communist Manifesto* (Cambridge: Cambridge University Press, 1960).

democratic governments. In much of the Third World, however, this "inevitable" progression toward pluralism, moderation, and democracy did not occur. Rather, economic and social change gave rise to radicalism on the one hand or authoritarianism on the other, at least as much as to democracy. Moreover, a good case can be made that the causation should be exactly reversed from what it was in the early development literature: that first a decent *political system* needed to be put in place, one that was really interested in and committed to economic development and pluralism (instead of simply using government power to attain personal wealth). In the short run at least, there was very little that was inevitable in the developing nations about economic growth automatically producing pluralism and a democracy that looked "just like ours."

The Sociologists

The next group to weigh in on development themes was the sociologists. Here one thinks primarily of Talcott Parsons,[7] Daniel Lerner,[8] Seymour M. Lipset,[9] and (although he was a political scientist) Karl Deutsch.[10] Parsons was a "grand theorist" at Harvard who never spent any time in the developing world but who nevertheless advanced a set of categories for comparing "modern" and "traditional" societies that he presented as having universal validity. He called these categories "pattern variables." Parsons suggested that traditional societies are based on ascription (birth, family name, clan or tribe), whereas modern societies are based on merit; that traditional societies are particularistic or parochial (closed, narrow, confined, limited) in their viewpoints, whereas modern societies are based on universal values; and that traditional societies are "functionally diffuse" (military, political, and economic functions may get all mixed up), whereas more developed societies are functionally specific and differentiated (see Table 3.1).

These are probably useful contrasts in some ways. In reality, however, most societies are complex mixtures of ascription and merit, of particularism and universalism, and of diffuseness and specificity. Nor in the Parsons scheme is there any indication of how societies move from one form to another (the assumption is, once again, inevitably, through economic development) or of why these three traits should be singled out and not others. In addition, the distinction between traditional and modern is too absolute, and it often produced

---

[7]Talcott Parsons, *The Social System* (Glencoe, IL: Free Press, 1951): Talcott Parsons and Edwards Shils (eds.), *Toward a General Theory of Action* (Cambridge, MA: Harvard University Press, 1951).

[8]Daniel Lerner, *The Passing of Traditional Society* (New York: Free Press, 1958).

[9]Seymour M. Lipset, "Some Social Requisites of Democracy: Economic Development and Political Legitimacy," *American Political Science Review* 53 (March 1959): 69–105.

[10]Karl Deutsch, "Social Mobilization and Political Development," *American Political Science Review* 55 (September 1961): 493–514.

Table 3.1 Parsons's Pattern Variables

Traditional Society	Modern Society
Ascription $\longrightarrow$	Merit
Particularism $\longrightarrow$	Universalism
Functionally diffuse $\longrightarrow$	Functionally specific

expectations about modernity that the developing countries could not possibly live up to. Nor, as with the economists, is there any mention by the sociologists of political factors; the processes involved are assumed to be inevitable. Parsons's goal was to present these "pattern variables" as "ideal types," but the result was some misplaced polarities in the study of the developing nations.

Lerner studied the effects of increased means of communications on modernization and development in the Middle East. His was a more detailed study than Parsons's grand theory, more down-to-earth and with real facts and countries involved. But Lerner's study rested on many of the same assumptions as did those of other sociologists writing during this period. He assumed that the process from traditional to modern was one-way, that the modernization brought on by new communications media produced inevitable political results (egalitarianism, democracy, and so on), and that these processes were universal. But the 1979 Islamic revolution of the Ayatollah Khomeini in Iran, and his use of tapes ("modern communications") to get his hateful, fundamentalist message across, should be sufficient to give us pause as to just how one-way, inevitable, and universal these changes produced by modern communications were.

In two seminal articles (see notes 9 and 10) published just as the interest in development was getting into high gear in the late 1950s and early 1960s, Seymour M. Lipset and Karl Deutsch focused, respectively, on "the social requisites of democracy" and "social mobilization." The two articles, though derived from distinct research, were remarkably parallel in their arguments. Both asserted that certain social requirements (high literacy, economic development, mobilization of peasants and workers, modern communications, education, consensus on the rules of the game, and so on) must be met before a society could become developed and democratic. Lipset and Deutsch were careful to argue that higher education levels do not cause democracy (in Franco's Spain, for example, new education campaigns were launched, but they taught authoritarianism rather than democracy), but they did argue that there is a close correlation between the two. However, their followers and disciples were not quite so careful as Lipset and Deutsch were, and in some circles the belief grew that social mobilization, education, and the like, *would* cause democracy to flower.

For a long time (and often continuing to today), these ideas of the causative relationship between economic and social change *and* democratization represented the ideological foundation of the U.S. foreign aid program directed at the developing countries. That program had largely been designed in the early 1960s by the economist W. W. Rostow, so we should not be entirely surprised to find these same assumptions prevalent. Rostow had presented an analysis of the several "stages" of economic growth. The stimulus in proceeding from one of Rostow's "aeronautical" stages (first preconditions for take-off, then take-off, next drive to maturity, eventually age of high mass consumption) to the next was economic growth. Economic growth, according to Parsons, Lerner, Deutsch, and Lipset, would inevitably produce social modernization and differentiation that would lead to democracy. All the United States needed to do, the argument ran, was to provide economic aid, aid to education, new communications media, aid to new social groups, and so on; democracy would presumably inevitably follow. And in terms of U.S. foreign policy and cold war considerations, such development would carry the country past the stage where it would be susceptible to Marxist-Leninist takeovers (Rostow's book had called communism a "disease" of the transitional stages; once the country got beyond that stage, communism was no longer viewed as a threat). So, not only would U.S. aid produce development (ethically and morally good), but it would also serve our foreign policy purposes. As we will see, there are some enormous holes in this argument.

The Political Scientists

The high point of this early period of the study of development was the publication in 1960 of *The Politics of the Developing Areas*, edited by Gabriel A. Almond and James S. Coleman.[11] In his introduction to the volume, which also included contributions by other experts with country or regional expertise, Almond set forth a framework for studying development that was to have enormous influence on the field. The main ingredients were the following: First, Almond accepted the emphasis on process, informal actors, and genuine comparison set forth by Macridis and other younger scholars in the 1950s. Second, Almond adapted for comparative politics the systems framework (input → governmental decision making → output) that David Easton had suggested a few years earlier. Third, Almond took Parsons's pattern variables (ascription → merit; particularism → universalism; functionally diffuse → functionally specific) and applied them to the political differences between developing and developed nations. And fourth, because, Almond reasoned, the same functions had to be performed in *all* political systems regardless of the institutions in place, he set forth a *functionalist model* of political activity that presumably would be universally valid—even though Almond later admitted that at that time he had never visited a developing country.

---

[11]Gabriel A. Almond and James S. Coleman (eds.), *The Politics of the Developing Areas* (Princeton, NJ: Princeton University Press, 1960).

On the input side, Almond had four functions:

1. *Political socialization*—how people learn about or are inculcated with political values and ideas
2. *Interest articulation*—how interests are articulated and set forth, which sounded like interest group activity
3. *Interest aggregation*—how interests are brought together and presented in the political system, which sounds like political party activity
4. *Political communications*—how interests and influences are conveyed to political decision makers

On the output side were three functions:

1. *Rule making*—who makes the rules or laws
2. *Rule execution*—carrying out and administering the rules or laws
3. *Rule adjudication*—deciding conflicts over rules within the system

A close look at these output functions reveals that they bear a striking resemblance (although called by different names) to the American system of tripartite separation of powers into legislative, executive, and judicial branches. However, Almond continued to insist that his categories had universal validity, that all these functions *had* to be performed by all the world's political systems.

Even at the beginning there was some skepticism of the Almond approach. Most Europeanists did not find his categories very helpful for their research on advanced societies. Similarly, senior Asia and Latin America specialists often felt the Almond design was an effort to stuff their countries into a set of categories that didn't really apply. Almond himself, meanwhile, had assumed the chairmanship of the important new Committee on Comparative Politics (CCP) established in the 1950s by the grant-making *cum* policy agency Social Science Research Council (SSRC); but even within this group not everyone accepted Almond's framework or the pattern variables of Parsons on which it was built. (The CCP/SSRC is discussed in more detail in the next section.) Nor did those with more experience in the field than Almond had feel that his categories fit all their countries very well.

Nevertheless, the Almond design and *The Politics of the Developing Areas* had an enormous influence in the early to mid-1960s, particularly on younger scholars and graduate students. The reasons for this were several. First, the Almond design provided a means to understand, and an outline presumably applicable to, *all* the world's disparate political systems. Second, it told those who were just starting in the field what to look for: interest aggregation, rule adjudication, and so on. Third, what made it attractive was that Almond's approach was not only "scientifically" valid (or so many thought at the time) but also morally good. That is, not only could it be used to study development systematically, but it also suggested what might be missing in a country's development, which comparative politics or U.S. foreign aid could presumably correct (Almond later admitted that his writings in the John F. Kennedy era of the early 1960s were infused with the do-gooder, "Peace Corps mood" of the times). That was the fourth reason for developmentalism's popularity: Not only was it scientifically sound and morally right, but it also, in this optimistic, romantic pre–Vietnam War period, was amenable to correcting by U.S. foreign aid. Who could resist an approach that had such an impressive combination of virtues?

So, armed with the Almond categories, a whole generation of young scholars went off to Asia, Africa, Latin America, and the Middle East to study "development." What they found, however, often bore little resemblance to what the Almond framework had suggested. We pick up the thread of why that was so and its implications later in the chapter when we review criticisms of the developmentalist approach, but first we must discuss the proliferation of developmentalist writings.

The Proliferation of Development Studies

During the 1960s studies of development proliferated, and the developmentalist approach became the dominant one in the field of comparative politics. The Committee on Comparative Politics of the Social Science Research Council (CCP/SSRC) led the way under Almond's leadership, producing seven influential volumes in the 1960s and early 1970s, all published by the prestigious Princeton University Press. These included volumes on political parties and political development, communications and political development, bureaucracy and political development, political culture and political development, education and political development, political modernization in Japan and Turkey, crises and sequences in political development, and the European historical experience with development.[12]

---

[12]Social Science Research Council series, "Studies in Political Development": Almond and Coleman, *Politics of Developing Areas;* Lucian W. Pye (ed.), *Communications and Political Development* (Princeton, NJ: Princeton University Press, 1963); Joseph LaPalombara (ed.), *Bureaucracy and Political Development* (Princeton, NJ: Princeton University Press, 1963); Robert E. Ward and Dankwart A. Rustow (eds.), *Political Modernization in Japan and Turkey* (Princeton, NJ: Princeton University Press, 1964); James S. Coleman (ed.), *Education and Political Development* (Princeton, NJ: Princeton University Press, 1965); Lucian W. Pye and Sidney Verba (eds.), *Political Culture and Political Development* (Princeton, NJ: Princeton University Press, 1965); Joseph LaPalombara and Myron Weiner (eds.), *Political Parties and Political Development* (Princeton, NJ: Princeton University Press, 1966); Leonard Binder, James S. Coleman, Joseph LaPalombara, Lucian W. Pye, Sidney Verba, and Myron Weiner (eds.), *Crises and Sequences in Political Development* (Princeton, NJ: Princeton University Press, 1971); Charles Tilly (ed.), *The Formation of the National States in Western Europe* (Princeton, NJ: Princeton University Press, 1975).

But that was just the beginning. In addition to its own work, the CCP/SSRC also commissioned a large number of studies by others. It brought over two hundred scholars in as contributors to its various books and deliberations. Almond, the group's chairman, also began publishing a series of textbooks in comparative politics that built on his framework and became best-sellers in the field. In addition to their work as members of the CCP/SSRC, such leading scholars as Lucian Pye, Myron Weiner, Joseph LaPalombara, Robert Ward, Sidney Verba, Leonard Binder, and James Coleman were also putting out a large number of studies on their own dealing with development themes.

The developmentalist approach soon spread far beyond the original CCP/SSRC group. The CCP/SSRC had served as a catalyst, but now a large number of other scholars were also publishing books dealing with modernization and other aspects of development. Entire bodies of literature soon sprang up around such popular themes as education and development, the armed forces and development, trade unions and development, religion and development, peasants or agrarian reform and development, and so on. A bibliography published in the mid-1960s contained over two thousand entries dealing with development themes; shortly thereafter, an entire book-length volume was published focusing exclusively on the topic of development.[13]

Development now shifted from being just one academic approach to being *the* approach underlying U.S. assistance programs for developing nations. Here Rostow had been the key person as one of the architects of the U.S. foreign aid program in the early 1960s, as head of policy planning under Kennedy at the Department of State, and later as national security adviser to President Lyndon Johnson. Once again the familiar developmentalist/policy assumptions were applied: If only we can provide enough economic assistance, the argument ran, then we can create middle-class, democratic societies that will be socially just and that can also resist the appeals of communism. To that end, a host of development-related programs—the Peace Corps, the Alliance for Progress, CIA aid to peasants and trade unions, aid to favored political parties, aid to education, aid in the development of mass communications, agrarian reform, community development, military assistance (the list goes on and on)—were put in place to help developing countries make the transition to modernity. It bears reemphasizing that such programs were designed to serve both the goal of assisting developing nations and U.S. foreign policy goals, which were seen as complementary; no possible contradiction between the two was seen at that time.

---

[13]John Brode, *The Process of Modernization: An Annotated Bibliography of the Sociocultural Aspects of Development* (Cambridge, MA: Harvard University Press, 1969); Saul M. Katz and Frank McGowan, *A Select List of U.S. Readings on Development* (Washington, D.C.: Agency for International Development, 1963).

Few disagree with the policy goals in the developing nations of supporting peasant and worker organization, encouraging community development,
building roads and highways, or helping with agrarian reform. The question
was whether the model set forth in Rostow's and others' writings, based so
heavily on the European and U.S. experiences, was really relevant in the particular circumstances of today's developing nations. For example, the model
of citizen participation advanced always came out looking like a New England town meeting; the agrarian reform model bore a striking resemblance
to conditions in rural Wisconsin. There was nothing inherently wrong with
these programs per se, but they should have better taken into account local
cultures and customs. Translated into U.S. aid policy, a manifest program of
political development often left a great deal to be desired.

In addition to providing foreign aid to a great number of Third World
countries, the U.S. government established a number of programs in American universities to advance the study of development. First, the CIA and then
more overt sources provided the funding for a number of centers for the
study of development. The U.S. government also provided stipends to some
major foundations and research institutes for them to provide funding for
other development projects. Various faculty members also received grants
from the government to study the different aspects of development. For
graduate students there was the National Defense Foreign Language
(NDFL) program to help channel young people into programs that combined language training with Third World area specialization. Such bland-
ishments provided enormous encouragement for the study of development.

Significantly, with all this encouragement of and money available for
the study of development, some subject areas were completely ignored. For
example, no one seriously studied business or entrepreneurship and development—possibly because in those days the assumption was that a centrally
planned or perhaps "mixed" economy was the best way to achieve development, and few academics thought seriously about the contribution of business to development. Another glaring omission was the lack of studies
of oligarchies or ruling classes and development—again, presumably, because this element was seen as inevitably fading away as development and
social justice were advanced and because the democratically inclined persons who studied development were uncomfortable with oligarchies and
ruling classes. But in the short run at least, these groups did not disappear,
and there was often precious little democratic advance; a strong case can
be made that if we are going to study development, we had better be well
informed about those elite groups with the capacity to control, coopt,
or frustrate it. A third omission was the lack of study of any alternatives to democracy and Marxism-Leninism as routes to development—
undoubtedly a result of the cold war preoccupations of the time. There was
no attention to such "third ways" or "halfway houses" as corporatism, bureaucratic-authoritarianism, or combined civil-military *juntas* in the process

of development—all themes that came to the fore later and that are discussed in the following chapter.

Another omission was the absence of a clear definition of what precisely political development meant. In the less divisive, more consensual atmosphere of the early to mid-1960s, people simply assumed they knew what it meant and that others of goodwill would arrive at the same understanding. In fact, however, the term had diverse meanings. Some, chiefly the political sociologists, thought political development meant the greater differentiation and specialization of functions—rather like Parsons's or Almond's categorization of functions. Others, mainly political scientists, thought political development meant the growth of institutions: interest groups, political parties, bureaucracies, and the like. Still others equated political development with democratization, which made the process and institutions involved look just like the United States. Within the U.S. government, which had foreign policy interests in advancing political development, the term implied stability and anticommunism as well as democratization. Political scientist Lucian Pye once counted over twenty distinct uses of the term.

Most of those who wrote about political development in these early days were not very precise about the term's meaning. Most scholars probably incorporated all of the meanings just noted—specialization and differentiation, institutionalization, democracy, stability—without being very exact about it. Such vagueness was not so bad as long as there was a good general understanding of what was meant. However, the very looseness of the concept provided an opportunity for the critics to attack it. Moreover, unlike economic development (which can be measured quite simply and precisely in terms of gross national product or GNP per capita) or social modernization (which can also be measured precisely as levels of literacy, degree of urbanization, and so on), political development had no exact measures. How would we know when a country was politically developed or not? Or when it began the transitional phase? The dilemma was that there was no way of knowing. If we look back at Table 1.1, we see that economic and social development can be measured according to various indices but there is not a single gauge for political development. These definitional and measurement problems would continue to plague the concept of political development.

Despite these omissions and the faults already hinted at, the developmentalist approach became *the* dominant approach in comparative politics in the 1960s. Thousands of articles and hundreds of books were written on development during that era, and hundreds of graduate students fanning out to all areas of the globe wrote doctoral dissertations during this decade on developmentalist themes. But what they found in their studies often had little to do with what Almond's famous analysis said they should find. Then came the protests against the Vietnam War, a war that seemed to demonstrate that the U.S.-favored development path was destructive and didn't work very well. By the late 1960s the criticisms of the developmentalist approach were mounting.

Criticisms of the Developmentalist Approach

The young faculty and graduate students who went out to the emerging na-tions in the 1960s armed with the developmentalist categories and came back to write their books, articles, and doctoral dissertations often became the foremost critics of that approach. Recall that Almond's had been an abstract, deductive design based on no actual field experience in the developing na-tions. Many young scholars, however, found that Parsons's pattern variables and Almond's functional categories had very little to do with their countries. The Almond design looked nice and logical on paper, but it had little to do with the realities these younger scholars observed in practice. The reality was usually not "interest aggregation" or "rule adjudication" but more likely caste, tribe, and clan politics and conflict, vast patronage networks, favoritism and special privileges, elite rule, military repression, a nasty scramble for power and money rather than happy pluralism, and so on. Instead of con-cluding that the political systems they were studying were "dysfunctional" according to the Almond paradigm, more and more of these young scholars came to the conclusion that the paradigm itself was faulty. These criticisms came increasingly to the surface in the 1960s and led eventually to a consid-erable rethinking of the entire developmentalist approach.[14]

A second major influence was the war in Vietnam in the mid-1960s. In South Vietnam the United States had tried all the programs that the devel-opmentalist school suggested: agrarian reform, aid to democratic trade unions and peasant associations, creation of political parties, reform and pro-fessionalization of the armed forces, assistance through the transition so the country would not be susceptible to communist revolution, and so on. But nothing the United States tried seemed to work successfully or well. Fur-thermore—and this was the main criticism—the United States, by engaging in a bombing campaign and heavily Americanizing the war, seemed to be

---

[14]The critical literature includes: Sidney Verba, "Some Dilemmas in Comparative Research," *World Politics* 20 (October 1967): 111–27; Mark Kesselman, "Order or Move-ment: The Literature of Political Development as Ideology," *World Politics* 26 (October 1973): 139–53; Philip H. Melanson and Lauriston R. King, "Theory in Comparative Poli-tics: A Critical Appraisal," *Comparative Political Studies* 4 (July 1971): 205–31; Geoffrey K. Roberts, "Comparative Politics Today," *Government and Opposition* 7 (Winter 1972): 38–55; Sally A. Merrill, "On the Logic of Comparative Analysis," *Comparative Political Studies* 3 (January 1971): 489–500; Robert T. Holt and John E. Turner, "Crises and Sequences in Collective Theory Development," *American Political Science Review* 69 (September 1975): 979–95; R. S. Milne, "The Overdeveloped Study of Political Development," *Canadian Journal of Political Science* 5 (December 1972): 560–68; Philip Coulter, "Political Develop-ment and Political Theory: Methodological and Technological Problems in the Compara-tive Study of Political Development," *Polity* 5 (Winter 1972): 233–42; Ignany Sachs, "The Logic of Development," *International Social Science Journal* 24, no. 1 (1972): 37–43.

destroying the country of Vietnam in the process. Given that so many of those (for example, Rostow) who were the architects of development theory were also among "the best and the brightest"[15] involved in the fashioning of U.S. policy in Vietnam, the souring Vietnam experience seemed to discredit the developmentalist approach. Out of Vietnam came the strong sense that the United States and developmentalism not only didn't have the answers but had provided the *wrong* and destructive answers.

A third blow to developmentalism came with the publication in 1968 of Samuel P. Huntington's influential *Political Order in Changing Societies*.[16] The earlier development literature had argued that economic growth, social modernization, and political development went hand in hand and were mutually reinforcing. But Huntington showed convincingly that rapid economic growth and social mobilization, rather than leading to stability and democracy, could be so upsetting of traditional ways that they produced chaos and breakdown. Social modernization leads people to have increased expectations for a better life often before their political institutions are capable of providing it, and the result is disappointment and frustration on a national scale leading to societal unraveling or even revolution. Huntington suggested that instead of focusing on social change, scholars and government officials should concentrate on building strong institutions capable of handling change, such as armies, bureaucracies, and political parties.

A fourth criticism of development growing mainly out of the experience of many young scholars studying development abroad in the 1960s was that it was biased and ethnocentric. The development categories, the stages of growth, and the processes involved all derived from the Western (European, U.S.) experiences with development, not from the developing areas themselves. The experience of many young scholars in non-Western developing nations often led them to conclude that the Western tradition was of doubtful applicability in Third World areas whose culture and history were quite different.[17]

Fifth, it was argued that the international context for development in the late twentieth century was also different from that prevailing in the early nineteenth century when most of Europe began its upward ascent. Then, nations could largely develop autonomously and in isolation. In today's world, however, the developing nations are much more involved in global markets, affected by world oil price changes, shaped by multinational corporations,

---

[15]After the title of David Halberstam's book *The Best and the Brightest*.

[16]Samuel P. Huntington, *Political Order in Changing Societies: The Governing of Restless Nations* (New Haven, CT: Yale University Press, 1968).

[17]A. H. Somjee, *Parallels and Actuals of Political Development* (London: Macmillan, 1986); Howard J. Wiarda, *Ethnocentrism and Foreign Policy: Can We Understand the Third World?* (Washington, D.C.: American Enterprise Institute for Public Policy Research, 1985).

and caught up in complex relations of dependency and interdependency. They cannot develop on their own but are inevitably involved in big-power relations and market forces over which they have no control.

Sixth, the timing, sequences, and stages of development that the West experienced cannot be repeated in today's developing nations. The West had a long time to develop and could do so gradually; but the people in today's developing nations are aroused, impatient, and unwilling to wait the several generations that it took for the West to develop. The sequences are also off: Whereas in the West industrialization drew people out of the countryside and into urban jobs, in the Third World urbanization is preceding industrialization and leading to high unemployment and immense social problems. As regards stages, the West went from feudalism to capitalism to in some countries various forms of socialism or social democracy, but in the developing nations these stages have been jumbled together with the result that feudalism, capitalism, and sometimes socialism often coexist side by side in confused, overlapping form.

Seventh, the developmentalist approach misrepresented the role of traditional institutions, such as the family, religion, the tribe, the caste, or the clan. Most of the development literature suggested that traditional institutions would either fade away or be destroyed as development proceeded. But many of these institutions are sources of pride and are quite functional in the developing nations. They often provide the "glue" that helps hold these countries together as they go through the wrenching process of transition. Moreover, in many developing nations, we have learned that rather than being swept aside as development proceeds, such traditional institutions as tribes and caste associations may be themselves capable of a great deal of modernization, often converting themselves into interest groups or political parties, and thus serving as bridges between tradition and modernity.

Eighth, within the developing nations there is a strong sense that the early development literature emanating from the West not only was biased but also raised false expectations and created unrealistic goals for these societies to achieve. The developmentalist literature portrayed the process of development in happy, peaceful, almost antiseptic phrases when in fact the process is often bloody and wrenching. By underestimating the difficulties involved and by forcing on the developing nations Western institutions and practices that had no root in their cultures, the developmentalist approach often led to conflict, bloodshed, and military takeovers.

A ninth criticism focused on the logic and methodology of the developmentalist approach. Few scholars accepted fully the pattern variables that were part of Almond's analysis, or his functionalist approach. There were additional problems in comparing or "adding up" apples (Africa), oranges (Asia), and pears (Latin America). These areas were so different culturally, sociologically, and in other ways that it was difficult to compare them using the same criteria, and many scholars were not convinced of the feasibility of using a single set of indices to compare all the world's nations.

Tenth, radical critics charged that the development approach was all part of a cold war strategy to keep the Third World under U.S. domination. That charge is probably too simplistic. The United States undoubtedly became more interested in the Third World because of cold war concerns, the U.S. government provided fellowships and helped fund some research centers devoted to Third World affairs, and most scholars of development saw no incompatibility between their work and U.S. policy goals in the Third World. But the way to achieve those policy goals was to *promote* Third World development, not hold it back, since that would produce the moderation and stability the United States wanted. So it is hard to make a convincing case of a concerted (U.S. government and development scholarship) effort to retard modernization.

An eleventh criticism of the developmentalist approach was that, inadvertently, it sometimes wreaked havoc in the developing nations. By consigning "traditional institutions" to the ashcan of history, for example, developmentalism sometimes undermined the institutions that gave coherence and stability to these nations and that might have enabled them better to bridge the transition to modernity. Or, by its policy of aiding the armed forces in many developing nations, the U.S. government may have assisted the one institution that did not need strengthening, and therefore helped encourage oppression and military takeovers.

One final criticism of the developmentalist approach involves the choices of scholars to be included within the prestigious publications that the CCP/SSRC, especially, was issuing. This criticism has to do with academic politics. Although the CCP/SSRC did make an effort to include some new persons, that was perceived as woefully inadequate by the rest of the field. Year after year as the CCP/SSRC volumes came out and as its conferences were held, the same scholars whose ideas seemed to be more and more shopworn were involved. Insufficient effort was expended to bringing in new, younger people who had new ideas. Eventually, these omissions bred resentments; quite a number of those not included in the CCP/SSRC's studies became among the strongest critics of the developmentalist approach.

These criticisms of the literature and approach of political development were powerful and devastating. Moreover, they were cumulative. By the end of the 1960s, the criticisms were so widespread and so many case studies had been written in which the developmentalist approach had been found wanting that the basic theory and its assumptions were under attack. As we see in the next chapter, new approaches came to the fore and developmentalism was eclipsed.

As in the 1950s, a generational factor was also involved. In that earlier decade, the traditionalist approach adhered to by an older generation of scholars had been strongly criticized by the "young Turks" who wanted to go in new directions. But by the late 1960s to early 1970s the former young

Turks were seen as older, part of "the establishment," and out of touch. A new generation of scholars that came of age during the civil rights and protest movements of the 1960s emerged. They had new ideas, a different agenda, and a variety of newer approaches that sometimes borrowed from but also often rejected developmentalism. This group and their new approaches would come to dominate the comparative politics field in the 1970s.

A Reassessment of the Developmentalist Approach

Developmentalism was the dominant comparative politics paradigm of the 1960s. Its dominance within the field corresponded to a number of trends within the broader society: the rise of the developing nations, the sense of hope and optimism that accompanied the Kennedy era, and the emergence of a new generation of scholars committed to new ideas and a new approach. But by the end of the 1960s, with the assassinations of John F. Kennedy and Martin Luther King, Jr., the Vietnam War, and both new pessimism about and widespread questioning of earlier assumptions, the developmentalist approach also came under strong attack. Eventually, in the 1970s, it was superseded by other approaches.

The developmentalist approach, while open to various criticisms, nevertheless contributed significantly to our understanding of Third World nations. In its systems approach, its focus on change and decolonization, its emphasis on dynamic factors and genuine comparisons, developmentalism added significantly to our knowledge of Third World change. While many of the criticisms later leveled against it seem valid, one should not lose sight of the many contributions it made. Too often in comparative politics courses and seminars the developmentalist approach is reviewed and dismissed in a single session. But there are in fact rich insights, valuable information, and intriguing concepts in the developmentalist approach from which we can still learn. A first step would be to disaggregate or differentiate among and between the different developmentalist contributions, separating out those that deserve the criticism they have received (Rostow, Lipset, some of Almond's earlier writings) from those that present more nuanced and sophisticated interpretations (Apter, Huntington, LaPalombara, Macridis, Pye, Rustow, Weiner).[18]

Two themes dominate our thinking at the end of this chapter. One is that,

---

[18]See, for example, David E. Apter, *The Politics of Modernization* (Chicago: University of Chicago Press, 1965); Myron Weiner and Samuel P. Huntington (eds.), *Understanding Political Development* (Boston: Little, Brown, 1987); *Comparative Politics* 1 (October 1968), articles by Rustow, Macridis, and LaPalombara; Lucian W. Pye, *Aspects of Political Development* (Boston: Little, Brown, 1966); Dankwart A. Rustow, *A World of Nations: Problems of Political Modernization* (Washington, D.C.: Brookings Institution, 1967); Roy Macridis, *Modern Political Regimes* (Boston: Little, Brown, 1986).

in the history of comparative politics that we have been tracing, the developmentalist approach is about to be supplanted in the 1970s by a number of other approaches, which are addressed in Chapter 4. The second is that, in the 1980s and 1990s, as democracy was reestablished in many of the developing areas and prosperity increased, the developmentalist correlations between literacy and democratization, social change and democratization, and economic development and democratization began to look better and better. Could it be that the Rostow/Lipset/Almond developmentalist school and approach, while wrong in the short run and containing many errors, might yet turn out to be correct in the longer run? And, if that is so, could a reformulated, nonethnocentric, and less problematic developmentalist approach be resurrected and provide us with valuable insights concerning the development process? That is a subject to which we return in Chapter 7.

4

Political Culture and Comparative Politics

Political culture may be defined as the basic values, beliefs, ideas, attitudes, and orientations that citizens of different countries have about their political systems.[1] Political culture refers to core values, not ephemeral ones: whether people accept the basic premises of their political system (democracy, separation of powers, civil liberties, etc.), not whether one approves or disapproves on a daily basis of how well the president is doing his job. Clearly, political culture can vary greatly from country to country, with some countries having a democratic, participatory, and more or less egalitarian political culture; others being more elitist, top-down, and authoritarian; others believing in Marxism and/or statism; and still others being traditional and parochial, with little interest or involvement in politics. It is the similarities as well as differences in beliefs and attitudes between countries and regions that stimulate comparisons and thus make political culture a subject of major interest to comparative politics.

The study of political culture gives rise to some very

---

[1]A particularly useful introductory comparative politics volume that employs a political-cultural approach while also integrating political culture into the larger political system is Gabriel A. Almond and E. Bingham Powell, *Comparative Politics: A Developmental Approach* (Boston: Little Brown, numerous editions).

large issues in political science and in the social sciences generally; those include the questions of what drives politics or what produces political change. Is it values, ideas, and beliefs (political culture), or is it class structure and ownership of the means of production and distribution (Marxism)? Is it institutions—political, social, or economic—that shape and determine values and beliefs, or is it the values and beliefs, or ideas, that shape or determine what our institutions look like? Or is it biology and genetic makeup that, according to the growing field of sociobiology, trump all these other explanations? Or, as most social scientists tend to believe, is it some complicated, constantly changing combination of all of these explanations? Obviously, when we study political culture, we are making a statement that we think values, beliefs, and ideas are important—not necessarily that they are the only or most important factor in explaining differences between political systems (although some students of comparative politics believe that) but that political culture provides one important explanatory factor among several, including class and social structure, institutions, level of economic development, and—who knows—perhaps biology as well, although few political scientists know much about that.

The study of political culture arose at about the same time—the 1960s—as the study of political development, and in fact the two are closely interrelated. Recall the discussion in Chapter 3 on development: while Rostow and the economists focused on economic growth and Lipset and the sociologists wrote about the social prerequisites of democracy, political scientists were mainly writing about political values or political culture. For example, the shifts that Gabriel Almond emphasized in his "pattern variables" from ascription to merit, from particularism to universalism, and from functionally diffuse societies to functionally specific *all* involved values and value changes. In other words, the political development approach believed that, to achieve modernization, it was necessary not just to change the economy and social institutions but to change values as well—maybe even *primarily* to change values. Indeed, most of those pioneering scholars on political development in the influential Social Sciences Research Council/Committee on Comparative Politics (SSRC/CCP) were also pioneers in the study of political culture and believed that ideas and values were either *the* or among the most important driving forces in history. The emphasis on values and ideas also served to distinguish the political culture approach from the Marxian model of class conflict; and since the cold war was also being hotly waged at that time, doubtless that was a factor as well. In any case, for a long time the study of political culture and the study of political development were closely intertwined.

History of Political Culture Approaches

When we say that political culture focuses on the ideas, values, and beliefs of a society, we are saying that the history, religion, and general sociocultural background and orientation of a country are important for understanding it. For example, it is probably no accident that modern capitalism and democracy arose in the Judeo-Christian West and that countries founded on Confucian, Buddhist, and Islamic principles took longer and have had a harder time becoming free-market democracies. Or, did the fact that Latin American politics had its roots in feudal and medieval Catholicism retard its historical development as compared with the relatively progressive Protestantism, Calvinism, pluralism, and freedom of religion of the British colonies in North America? Here we have some classic political culture issues, involving the interrelations between religion and politics or religion (values) and economic development. We can also gain insight into the political culture by studying a country's music, literature, advertising, and television.

One of the first to study comparative political culture in a serious and systematic way was the great German sociologist Max Weber. In the late nineteenth century Weber embarked on a massive project to study the relations between religion and economic development.[2] He wanted to know why the countries of Europe, especially Northwest Europe (England, Holland, Germany), had so far outdistanced the countries of Asia and the Middle East in terms of economic growth. He was also interested in why the Protestant countries of Northern Europe had done better than the Latin or Mediterranean countries of the south. So he comparatively studied the values embedded in Buddhism, Catholicism, Confucianism, Islam, and Protestantism to get at the roots of these differences. His conclusion was not the simplistic one that people who have never read Weber often spout, that Protestants are good guys and that all these others are bad. Instead, his research revealed that in Protestantism, especially in its Calvinist variant in the Netherlands and other countries, the God-ordered emphasis on hard work, honesty, seriousness, and the thrifty use of money and time (both of these latter *lent* to us by God) was particularly conducive to business and capital accumulation. Other societies based on different religions lacked these qualities. Here, then, are a set of values—religious values—that provide a powerful explanation for why some countries forged ahead and others lagged behind.

More recently David S. Landes has embarked on a similar quest in his important book *The Wealth and Poverty of Nations: Why Some Are So Rich and Some So Poor.*[3] Like Weber, Landes is interested in explaining why some countries have done so well and others remain undeveloped. And like Weber he is a careful researcher, emphasizing such geographic factors as climate, resources, and rainfall and such economic ones as trade and manufacturing. But the main factor, Landes argues, in explaining early industrialization in

---

[2]Max Weber, *The Protestant Ethic and the Spirit of Capitalism* (New York: Scribner's, 1958).
[3]New York: Norton, 1998.

Western Europe and the relative lack of success of other areas, as well as the differences between Northwest Europe (Holland, England) and Southern Europe (Spain, Portugal, Greece) is *cultural*.

In Landes's view, the industrial revolution occurred first in Northwest Europe for three reasons, all of them cultural: (1) autonomous intellectual inquiry was allowed to flourish regardless of any religious orthodoxies, (2) Europe was the leader in scientific experimentation that combined empirical observation and measurement, and (3) independent research was routine and respected and rewarded there as nowhere else. Landes ultimately comes to the same basic conclusion as did Weber: that it is ideas, values, and culture that both are the driving forces in change and that explain differences between countries, and not so much—at least initially—economic or institutional causes. In other words, in answer to the chicken-egg question posed earlier, both Weber and Landes argue that it is cultural factors that mainly explain political and economic outcomes, and not, as Marx argued, economic factors that undergird the cultural "superstructure."

Political culture studies achieved widespread acceptance and popularity between World Wars I and II through the emerging field of cultural anthropology. Some of the most prominent cultural anthropologists—Franz Boas, Margaret Mead, and Ruth Benedict—became household names during this period, and their books about exotic places with often exotic cultural beliefs and practices became best-sellers.[4] Cultural anthropology sought to study distinct cultures on their own terms, in their own languages, and within their own setting, without imposing on them the scholars' own (usually North American) lenses or making ethnocentric value judgments. The *political* uses and implications of cultural anthropology were exemplified during World War II when Benedict was commissioned to write a book about Japanese culture that could be utilized by the American government in the war effort.[5] A few years later Nathan Leites and his colleagues at the RAND Corporation, an Air Force think tank, completed a similar political culture–based study of the Soviet Communist elite that was used in the cold war.[6]

World War II proved to be a turning point in political culture studies, however. By this time, in the press and in popular books, serious studies of cultural anthropology and political culture were being supplanted by what were called "national character studies" that often involved dangerous stereotyping. We are all familiar with the stereotypes involved: all Germans are

---

[4]Franz Boas, *Anthropoloty and Modern Life* (New York: Dover, 1986); Margaret Mead, *Coming of Age in Samoa* (New York: Morrow, 1961); Ruth Benedict, *Patterns of Culture* (New York: Mentor Books, 1957).

[5]Benedict, *The Chrysanthemum and the Sword: Patterns of Japanese Culture* (London: Routledge & Kegan Paul, 1967).

[6]Nathan Leites, *The Operational Code of the Politiburo* (Santa Monica: RAND, 1951).

authoritarian, all Frenchmen are great lovers, all Italians eat pizza, all Latins practice *machismo*, Arabs are all terrorists, and so forth. And within this genre, there were actually some good books written: Luigi Barzini's *The Italians*[7] and Salvador de Madariaga's *Englishmen, Frenchmen, Spaniards*.[8] But in less careful hands or among those with a political agenda, such national character studies can become the basis for ethnic slurs, prejudice, racism, hate crimes, and—in the eugenics movement of the pre–World War II period—selective human breeding.

Stereotyping people by religion, ethnicity, race or national origins can be both dangerous and destructive, as, for example, when applied to Jews and Gypsies by the Nazis during World War II. Or in the enmity between Greeks and Turks, Serbs and Croats, Jews and Arabs, French and Germans, Japanese and Chinese, Hutus and Tutsis, and a large number of other ethnic, religious, and nationality groups. Such stereotypes are not only inaccurate (it is false to say that *all* English or Dutch are this or that), but they frequently result in discrimination, pogroms, genocide, and mass slaughter being carried out by one people or nationality against another people or nationality. World War II and the Nazi experience as well as the various genocides that have followed brought these issues to a head.

In the aftermath of the war such national, ethnic, or racial stereotyping was denounced and discredited. Journalists (such as Barzini) often continued to produce books involving nationality traits on individual countries and most scholars in comparative politics remained convinced that individual country or culture area differences in values, history, religion, and ideas were important. After all, when one travels to France, Germany, Italy, or Spain, or to Asia, Africa, Latin America, or the Middle East, one knows *immediately* from the sights, sounds, smells, and colors that one is in one particular country or region, and not in another. So culture studies remained important, even though it was hard to do them systematically and without prejudice, with the result that for a time after World War II studies of political culture were often discredited and went into eclipse.

The Civic Culture

A major breakthrough in the study of comparative political culture came with the publication in 1963 of Gabriel A. Almond and Sidney Verba's book entitled *The Civic Culture: Political Attitudes and Democracy in Five Nations*.[9] The

---

[7]Luigi Barzini, *The Italians* (New York: Atheneum, 1964).

[8]Salvador de Madariaga, *Englishmen, Frenchmen, Spaniards* (New York: Hill & Wang, 1969).

[9]Princeton NJ: Princeton University Press, 1963.

book was a pioneering work for a number of reasons: first, it contained a so-phisticated discussion of political culture; second, it involved a genuinely comparative study of five nations (Great Britain, United States, West Germany, Italy, and Mexico); and third, rather than being based on impressionistic interpretation as in the old national character studies, it was grounded on hard data generated from detailed public opinion surveys carried out by the investigators in each of the five countries. This last was particularly important because it enabled researchers to move away from dangerous national stereotyping and toward a more empirical or scientific examination of *patterns* of behavior.

The term *culture* can be obviously used in a variety of ways and with a variety of meanings. It encompasses music, literature, and art as well as how people conduct themselves and what they believe, think, and do. Almond and Verba indicate that they are particularly interested in the *psychological orientation* of peoples toward their political system, in the values and attitudes of citizens as they affect politics. By *political culture*, thus, they mean the cognitions, feelings, and attitudes of people toward politics. The political culture of a nation is the "particular distribution of patterns of orientation toward political objects among the members of the nation."

Almond and Verba go on to distinguish three types of political cultures. *Parochial political cultures* are generally found in poor, illiterate, underdeveloped societies where people may focus on their own narrow (parochial) family, village, or tribe but have little sense of, or participation in, the larger, national political system. A *subject political culture* is one in which people are becoming aware of the larger political system but are not themselves participants in it; they are *subjects* of the state, which is usually top-down and authoritarian, but they have few rights to involve themselves in its decision making. The third type is called *participatory* or *"civic."* By this, Almond and Verba mean a democratic political system where citizens can vote, have rights that are protected, and participate fully in the political process. It is clear that Almond and Verba (and most of the rest of us) prefer the third or civic type; moreover, there is a progression of types here that reflects our earlier discussion of development. That is, parochial political cultures are most often associated with the less developed nations; subject political cultures, with transitional regimes; and civic political cultures, with the developed, democratic countries.

The Civic Culture took over five years to research and write; it included interviews with over five thousand persons in the five nations represented. These were in-depth interviews that called for responses on a great variety of issues relating to politics and the political system. The results were not entirely surprising: that Great Britain and the United States were the most participatory, civic, and democratic of the five countries studied; that Germany and Italy occupied intermediary levels on these scales; and that Mexico was the least democratic with large numbers of peoples falling into the parochial and subject categories.

While the results were not surprising to people who know these countries, what was impressive was the systematic and precise quantitative measures that the authors could give to the comparative study of political culture. Henceforth, it would not be acceptable to base political culture explanations of different countries on the researcher's impressions alone; instead, survey results were needed to give such studies a more scientific base and to measure *patterns* of beliefs, not just stereotypes. For example, a country such as Mexico might be partly parochial, partly subject, and partly civic; and by carrying out surveys such as this, we could tell the relative balance among these diverse orientations within Mexico. We could also compare Mexico with the patterns in other nations. As a practical matter, most scholars sought to combine such survey results with other measures of political culture, such as historical studies, to arrive at a full and complete picture of political culture.

In the years following publication of Almond and Verba's book, studies of political culture blossomed. There were studies of political culture in Africa, Asia, Latin America, and the Middle East;[10] studies of Confucian, Hindu, Islamic, and Roman Catholic political cultures;[11] of the relations between political culture and religion;[12] of how political culture values were transmitted through the family or the school system;[13] of the relations between literature and political culture;[14] and between types of legal systems and political culture.[15] Other scholars studied how political culture changed or even under-

---

[10]George Ayittey, *Indigenous African Institutions* (New York: Transnational, 1991); Sangbok Han (ed.), *Asian Peoples and Their Culture: Continuity and Change* (Seoul: Seoul National University Press, 1986); Anwar Syed, *Pakistan: Islam, Politics and National Solidarity* (Lahore: Vanguard, 1983); Lloyd I. and Suzanne Rudolph, *The Modernity of Tradition* (Chicago: University of Chicago Press, 1967); Howard J. Wiarda (ed.), *Non-Western Theories of Development* (Fort Worth, TX: Harcourt Brace, 1998).

[11]Peter Moody, *Tradition and Modernization in China and Japan* (Belmont, CA: Wadsworth, 1995); Glen Dealy, *The Public Man: An Interpretation of Latin American and Other Catholic Countries* (Amherst: University of Massachusetts Press, 1977); A. H. Somjee, *Development Theory: Critiques and Explorations* (London: Macmillan, 1991); and Ahmet Davutoglu, *Alternative Paradigms: The Impact of Islamic and Western Weltanschauungs on Political Theory* (Lanham, MD: University Press of America, 1994).

[12]Donald E. Smith, *Religion and Political Development* (Boston: Little Brown, 1979).

[13]Richard K. Dawson, Kenneth Prewitt, and Karen Dawson, *Political Socialization* (Boston: Little Brown, 1977); Ola Westin, *On Political Socialization and Education* (Uppsala, Sweden: Uppsala University Press, 1981).

[14]Doris Somner, *Foundational Fictions* (Berkeley: University of California Press, 1991).

[15]John Henry Merryman, *The Civil Law Tradition* (Stanford, CA: Stanford University Press, 1969).

went revolutionary transformation,[16] while still others studied the clash and conflict between two or more political cultures within a single political system, possibly leading to bloodshed or even civil war.[17] Meanwhile, the theoretical underpinnings of political culture studies and their relations to broader development themes also became more sophisticated.[18]

Recall, however, that in our model of the political system presented in Chapter 1, political culture was only one part, one aspect, of a larger system and process. In the section on "Approaching the Subject," political culture and political history constituted only two of the twelve subject matters listed. That means, in the author's view, that while political culture is one important part of a full-length study of the political system, it is not the only part, nor is it necessarily or always the most important part. Other factors or "variables," we have insisted, such as class and social structure, interest groups and political parties, government institutions and decision making, and public policy outputs, may be just as or, depending on the circumstances, more important.

The author's views on the issue probably come close to representing a consensus or majority view among students of comparative politics, but they are not the only views on the subject. I see political culture as an important factor but not the only factor in explaining comparatively the differences among nations. Political culture is thus a necessary subject of inquiry but not a sufficient one, in the sense that the researcher also has to consider other explanatory factors. But this position stands in contrast to the views of some scholars who want to elevate political culture into the sole, all-encompassing, and *only* explanation of national political differences and of other scholars who want to eliminate political culture explanations altogether, presumably in favor of a class-based or some other single-cause explanation. To most of us in comparative politics, both of these alternative positions seem too rigid, too absolute, too driven by ideological considerations, and probably with too many axes to grind. Instead, most of us favor a middle position is which political culture is seen as important but not all-important, in which a sophisticated political culture explanation is viewed as a complement to other explanations and is used in conjunction with them.

---

[16]Richard Fagen, *The Transformation of Political Culture in Cuba* (Stanford, CA: Stanford University Press, 1969).

[17]Marc Belanger, *Rethinking Political Culture: Counterinsurgency, Democracy, and Political Identity in Guatemala*, Ph.D., Department of Political Science, Amherst, University of Massachusetts, 1993.

[18]Lucian Pye and Sidney Verba, *Political Culture and Political Development* (Princeton, NJ: Princeton University Press, 1966).

Criticisms of the Political Culture Approach

During the 1960s and on into the 1970s, the study of political culture flourished. Ideas, values, beliefs, and overall political culture were all thought to be important and worthwhile subjects of inquiry, either by themselves or in conjunction with other factors. Political culture was thought to be particularly useful in studying as well as assisting the developing areas. Many scholars believed that unless and until these countries got their political cultures reoriented toward honesty, fairness, egalitarianness, and serving the public good rather than the private self-enrichment of their ruling elites, no amount of economic aid or investment would do them much good.

Political culture's rise and decline ran parallel to that of the political development approach, with which it was closely related. Both of these approaches emerged as major breakthroughs in comparative politics. But then came Vietnam, assassinations of leading political figures, protest movements, Nixon, and Watergate. Both political development and political culture were strongly attacked. New and more radical approaches came to the fore. The political development approach went into a tailspin from which it never fully recovered—although much of U.S. government foreign aid is still based on this approach as is the emphasis on Transitions to Democracy (see Chapter 6). Political culture also suffered, and for quite a number of years no new or significant breakthrough occurred in that field. Most scholars continued to use political culture as one important explanatory factor among several, but political culture lost its place as an exciting new concept. First, we deal with criticisms that have been leveled against political culture; next, we treat the quite remarkable renaissance that political culture studies have recently experienced.

The main criticisms leveled against the political culture approach include the following:[19]

1. Political culture is used as a "residual category." That is, whenever we can't find any other explanation for a country's behavior, we blame it on "political culture." If a regime is corrupt or patronage dominated or a country is unstable or authoritarian, the temptation may be strong to say, "Oh, it's just the political culture." But that is a form of circular reasoning that really explains nothing; obviously, more information and more explanation are necessary. In other words, political culture cannot be used simply as a "dumping ground," an explanation to fall back on when we

---

[19]For the criticisms, see Carol Pateman, "Political Culture, Political Studies, and Political Change," *British Journal of Political Science* 1 (1973); and Robert C. Tucker, "Culture, Political Culture, and Communist Society," *Political Science Quarterly* (January 1973): 173–90.

don't know what else to say. More details and greater precision are needed to make the link between the corruption, patronage, or instability that may be readily visible, *and* the aspects of political culture that explain those features. This criticism is directed at careless users of the political culture concept; careful, clear, and specific use of the concept can overcome the problem.

2. The concept of political culture is too vague. It seems to include everything: literature, art, music, values, political ideas, religion, history, behavior, whatever. In this sense, political culture becomes a kind of grab bag of everything, and, when one throws everything into an explanation, one is left with really nothing. Once again there are elements of truth in this criticism. Political culture does cover a lot of territory. And one must be careful and discriminating in its use. But remember, political culture asks us only to consider the specifically *political* aspects of art or literature. Moreover, by the careful weighing of facts and evidence, it *is* possible to draw out of all these background factors the specific traits that help us explain modern-day politics. But great care, circumcision, and discrimination must be used.

3 In its focus on culture, the political culture approach was accused of ignoring *structure*. *Structure* in this case meant the class system and the ownership of the means of production and distribution. This was, in other words, the Marxist critique. Now, it is true that in their enthusiasm to study political culture, some scholars, naturally enough, overemphasized cultural factors; a handful ignored structural factors altogether. Most of us in the field, however, believe that *both* structure and culture are important, although we may still differ as to precisely how much weight to assign to each of these important explanations; the real challenge is to weave together both cultural and structural as well as other explanatory variables. If some scholars want, however, to focus their attention on the study of political culture because they find it interesting or important or both, that should not bother us too much—as long as we recognize that political culture is not the only answer as to why nations behave as they do and that other factors also need to be taken into account.

4. Another criticism of political culture was that it ignored international influences. Indeed, the focus in the early political culture literature was almost exclusively on domestic values and influences shaping political culture. But remember that all this early political culture literature was written before the onset of globalization; it was also written before most of the developing nations had very many radios or TVs and before VCRs, satellites, and cable television. So we should not expect too much. On the other hand, even in these early days, MIT political scientist Lucian Pye was writing about the "world political culture" (rock music, Coca-Cola,

blue jeans, American TV, and—along with these others—freedom and democracy).[20] And, of course, by now, with the incredible spread of mass communications including in the Third World, we would want to emphasize these factors even more. This criticism, therefore, seems valid but has since been corrected.

5. Political culture was also criticized as being ethnocentric. The values and ideas that were set forth as "most developed" or "most modern" always seemed to bear an uncanny resemblance to the United States or Great Britain and their democratic, participatory political cultures. This was particularly true of *The Civic Culture* volume in which the most valued traits—the "civic" culture—corresponded exactly to the United States and Great Britain while other countries lagged behind. The "ethnocentrism" charge leveled against political culture was exactly parallel to the same charge raised in regard to political development.

In response, it should be said that, as committed democrats (small *d*), most of us don't mind terribly if a democratic, egalitarian, participatory political culture and system come out as the model system for others—authoritarian regimes, totalitarian regimes, subject or parochial regimes—to live up to. At the same time, there is a lot of truth to the ethnocentrism charge. The ideal "civic" political culture does look exactly like the United States; moreover, it is in the longer view an idealized, even romantic, almost unrecognizable picture of the United States. In addition, the authors of *The Civic Culture* portray only one path to development when, in fact, there are multiple routes as well as many different kinds of democracies. So this criticism of *The Civic Culture* as being ethnocentric also seems valid—even though such criticism of one particular volume does not detract from the overall value of the political culture approach, nor should it obscure that it was precisely students of political culture who themselves analyzed the several different forms and processes that development may take.

6. Finally, *The Civic Culture* was criticized for its methodology. Five thousand persons were interviewed for this book, which sounds like a large sample; but remember that five countries were involved, resulting in an average of one thousand persons interviewed in each. That is probably not a large enough sample for the size and complexity of the five countries studied. In addition, the samples overrepresented urban persons, particularly in the Mexico case, thus leaving rural persons and peasants woefully underrepresented. These methodological problems obviously need correcting; on the other hand, it should also be recognized that in many quarters this study was praised for its pioneering and innovative

---

[20]*Aspects of Political Development* (Boston: Little Brown, 1965).

methodology. For this was the first major comparative politics survey of political culture attitudes in five countries using such a sophisticated methodology, a cross-country research design, and a particularly detailed theoretical treatment of political culture itself.

The Renaissance of Political Culture

During the 1970s and a part of the 1980s, political culture studies were often discredited in some quarters. In part, this reflected the criticisms listed earlier. But, in part, it reflected the times: Vietnam, Nixon, Watergate, protests, oil crises, recession, Jimmy Carter's "malaise." Many persons, particularly in the academic community, had become disillusioned with or lost faith in America and America's future; and, if we could not get our own house in order, who were we to foist off our versions and models of political development or political culture to the rest of the world? If during the 1970s much of the country was in a funk, why should we expect comparative politics and its main approaches to be immune from these influences?

A third factor accounting for the decline of political culture studies was the rise during this period of new and alternative approaches (treated in detail in the next chapter). These included dependency theory, political economy, and a revived Marxism. All these approaches reflected, in part, the protest movements of those times; all focused on "structural" (class, economic) approaches to development and overall comparative politics; and in none of them was there much room for political culture. At the same time, we also need to recognize that, during this same period, there were some new and pathbreaking studies of political culture in Africa, Asia, Latin America, the Middle East, and Europe, which, however, required a change in the times and academic atmosphere to be given due recognition.

The renaissance in political culture studies began in the 1980s with the publication by Almond and Verba of a new edition of their pioneering work entitled *The Civic Culture Revisited*.[21] In this new edition, Almond and Verba tried to answer the theoretical and methodological criticisms of their book raised over the nearly twenty years since its initial publication. They even invited some of the most vociferous critics to contribute chapters to the new edition! And they solicited chapters from experts on each of the five countries covered in their original volume dealing with the political culture of those countries, providing more refined analysis, and updating the materials presented. The result was more than a new edition; it was almost a completely new volume—although it had less of a splashy pathbreaking impact than did the original *Civic Culture*.

---

[21]Boston: Little Brown, 1980.

The revised or "revisited" volume of Almond and Verba was followed by a variety of new political culture studies by some of the leading figures in American Political Science. In 1981 Professor Samuel P. Huntington of Harvard University published a superb study entitled *American Politics: The Promise of Disharmony*[22] in which he moved away from his earlier emphasis on political institutions and, in looking at the American political system from a comparative perspective, toward a focus on political cultural factors. That was shortly followed by his work on transitions from authoritarianism to democracy in which Huntington clearly saw changes in political culture as *the* crucial factors in the transition.[23] Huntington, as well as another former American Political Science Association president Aaron Wildavsky and leading comparativist Harry Eckstein, published major articles on political culture in a short time span.[24]

At about the same time, MIT professor Lucian Pye, one of the early pioneers in the political culture approach, published a major work on Chinese political culture.[25] Pye argued that much of traditional Chinese political culture, founded on the Confucian belief system, had persisted into the modern era and continued to bind and limit China's Marxist-Leninist leadership from changing the system as rapidly as they wished. Pye focused particularly on the psychological constraints on Chinese political behavior. As a serious scholar, Pye made clear at the outset that in emphasizing cultural considerations he had no intention of disparaging other approaches to the study of politics. Nevertheless, he insisted on the importance of political culture as one key factor among several—and perhaps the most important one.

A variety of studies, both interpretive and quantitative, were published during this period on Latin American political culture. The interpretive studies suggested that, even though Latin America was mainly "Western" in its political beliefs and institutions, as a product of feudal, medieval Spain and Portugal, Latin America was governed by very different norms than is North American democracy. Latin America represented a fragment of the West from sixteenth-century Iberia—two-class, elitist, authoritarian, hierarchical—and, therefore, its political institutions and practices were quite different from

---

[22]Cambridge, MA: Harvard University Press, 1981.

[23]*The Third Wave: Democratization in the Late Twentieth Century* (Norman: University of Oklahoma Press, 1991).

[24]Wildavsky, "Choosing Preferences by Constructing Institutions: A Cultural Theory of Preference Formation," *American Political Science Review* 81 (March 1987); Harry Eckstein, "A Culturalist Theory of Political Change," *American Political Science Review* 82 (September 1988) 789–804.

[25]*The Mandarin and the Cadre: China's Political Cultures* (Ann Arbor: University of Michigan Press, 1988).

U.S.-style liberalism, pluralism, and democracy.[26] Empirical studies refined this analysis, provided empirical tests of its validity, and pointed out variations, both within and between countries.

In Asia the debate waxed strong over the emphasis on what were termed "Asian values."[27] Particularly as the Asian nations became more prosperous, successful, and economically powerful, Asian leaders and intellectuals began to reassert and champion their own values (largely Confucian in origin) and to tell American and other critics of their political systems that they had no right to tell Asians how to govern themselves or to give them unwanted lectures on human rights. In some cases, the assertion of Asian values was a smokescreen for justifying authoritarian practices; but it also represented a widespread Asian resentment of Western criticism, of the U.S. and others telling Asian nations what to do, as well as an assertion by Asia of the importance of its own traditions and ways of doing things. Here we have political culture debates carried to the level of high national and international policy.

Much the same thing occurred in the Middle East and Africa. The Islamic fundamentalist revolution in Iran in 1979, and the impact of some of the same cultural nationalistic ideas subsequently in other countries, emphasized and sought to propagate an Islamic political culture and model of development. Edward Said's *Orientalism*[28] and numerous other studies similarly asserted Islamic cultural and political values as well as criticizing the West—including Western models of development—for attempting to impose its values and model on the area. Similarly, in Africa: rejecting that their political culture was "traditional" or "parochial," as much U.S. social science and political culture literature had asserted, many African leaders and intellectuals sought to fashion an African model of development and to emphasize indigenous institutions rather than ill-fitting imported ones.[29]

Perhaps the most impressive of the new political culture projects done during this period was the comparative study carried out by Professor Ronald Inglehart.[30] Like the original *Civic Culture* volume, Inglehart's study combined a sophisticated theoretical discussion of political culture with particularly rich public opinion survey data. Inglehart found that the peoples of different

---

[26]Howard J. Wiarda (ed.), *Politics and Social Change in Latin America*, 3rd ed. (Boulder, CO: Westview, 1992).

[27]For example, Raul S. Manglapus, *Will of the People: Original Democracy in Non-Western Societies* (Westport, CT: Greenwood, 1987).

[28]New York: Vintage, 1978.

[29]Ali Mazrui, *The African: A Triple Heritage* (London: BBC Publications, 1986).

[30]The Renaissance of Political Culture," *American Political Science Review* 82 (December 1988): 1203–30; also by Inglehart, *Culture Shift in Advanced Industrial Societies* (Princeton, NJ: Princeton University Press, 1990).

countries and areas not only have quite durable political-cultural attributes but that these often have major economic and political consequences as well. Importantly, he found that political culture was a crucial link in explaining the relations between economic development and democracy and that, if one asks why some economically developed or developing countries have democracy and others do not, the answer is to be found in their differing political cultures. Perhaps most important for our discussion here was Inglehart's conclusion that, when empirically tested against other explanatory variables, the political culture explanation was a powerful tool of understanding.

The end of the cold war in the early 1990s served as a further impetus to political culture studies. For one thing, the decline of strategic factors in international politics enabled students of comparative politics to concentrate more on cultural differences. For another, the end of the cold war brought ethnic, cultural, and nationality issues long bottled up by the superpowers to the forefront. Third, the collapse of Marxism-Leninism in Russia and Eastern Europe; the failure of Marxist regimes in Cambodia, Cuba, and North Korea; and the abandonment of Marxian economics in China and Vietnam combined to lead to a general discrediting of Marxist or "structuralist" explanations and, hence, to a new emphasis on cultural factors.

One of the most important of the post–cold war books was Samuel P. Huntington's *The Clash of Civilizations*.[31] Huntington argued that, with the cold war over, future international conflict would involve not so much clashes between superpowers but clashes between civilizations, or cultures. He identified the major civilizations as Western, Confucian, Japanese, Islamic, Hindu, Slavic Orthodox, Latin American, and African. He said that cultural differences between these civilizations are far greater than the political, ideological, or economic differences. Writing at a time of particular conflict between the United States and Japan and between the United States and fundamentalist Islam, Huntington saw the cultural differences as being paramount; as evidence he offered the clash between Slavic Orthodox Serbs and the Muslims in the former Yugoslavia, ethnic and religious conflicts in many areas of the globe, as well as separatist movements in many Western nations. The Huntington thesis was controversial and probably overstated (can one really imagine a war between the United States and, say, Japan over cultural issues?), but it certainly stirred debate and served to reemphasize the growing importance of cultural explanations.

A second pathbreaking study that similarly emphasized cultural factors in explaining development differences was by Robert Putnam, another Harvard political scientist.[32] Putnam's country of interest is Italy, but his study, like

---

[31]New York: Simon & Schuster, 1996.

[32]*Making Democracy Work: Civic Traditions in Modern Italy* (Princeton, NJ: Princeton University Press, 1993.

other major works in comparative politics, is far more than a single-country case study. Putnam is interested in the larger question of what makes democracy work or not work, and he uses Italy's various regional governments to test his hypothesis. He concludes that democracy works best in those regions with high levels of "civic community," by which he means patterns of social cooperation based on tolerance, trust, and widespread norms of active citizen participation. All of these are essentially cultural attributes. What makes Putnam's study so valuable is not only his findings but the fact he also fairly and in a balanced way assesses other explanations (structural, institutional, class based) before arriving at an assessment stressing cultural factors.

A third major work emphasizing cultural themes is that of Francis Fukuyama. Two of Fukuyama's books are of particular interest. The first, provocatively entitled *The End of History*,[33] argues that, with Marxism-Leninism vanquished and authoritarianism in decline in Asia, Latin America, and other areas, democracy was the only viable and legitimate form of government; that with the triumph of democracy, the great systems debate in comparative politics between Marxist-Leninist, authoritarian, and democratic regimes was over. By his title (and it is often misinterpreted mainly by people who have not read the book), Fukuyama did not mean literally that history was over, only that the struggle between grand political ideas had largely ended and that democracy was the system of government that virtually all peoples everywhere desired. In a subsequent volume entitled *Trust*,[34] Fukuyama elaborated on these themes and emphasized much like Putnam that mutual trust and civic responsibility were the keys to good government.

Although many other good books and articles on political culture have been published in recent years, students should also be aware that there are many bad books out there as well. I cite only one here (actually two but by the same author) as an example of how *not* to do political culture research and analysis. These are Laurence Harrison's *Underdevelopment Is a State of Mind* and *The Pan-American Dream*.[35] In these two volumes (one cannot call them studies), Harrison tries to explain the differences between the United States and Latin America (as well as the situation of African-American and ethnic and racial differences everywhere) by emphasizing cultural traits. He blames Latin America's relative lack of development on Catholicism, its Spanish background, and its lack of a work ethic. He wants Latin America to jettison its entire cultural history and adopt U.S. values—as

---

[33] *The End of History and the Last Man* (New York: Maxwell Macmillan International, 1992).

[34] *Trust: The Social Virtues and the Creation of Prosperity* (New York: Free Press, 1995).

[35] *Underdevlopment Is a State of Mind: The Latin American Case* (Lanham, MD: University Press of America for the Harvard Center for International Affairs, 1985); *The Pan-American Dream: Do Latin America's Cultural Values Discourage True Partnership with the United States and Canada?* (New York: Basic Books, 1997).

if culture is something that one puts on anew every day like a pair of socks. Harrison's argument is flawed by ill logic, *ad hominem* arguments, cultural stereotyping, prejudice, simplistic arguments, the elevation of a useful but still simple explanation into an exclusive and all-encompassing one, and strong prejudice. There are many good studies extant of political culture; unfortunately, Harrison's books are not among them.

A Summing Up

In the right hands, and with a balanced point of view, political culture can be a powerful explanatory tool. All of us know that political culture is important in explaining differences and similarities between countries; the question is how to use this tool of analysis in the most analytic, balanced, and nonprejudicial way.[36]

We, therefore, conclude this chapter with a number of cautionary admonitions:

- Use political culture but with caution.
- Keep in mind that political culture is dynamic; it is not fixed but changing, usually in conjunction with larger social, economic, and political changes.
- A country may have more than one political culture, and these may be in conflict.
- Political culture is often manipulated by different political elites for their own advantage—another reason to be cautious.
- Political culture provides a useful but still partial explanation; avoid elevating it into a single, monocausal, all-encompassing explanation; remain open to other explanatory factors.
- Avoid ethnic or religious stereotyping and racism; use tendency statements; utilize survey data as much as possible and give the percentages; always remember that within any group no one ever conforms entirely to the general patterns observed.

---

[36]A good recent collection is Larry Diamond (ed.), *Political Culture and Democracy in Developing Countries* (Boulder, CO: Reinner, 1994).

5

Challenges and Alternatives to Development

Bureaucratic-Authoritarianism, Dependency Theory and World Systems, Corporatism, Political Economy, State–Society Relations, Indigenous Theories of Change, Rational Choice Theory, and the New Institutionalism,

Major changes in comparative politics have often corresponded to the changes of the decades. The traditional, formal-legal approach dominated the field through the 1950s: until Macridis's critique had time to sink in, the discipline of political science had emphasized more informal political processes, and a host of new and developing nations had emerged on the world scene. Then, the political development approach was dominant during most of the 1960s—until the Vietnam War, the student protests, and the rise of a new generation of young, often more radical, nonestablishment comparative politics scholars. These more critical approaches dominated during the 1970s and on into the 1980s when a new consensus began to emerge.

The crisis of the political development approach began when more and more young scholars began to report back in their doctoral dissertations and published works that the categories and concepts advanced in the general theoretical literature by Rostow, Almond, and others failed to correspond to what they had observed in the developing nations. Eventually, these individual expressions of discontent came together in a more general critique that suggested strongly—much to the consternation of the now-senior scholars who had earlier championed developmentalism—that maybe the whole theory of development was wrong or misapplied. To these discontents were added the general discontents of the time: Vietnam, the assassinations of Martin Luther King, Jr., and Robert Kennedy, the presidency of Richard Nixon, Watergate, global economic downturn, heightened cold war tensions, and so on. This was a period when all established institutions including motherhood and the family were under fire; we should probably not expect that comparative politics would be immune from the critical spirit.

The criticisms of the political development approach were strong and devastating. As the political development approach declined in popularity, a number of new approaches—dependency theory and the world systems approach, corporatism, bureaucratic-authoritarianism, political economy, state–society relations, indigenous theories—rose up to replace it. None of these acquired the position of dominance in comparative politics that developmentalism had enjoyed, but they certainly competed with it for influence. To these approaches were now added in the 1980s rational choice theory and the new institutionalism. Hence, by the 1990s, instead of one single approach in the field, there were now several—each with its own literature, apostles, theories, leading spokespersons, and disciples. The older scholars in comparative politics sometimes found this competition disquieting; others looked on the new diversity as healthy for the field. In any case, comparative politics had now become more divided and fragmented, with a greater variety of approaches, than ever before.

Dependency Theory and the World Systems Approach

Dependency theory and the world systems approach arose in the late 1960s and achieved considerable popularity especially—but not exclusively—among students on the left of the political spectrum. Indeed, that was part of the problem with these new theories: it was not always clear whether dependency and world systems were new and serious approaches in comparative politics or expressions of ideological positions.

Dependency theory arose from two major sources, which helps explain the confusion as to what it represented. One strong influence was Marxian thought. Marxism was a small minority current in comparative politics, and for a long time it had wielded little influence because of the overwhelming dominance of the political development approach. However, with the U.S. military intervention in the Dominican Republic in 1965, the Vietnam War, and the student protests of 1969–1970, the Marxian approach began to attract more attention. It focused on the contradictions between U.S. interests in the developing nations and the interests of the developing nations themselves, as well as on the contradictions and conflicts within these countries. In contrast, development theory had stressed the peaceful, evolutionary process of modernization and the harmony between U.S. interests and those of the developing nations. An early statement of the Marxian dependency alternative and approach to development was André Gunder Frank's book *Capitalism and Underdevelopment in Latin America*, a book published at the height of the Vietnam War protests in 1969 and one that, while often misrepresenting facts and making erroneous interpretations, nevertheless set forth a strong Marxian position.[1]

The other influence in dependency theory came from non-Leninists who were interested in the politics of the developing nations but were critical of what the prevailing development theory had left out of its analysis. For example, development theory had not paid any attention to international actors in the field of development; it had not examined the role of international markets and capitalism in the processes of development; it had not addressed class conflicts or exploitation; and it had not talked about the role of multinational corporations. All of these are fundamental elements in the development process, or the lack thereof, and yet none of them were analyzed in the prevailing development theory. Hence, it was agreed that developmentalism must pay attention to these "dependency" factors—factors that make one country's development dependent on another's—and must analyze a country's or group of countries' "relations of dependency" to the industrialized world. These suggestions came often from writers in the Third World who had experienced such dependency—from social democrats and independent Marxists (but not necessarily from Leninists). The most prominent book written from this perspective was Enzo Faletto and Fernando Henrique Cardoso's *Dependency and Development in Latin America*.[2]

The dependency approach was considered a serious corrective to the developmentalist approach. Instead of modernization in the industrialized world and the developing world going forward smoothly and together as developmentalism posited, dependency theory posited that development in the Third World was *dependent* on development in the already developed nations. Unfortunately, these two processes may not always be in harmony. Indeed, the First World may exploit the Third World, may intervene militarily there, may allow its multinationals to drain Third World resources or attempt to control the government, and so on. In its more radical expressions dependency

---

[1] André Gunder Frank, *Capitalism and Underdevelopment in Latin America* (New York: Monthly Review Press, 1969).

[2] Enzo Faletto and Fernando Henrique Cardoso, *Dependency and Development in Latin America* (Berkeley: University of California Press, 1979).

theory suggested that development in the First World came at the expense of development in the Third World, that First World development often exploited the Third World, and that Third World development was incompatible with First World development and could only take place when the First World and its capitalistic economic system was destroyed.

Dependency theory, therefore, is not one single school of thought. Rather, it presents a range of perspectives, some of which are neutral and scholarly and others of which are more partisan and ideological. Admittedly, the developing nations *are* often dependent on the developed ones, international market forces largely controlled by the developed world *do* sometimes retard Third World development, multinationals and other international actors *do* at times muck around in the internal affairs of other nations, and the United States has and *does* sometimes intervene militarily and in other ways in the Third World. One can pragmatically acknowledge these facts of life, however, as some writers about dependency have done,[3] without necessarily becoming an ideologue of *dependencia*. In other words, one can recognize that there are various relations of dependency in the world without elevating that into a single-causal explanation of all the world's ills or using dependency analysis simply to blame some scapegoat (the United States, multinationals, capitalism) for Third World underdevelopment.

More sophisticated dependency analysts have focused not just on the role of outside actors in internal Third World development but also on the interrelations between such outside influences and local elites within the developing nations.[4] For example, one might research the interactions of U.S. sugar companies, mining interests, or manufacturing concerns *with* local, Third World entrepreneurial groups, elites, and the government—often involved in an interlocking relationship. Or one might focus on the relations among the armed forces of a developing country who may happen to be in power, the civilian technicians who help manage the national accounts for them, *and* U.S. or other international investors who need a "favor" (tax breaks, import licenses, export permits) from these same groups. In short, dependency relations are often complex, including not just the actions of foreign concerns or governments but also local actors and institutions.

The world systems approach was frequently closely associated with dependency analysis. Its foremost advocate was political scientist/political economist Immanuel Wallerstein. Wallerstein went beyond specific dependency

---

[3]See Theodore H. Moran, *Multinational Corporations and the Politics of Dependence* (Cambridge, MA: Harvard University, Center for International Affairs, 1975); or Howard J. Wiarda, *Dictatorship, Development, and Disintegration: Politics and Social Change in the Dominican Republic* (Ann Arbor, MI: Xerox University Microfilms Monograph Series, 1975), chaps. 11–12.

[4]Peter Evans, *Dependent Development: The Alliance of Multinational, State, and Local Capital in Brazil* (Princeton, NJ: Princeton University Press, 1979).

relations between two countries or two areas and argued for an approach that emphasized a *world* system of dependency and exploitation. According to Wallerstein's theory of center-periphery relations, countries in the "center" of the world system (first, Western Europe; then, the United States) have exploited and gotten rich off the "periphery" (Eastern Europe; Southern Europe; colonies in Africa, Asia, and the Middle East; Latin America) at least since the great wave of European colonization and emerging global dominance in the sixteenth century. Wallerstein's approach thus involved studies of global colonialism and imperialism as well as dependency. While incorporating a dependency approach, Wallerstein went beyond dependency to construct a breathtaking, worldwide theory of exploitation, imperialism, and neocolonialism.[5]

The contributions—and limitations—of the dependency and world system approaches are several. First, the contributions: they oblige us to focus on international actors in ways that development theory did not; they emphasize world market and financial trends over which the developing countries often have little control; they talk of multinational corporations and other transnational actors who sometimes have considerable influence in developing nations' internal affairs; they bring in U.S. intervention, the role of capitalism, and other international factors about which earlier development theory had little to say. These are all important subjects with which comparative politics ought to be concerned. These dependency and world system factors ought to be seen as supplements to earlier comparative politics work, however—elements that the earlier work left out—not necessarily as complete, all-encompassing, new approaches, which is probably claiming too much for them.

Next, the limitations: first, dependency theory and the world system approach take the blame for underdevelopment off the shoulders of the developing nations and place it squarely on those of the already industrialized nations—surely an overstatement but a factor that helps explain these theories' popularity, especially in the developing nations. Second, and related, dependency analysis and world systems tend especially to blame the United States for the world's ills—again a vast overstatement. Third, the dependency and world system approaches are not even-handed: they tend to concentrate on countries that are dependent on the United States but to ignore countries that were dependencies of the former Soviet Union—for example, the former Soviet satellites in Eastern Europe, as well as Afghanistan, Ethiopia, Vietnam, Cuba, and Nicaragua. And fourth, also related to these others, dependency theory and world system theory have generally had a leftist, Marxist, or Marxist-Leninist thrust, which means that their utility as a tool of scholarly analysis is often limited by this heavy ideological baggage.

---

[5]Immanuel Wallerstein, *The Modern World System* (New York: Academic Press, 1976).

In serious, scholarly hands, dependency theory as well as the analysis of world systems can be a useful tool of analysis because out there in the "real world" there are genuine relations of dependence as well as complex patterns of interdependence. But in less sophisticated hands, dependency and world systems analysis has a tendency to spin off in ideological directions in order to criticize the United States.

Corporatism

The corporatist approach arose out of the selfsame unhappiness with development theory that gave rise to dependency theory—and at about the same time (late 1960s to early 1970s). It also suggested that the prevailing development theory was focused on the wrong subjects—or that its analysis was incomplete.

Corporatism was in some ways a strange term to use, and some of the scholars of this approach have expressed the wish that another term had been used. *Corporatism* often carries unfortunate connotations, because that was the term used to describe Mussolini's political-economic system in Italy and that of the National Socialists in Germany. Corporatism therefore carries an often very emotional association with fascism, which limits its effectiveness as a neutral social science term.

Actually, fascism is only one form that corporatism may take; there are also Christian democratic, liberal, social democratic, socialist, and bureaucratic forms. We should also list the other things that corporatism is not: corporatism is not like a modern joint stock company; corporatism is not the same thing as a business corporation; nor is corporatism a form of industrial organization.

Corporatism may be defined as a structure of national sociopolitical organization in which the major societal units (armed forces, religious bodies, employers, labor) are integrated into, and usually subordinated to, the state. This stands in contrast to liberalism or interest group pluralism in which the major societal units and interest groups are separate and independent from the state. Under corporatism, for example, state, labor, and business groups may enter into a formal alliance to avoid strikes while at the same time raising wages and productivity; or labor, business, and perhaps other groups will be incorporated into the state's regulatory bodies so as to guarantee them a voice in policy making; or perhaps these groups will have formal or de facto representation in parliament. In short, the corporative system, which integrates government and societal or interest groups, exists alongside, or parallel to, and may be as important as the electoral system, political parties, the parliament, and other institutions of a liberal/pluralist character with which we are more familiar.

Scholars began paying serious attention to corporatism in the late 1960s and early 1970s, when it became apparent that a large number of political phenomena could not be adequately explained simply by concentrating on elections, party or interest group competition, or the legislative or executive arenas. The corporatist approach seemed to offer a useful way to examine a variety of interesting political activities—modern industrial relations in which the state plays a large role alongside labor and capital, the incorporation of specific interest organizations into actual decision making, the implementation of public policy by hitherto private groups—that interest group theory and other approaches could not adequately explain.

From the beginning there were two approaches to the study of corporatism, which seemed often and needlessly to be in conflict. In one interpretation corporatism emerges from the political culture; is usually found in neofeudal societies (such as those of Latin America); stems from earlier, historical forms of corporatism (the "organic laws" governing the relations of military orders, towns, and so on, to the state); and often connotes the political worldview of the historical Aristotelian-Thomistic syntheses (emphasizing order, hierarchy, and the close integration of society into the state), which has now been updated to deal with the newer realities of a more industrialized and modern world. Corporatism in this sense is a historical tradition, an ideology, a sociocultural pattern, and a system of political understanding just like its alternatives, liberalism and Marxism. Because of their history and traditions, the Southern European and Latin American regions have been especially impacted by this particular political pattern. Hence, a proper understanding of Southern Europe and Latin America must begin by examining historical cultural traditions and societal assumptions rather than operating from the point of view of the liberal, pluralist, individualistic Anglo-American nations, which share a different cognition.[6]

A second view sees corporatism as a general institutional model of the political system with no particular cultural, regional, or ideological links.[7] In this view corporatism can exist in Europe, Japan, the United States, or other areas. Corporatism in this conception means a way of structuring national politics and of integrating labor and capital into state decision making, regardless of prior culture or history. Corporatism may still take a variety of forms in different countries, but it remains fundamentally different from liberalism. There are, in addition, authoritarian and bureaucratic forms of corporatism as well as more open and democratic forms.

---

[6]For examples from both Iberia and Latin America, see Howard J. Wiarda, *Corporatism and Development: The Portuguese Experience* (Amherst: University of Massachusetts Press, 1977); and Wiarda, *Corporatism and National Development in Latin America* (Boulder, CO: Westview, 1981).

[7]Philippe C. Schnitter and Gerhard Lehmbruck (eds.), *Trends toward Corporatist Interest Intermediation* (Beverly Hills, CA: Sage, 1979).

Most scholars see no contradiction between these two forms of or approaches to corporatism. There is clearly a *tradition* of corporatism that, because of historical religious factors, the legacies of feudalism, and a certain cultural history, is particularly strong in Southern Europe (especially the Iberian region) and Latin America. But other developing nations that may have legacies of tribal, caste, and clan associations may also be organized on a corporatist basis. At the same time, modern or "neo" corporatism, which is particularly strong in Western Europe and Japan, grows out of the bureaucratization of the modern state and the need to link labor and capital together for coordinated national development. The older cultural and historical forms of corporatism may evolve into the more modern kind or the newer forms of corporatism may develop without prior cultural traditions.[8]

Currently, there is widespread agreement that corporatism involves a special pattern of relations between the state or government and other social or political institutions and associations, one in which the state plays the role of architect and regulator of the political order. The state helps define, structure, and delimit the scope of class and interest group activity, coordinates the activities of private and professional associations, and creates mechanisms of direct sectoral interest representation in decision making. Corporatism is, therefore, a system of interest group representation based on noncompeting, officially sanctioned, state-supervised groups. Unlike liberalism, the state is not merely a referee of the interest group struggle but is itself an active force imposing design and structure on the political system. But unlike totalitarianism, corporatism (except in its fascist variant) does not entail "total" mobilization and politicization of society.

The corporatist approach is especially useful in analyzing modern labor relations, the relations of interest groups to the state, to parliaments, and to one another, the regulatory apparatus and policy making of the modern state, social security and social welfare legislation in which labor and the state are involved, and the relations in general between decision making and public policy. It should be noted also that corporatism makes no claim to being a complete explanation of political behavior; instead, it may be thought of as a complement to other explanations. The corporative structure usually stands parallel to and alongside other political institutions and arenas (the electoral arena, the military arena, the political party arena); seldom is a political system completely corporatively based (the New State of Antonio Salazar in Portugal in the 1930s came the closest). Hence, where explanations based on corporatism and corporative structures are useful, by

---

[8]Howard J. Wiarda, *Corporatism and Comparative Politics: The Other Great "Ism"* (New York: M. E. Sharpe, 1997).

all means let us utilize them; but where other explanations are called for (for instance, in discussing electoral behavior or political parties), by all means let us use them also. Our goal, after all, is to understand comparative political systems as fully as possible, and whatever helps us do that ought to be used.

This pragmatic approach to corporatism is now widely accepted in comparative politics. A few flag wavers still brandish corporatism as an ideological banner in one form or another, but most scholars do not use the corporative approach that way. Rather, corporatism is seen as a useful approach to understanding political phenomena that other approaches—developmentalism or liberalism—spoke to only weakly or not at all. Hence, corporatism is no longer so controversial a concept as it once was or as dependency analysis still is. It has been widely incorporated within the comparative politics field, although its limits (it is a partial but not a complete explanation) are also recognized. The debate over corporatism has thus died down; everyone recognizes that it has its useful aspects, and the impassioned controversies about it of a few years ago have faded.

Bureaucratic-Authoritarianism

Bureaucratic-authoritarianism, or B-A as it is popularly called, is yet a third approach that grew out of the late 1960s' disillusionment with developmentalism. Developmentalism, recall, had posited a close correlation between economic growth and political democracy; as economic development went forward, democracy was supposed to follow. But in Africa, Asia, and especially Latin America in the late 1960s, one democratic regime after another gave way to military-authoritarianism. The B-A approach was launched as an effort to try to explain what went wrong, why development produced not democracy but breakdown and authoritarianism.

As with the other approaches previously mentioned, the B-A approach can be utilized at several different levels. First, there is the issue of bureaucratic-authoritarianism. This term was used to indicate that military takeovers, especially in Latin America, were no longer just simple one-man affairs but had become far more involved than that. In the new, more complex societies of Latin America, *coups d'état* are usually carried out by the military acting as an institution, not just by a single disgruntled officer. Or, typically, they are carried out with both civilian and military participation, again implying a more complex process and structure than an old-fashioned military takeover. For these reasons, the military regimes in such more developed and complex countries as Argentina, Brazil, and Chile required analysis at a complexity level commensurate with their own level of modernization—hence the term *bureaucratic-authoritarianism.*

At a second level, B-A as articulated by its foremost exponent, Guillermo O'Donnell, was closely related to, and an extension of, dependency theory.[9] According to O'Donnell, the dependent position of the Latin American economies placed strong limitations on the region's capacity for economic growth. As economic expansion declines, discontent grows, especially in the lower classes. The ruling elites, including the military, then have a clear-cut choice: they can curtail growth, or they can continue to pursue it by squeezing and repressing the workers, through wage reductions, belt tightenings, and general austerity. When faced with this stark choice, the elites have consistently opted to continue growth. To control the lower classes, however, they have required a repressive military regime in power. Hence, the alliance of civilian elites and the military brought together in a concerted effort— bureaucratic-authoritarianism—to control the lower classes.

At a third level, B-A became a rather vague and unclear argument based on economic determinism. In O'Donnell's argument B-A was produced by what he called the "crisis of import substitution." He argued that Latin America's industrialization, which took the form of manufacturing local products as substitutes for those historically imported from abroad (hence the term *import substitution*), had reached a point of saturation and could not be continued. Why this was so was not clear in O'Donnell's writing. In any case, the crisis of import substitution led to a slowing of economic growth, rising discontent from below, and hence a rash of military takeovers. In a subsequent formulation, however, O'Donnell used the selfsame crisis of import substitution to account for the transitions away from authoritarianism and toward democracy in the region. Now, you can't have it both ways: either the crisis of import substitution leads to authoritarianism or it leads to democracy, but it cannot lead to both. In addition to containing this logical flaw, O'Donnell's analysis was now subjected to a polite but devastating critique that suggested powerfully that its economics were wrong.[10]

The general assessment of most scholars at this stage is, first, that the focus on *bureaucratic*-authoritarianism is correct—these are (or were) more complex bureaucratic regimes than the one-man dictatorship of the past. Second, there *was* a social and economic crisis in Latin America in the 1960s that threatened the elites and middle class, who then turned to the military to protect their interests. But third, O'Donnell's attempt to impose an economic determinist interpretation on these events will not stand up. Here the

---

[9]Guillermo O'Donnell, *Modernization and Bureaucratic-Authoritarianism: Studies in South American Politics* (Berkeley, CA: Institute of International Studies, University of California, 1973).

[10]David Collier (ed.) *The New Authoritarianism in Latin America* (Princeton, NJ: Princeton University Press, 1979).

analysis is flawed both economically and politically. So let us accept the B-A phenomenon, and let us also accept that there was a sociopolitical crisis in the 1960s that threatened the governing elites and made them turn to the military for allies; but let us reject the economic determinist elements, which do not do the B-A theory any good and in fact detract from its usefulness.

In the meantime, most of the B-A regimes of record have since undergone transitions to democracy, a phenomenon that has by now rendered the B-A theory mostly of historical interest. These transitions to democracy and the literature they have spawned are taken up in Chapter 6.

Political Economy

Political economy (PE) as an approach has been around for a long time. Aristotle and Machiavelli, though known as political scientists, also paid close attention to economic factors; Adam Smith and Karl Marx, though economists, similarly saw the importance of political variables. The PE approach, essentially, tries to scale the barriers of our academic disciplines by focusing on both politics and economics, and particularly on the interrelations between the two.

A number of influences came together in the 1960s and 1970s that help explain the revival and rising importance of the PE approach. The first and simplest was the discrediting and decline of developmentalism as the main and, to that point, predominant alternative. As developmentalism appeared less attractive, the political economy approach gained more adherents.

The second reason was the rising influence of Marxist interpretations in American college and university faculties from the time of the Vietnam War, the student protests of the late 1960s, and Watergate. Many faculty members were radicalized by these events; quite a number of the radical student leaders also went on to earn advanced degrees and then to join university faculties. Whereas in the 1950s and 1960s Marxism had been such a minority strain in American colleges that its influence was slight (despite the effort by some politicians to get political mileage out of investigating it), by the 1970s the Marxist influence had become considerable and was still rising.[11] Of course, not all political economy analysis was on the left (witness Nobel Prize winner Milton Friedman and the Chicago School), but for a time at least that was the prevailing position.

A third reason for PE's growing influence was simply pragmatic: the increasing importance of international economic issues in world affairs. With

---

[11]Fun reading, though by no means a complete picture, is Roger Kimball, *Tenured Radicals: How Politics Has Corrupted Our Higher Education* (New York: HarperCollins, 1990).

the rise of Japan to economic great-power status, the emergence of the other East Asian economic "tigers" (Hong Kong, Singapore, South Korea, Taiwan), the great oil crises of the 1970s, the increasing influences of multinational corporations, globalization, and the rising sense of the United States' own dependence on imports and trade, economic issues became more and more important. In some circles it seemed that economic issues had surpassed political, diplomatic, and strategic ones as the most important in international politics. As economic issues gained greater salience, students of comparative politics began to focus more on international economic interrelationships and on domestic economic policy making than they had previously.[12]

One other factor helped explain this new focus on political economy: professional economists seemed often to be doing a poor job of analyzing these new international economic or political-economic forces. Whereas before, comparative politics scholars had largely concentrated on studying *political* institutions and had left economics to the economists, now, for the questions in which they were interested—the role of multinationals, the political implications of international trade, changing power relationships derived from economic rather than military might, the political role of labor unions, the international debt issue, central planning versus privatization, and many others—political scientists often discovered that they would have to do their own economic studies. Either there was no literature on these subjects from economists, or else what there was proved less than useful for the purposes of comparative political analysis. So specialists in comparative politics began reschooling themselves in economics and employing the tools of economics to probe the issues they wished to explore.

The result was a flurry of studies by comparative politics scholars of various political economy issues. Some scholars studied the incidence and impact of labor strikes in such turbulent countries in the 1970s as Italy, France, and Spain.[13] Others examined comparative policy making in such areas as housing, health care, and social security.[14] Still others focused on the role of multinational corporations or—making the link to dependency theory—on the impact of changing terms of trade on different political systems.[15] The comparative study of socialist and capitalist economic performance was

---

[12]Some of the better literature includes Stephen D. Cohen, *The Making of United States International Economic Policy* (New York: Praeger, 1988); and Joan Edelman Spero, *The Politics of International Economic Relations* (New York: St. Martin's, 1977).

[13]Douglas Hibbs, "On the Political Economy of Long-Run Trends in Strike Activity," *British Journal of Political Science* 8 (1978): 153–75.

[14]Arnold Heidenheimer et al., *Comparative Public Policy: Policies of Social Choice in Europe and America* (New York: St. Martin's, 1975).

[15]Stimulating reading is Mancur Olsen, *The Rise and Decline of Nations* (New Haven, CT: Yale University Press, 1982).

another main topic, as were government planning, the transition from social-ism to capitalism (as in Eastern Europe and the former Soviet Union), and issues of privatization of state-run enterprises.[16] During the 1970s and 1980s, a veritable flood of PE studies emerged in books and scholarly journals, and PE developed as one of the major approaches in comparative politics.[17]

The political economy approach is clearly related to some of the other ap-proaches already analyzed. The explanation for bureaucratic-authoritarianism, for example, could be seen as a type of PE analysis, as could corporatism with its focus on socioeconomic interests and their relations to the state. Depen-dency analysis, too, is clearly a type of PE approach applied particularly to the developing nations. Political development and political economy are also related (economic growth is the motor force that helps drive political devel-opment); but because PE has often had a Marxist thrust and political devel-opment was conceived in part as a non- or even anticommunist approach, these two have often been at loggerheads.

That fact leads to our final comments about PE. On many university cam-puses and in quite a bit of the writing on the subject, political economy has often been identified with a Marxist approach. To the extent that is true, an ideological component and political bias have been added to PE analysis. Be-cause many scholars do not find that particular ideology congenial or even useful, PE as an approach has sometimes suffered as a result of its association with Marxism.

But such an automatic connection between Marxism and PE need not necessarily be made, and in fact some of the most sophisticated work in com-parative politics is now being done using a political economy approach, inde-pendent of ideology. The argument is similar to that regarding dependency theory: both PE and dependency theory can take Marxist or non-Marxist di-rections. Shorn of its ideological blinders, PE (like dependency analysis) can be an exceedingly useful approach; but to the degree it takes on political over-tones from either the right or the left, PE (again like dependency) becomes mainly a political instrument rather than a serious tool of analysis.

State–Society Relations

State–society relations as an approach in comparative politics is in some senses akin to corporatism. That is, it is not meant as a full and complete approach in itself but as a useful complement to some other approaches. At the same time, it is not as ideological or as controversial as some of the other approaches

---

[16]Raymond Vernon, *The Promise of Privatization* (New York: Council on Foreign Rela-tions, 1988).

[17]The leading journal of political economy studies is *International Organization*.

analyzed here. Rather, the state–society approach has been largely accepted within the field without giving rise to the academic brawls that some other of the newer approaches do.

The state–society approach deals with the interrelations between the central state and the various units (classes, interest groups, private associations) that make up a society. This approach arose from the fact that in much of social science, both Marxian and non-Marxian, the state was not viewed as a major actor. In Marxian theory the state is seen as part of the "superstructure," which is determined by economic and class factors. In non-Marxian interest group theory, the state is a kind of neutral referee that umpires the interest group struggle but is not itself a major player. In both of these conceptions the state is a minor player, relegated to the position of being a "dependent variable"—dependent, that is, on the classes or the interest group struggle.

By contrast, the state–society relations focus seeks to "bring the state back in" as a major factor.[18] The state is seen as being a key regulator of interest group activity, of political parties, and of the policy-making process. The state is now viewed as being an "independent variable," or at least mostly so. The state is pictured as having varying degrees of autonomy from the society and as having a dynamic relationship with that society. Of course, it must be noted that many scholars of comparative politics have always believed the state or government to be an independent variable. They did not need to be reminded of the state's autonomy and independence in making some decisions, and they argue it is mostly economists and sociologists—neither of whom have been prone to acknowledge the independence of political variables—who have been responsible for the *revival* of the state–society approach, when in fact political scientists have always recognized a leading role for the state.

Actually, several different approaches to studying state–society relations have been advanced. In Latin American studies, state–society relations have been usefully employed as a way of emphasizing the strong, integrative, often organic role of state in that area, along with such strong societal groups as the Catholic Church and the armed forces, as well as the changing balance between them over time.[19] In this focus, state–society relations is closely related to the corporatist approach. In other developing nations the state–society focus has been used to study the relations of the clan, the tribe, or the caste association with the state, and the ways these relations have changed as the society moved from a feudal-agrarian-rural type to an urban-industrial

---

[18]Theda Skocpol (ed.) *Bringing the State Back In* (Cambridge: Cambridge University Press, 1985).

[19]Alfred Stepan, *State and Society: Peru in Comparative Perspective* (Princeton, NJ: Princeton University Press, 1978).

type.[20] In still other scholars' hands the state–society focus has been used to study revolutions, the disjunctions that may exist between state policy and societal needs or demands, and the processes of policy making—or breakdown—in the modern state.[21] In these areas the state–society focus often overlaps with the corporatism approach.

Most of us in comparative politics rather like the state–society approach. It claims neither too little nor too much. It is an important focus, but it does not presume to be a complete or all-encompassing one. At the same time, the state–society focus emphasizes political factors as well as social and economic ones. It provides important links to such other approaches as corporatism, dependency, and development. Thus, the state–society approach has been largely accepted in the field without great fanfare.

Indigenous Theories of Change

As developmentalism waned in the 1970s as a model for Third World modernization, and because in many areas Marxism-Leninism was also unacceptable, a number of developing areas and nations began to put forth their own, or indigenous, theories of change. They wanted a model of development based on local, home-grown institutions, not on ideas inspired from abroad or based on imported institutions that were not appropriate in their own context.[22]

The emphasis on indigenous, Third World models of change was accompanied by a strong critique of earlier models.[23] Many in the Third World argued that both developmentalism and Marxism-Leninism were European or American ideas, that they were based largely on the European experience with development, and that they were more or less irrelevant to their own countries. They asserted that their cultures, histories, and traditions were fundamentally different from those of the West, that the times and international contexts were different, and therefore that they needed a framework of development adapted to their own circumstances and ways of doing things.

This was heady stuff. It reflected widespread Third World disillusionment with the development models then current, both Marxian and non-Marxian,

---

[20]Joel Migdal, *Strong Societies and Weak States* (Princeton, NJ: Princeton University Press, 1986).

[21]Theda Skocpol, *States and Social Revolutions: A Comparative Study of France, Russia, and China* (New York: Cambridge University Press, 1979).

[22]Howard J. Wiarda (ed.), *Non-Western Theories of Development* (Fort Worth, TX: Harcourt Brace, 1998).

[23]A. J. Somjee, *Parallels and Actuals of Political Development* (London: Macmillan, 1986); Howard J. Wiarda, *Ethnocentrism and Foreign Policy: Can We Understand the Third World?* (Washington D.C.: American Enterprise Institute for Public Policy Research, 1985).

and an effort to go off in their own directions. Who could not be sympathetic to the Third World's efforts to find its own way, true to its own culture or cultures, rather than continuing to struggle along as pale imitations of Western ways? Such a formulation also meant that we would have, presumably, an Islamic model of development, a Latin American model of development, a sub-Saharan African model of development, a Confucian model of development, a Hindu model of development, and many others. Relying on local institutions for such indigenous models, in addition, implied that tribal or ethnic associations would serve as the basis for social and political organization in some parts of Africa and the Middle East, as would caste associations in India, and organic and corporatist institutions in Latin America (at least before the recent openings to democracy there). This is not only heady stuff but it is, potentially, downright controversial.

Helping give fuel to this movement for what was called a "nonethnocentric theory of development" were some dramatic events of these times. The Iranian Revolution of 1979 that toppled the Shah and brought the Ayatollah Khomeini and the Islamic fundamentalists to power, while often lamented and even ridiculed in the West, gave rise throughout the Middle East to the notion that there might be a genuinely Islamic model of development applicable to the entire area.[24] In India the caste associations were being reconsidered, no longer as "traditional institutions" as they were in development theory, bound to wither away as modernization proceeded, but as agencies of modernization that, akin to political parties, link the state and the society.[25] Similarly, in Africa the tribal grouping was no longer viewed as a backward institution certain to disappear under modernization's impact but as a viable agency capable of providing social services, police protection, and a sense of community.[26] In Latin America, again before the 1980s' swing toward democracy, the historical institutions based on corporatism and organicism were being touted in some quarters as providing for a genuinely Latin American model of development.[27]

But then a lot of things turned sour. The Iranian Revolution proved nasty, brutish, and far less popular than expected even in the Islamic world. The African experiments with "communalism" and other indigenous models often degenerated into authoritarianism and helped produce mass starvation. The

---

[24]See Edward Said, *Orientalism* (New York: Pantheon, 1978).

[25]Lloyd I. Rudolph and Susan Hoeber Rudolph, *The Modernity of Tradition: Political Development in India* (Chicago: University of Chicago Press, 1967).

[26]Keith B. Richburg, "Tribalism Still Shapes Kenyan Political Life," *Washington Post*, December 5, 1991, p. A42.

[27]Claudio Veliz, *The Centralist Tradition in Latin America* (Princeton, NJ: Princeton University Press, 1980); Howard J. Wiarda, *The Political Theory and Political Tradition of Latin America* (forthcoming).

indigenous models set forth proved to be the creation of elites and were far less popular with the masses in these areas than with the intellectuals that formulated them. Latin America, upon reflection, also decided that it didn't want to base itself on corporatist or organicist institutions but on democracy and representative government. Nowhere did indigenous models work well or as expected.[28]

During the 1980s, the idea of an indigenous model or models of development was further undermined by the triumph of democracy. With the decline and unraveling of Marxism-Leninism in Eastern Europe and the Soviet Union, and the overwhelming triumph worldwide of the democratic ideal, the notion of finding a third way, an indigenous route, between democracy and Marxism-Leninism also went into a tailspin. Western culture—Coca-Cola, blue jeans, rock music, consumerism, *and* democracy—has so overwhelmingly triumphed globally that it is virtually impossible to convince people that they should try something new, as yet unproven, indigenous, perhaps unworkable, and perhaps the product of intellectual elites and not of the masses. For good or ill, Western ways and "things" are what most people want; the notion of an indigenous model of development has faded into the background.

At this stage it may be hoped that various Third World countries will be able to preserve *something* of their historical indigenous culture under the onslaught of Westernism, or that they can perhaps blend, filter, and be somewhat selective in allowing that which is valuable in the West, while also preserving their own ways. Japan has been able to accomplish this and is, so far, the only non-Western country to "make it" to the top ranks of developed societies. Japan has borrowed and adopted from the West, but it has also preserved much of its own culture intact. One fears that other, weaker Third World cultures may not be so selective, however; they may well be overwhelmed by Western power, culture, and ways of doing things rather than successfully combining the new imported ways with their own traditional ones. Hence, the idea of an indigenous, home-grown route to development, or one for each major country or culture area, remains at this stage highly problematic.

Rational Choice Theory

Rational choice theory in comparative politics grew largely out of voting behavior studies in the United States, and from the effort to explain all politics in scientific, "rational" terms. This quest, in turn, derived from economics and the attempts by political scientists to fashion a universal science of politics that would parallel economics' focus on rational, self-interested actors operating to their own best advantage. Rational choice theory sought similarly to

---

[28]V. S. Naipaul, *Among the Believers: An Islamic Journey* (New York: Knopf, 1982).

develop a model of political behavior based on rational or self-interest and to use that as a means to explain individual electoral choice, congressional voting behavior, interest group politics, and governmental decision making.

Most scholars of comparative politics have so far been skeptical of the rational choice approach. They argue that politics is too complex and multilayered to be amenable to any single causal explanation. They say that even if rational choice theory explains *some* aspects of *American* political behavior, the world is too diverse for *all* the world's political systems to be explained in this way. Comparativists, as we have seen, have given a lot of attention to the study of political culture; but if cultures vary widely from area to area, how can one single explanatory model apply to all of them? In addition, rational choice theory assumes a certain stability of institutions; but in many countries instability, revolution, and chaos characterize the political system, so how can a theory based on stable institutions be of use? The result is that in no other field of political science has the rational choice approach been less favorably welcomed than in comparative politics. To the extent comparative politics remains oriented toward interpretation and toward explaining cultural differences, it has not been very receptive to the rational choice approach.

More recently the advocates of rational choice, acknowledging the importance of cultural differences, have tried to advance the argument a step further toward their approach. They may grant that different cultures and different political systems have different institutions, different values and beliefs, and different ways of expressing political preferences—for example, through a *coup d'état* rather than through the ballot box. Even granting these differences, however, the rational choice approach suggests that such diverse events as *coups d'état* in Latin America, ethnic conflict in the former Yugoslavia, decision making on economic policy in a variety of culture areas, and interest group competition can all be explained using this method. Combining both cultural and rational choice approaches, it is suggested that one *first* immerse her- or himself in the culture so as to thoroughly understand the context and uniqueness of the case, and *then* use rational choice to give the study a greater scientific and comparative basis.

Comparative politics and rational choice theory have often been at loggerheads in the past, and even today there are major differences between them. But there are also trends toward compromise in the two positions and ways to accommodate rational choice to comparative politics and vice versa. Both the tensions as well as the efforts to fuse the two will likely continue into the future.[29]

---

[29]George Tsebelis, *Nested Games: Rational Choice in Comparative Politics* (Berkeley: University of California Press, 1990); Robert Bates and Barry Weingast, "A New Comparative Politics: Integrating Rational Choice and Interpretivist Perspectives," Center for International Affairs, Harvard University, Working Papers No. 95-3, April 1995.

The New Institutionalism

In recent years students of comparative politics have rediscovered institutions. The new approach is called "the new institutionalism," but no one is quite sure what is new about this focus or if it is mainly a case of "old wine in new bottles." After all, fifty years ago institutions were the main and virtually only thing that comparative politics studied—that is, before the attack on the institutional approach in the 1950s launched by Macridis and the "young Turks." Have we now come full circle, or is there really something new about the "new institutionalism"?

Several influences are operating in this rediscovery of institutions by comparative politics. One is that, after nearly half a century of studying political process, political behavior, and decision making, political scientists have rediscovered that institutions and institutional arrangements—legislatures, judiciaries, executives, bureaucracies, elections, federalism, local government, and so forth—really do count. Second, the renewed emphasis on institutions reflects the resurgence in comparative politics in the study of developed nations—North America, Europe, Japan—where political institutions tend to have greater importance. Third, the new institutionalism is related to the focus on state–society relations, corporatism, and rational choice theory, all of which emphasize institutions. Fourth, the transition to democracy in so many areas of the globe in the 1980s and 1990s has meant a renewed emphasis on getting the institutions right. And fifth, there are numerous interesting issues out there—welfare reform, centralism versus local government, presidentialism or parliamentarism, many others—in which institutions play a key role.

Many of the issues and concepts in the new institutionalism were first raised in quite sophisticated form by the "old" institutionalists. Students of comparative politics may wish to go back and read some of these post–World War II classics, such as the books by Maurice Duverger, Herman Finer, Carl Friedrich, or Karl Loewenstein.[30] There one will find extensive treatments of such subjects as constitutionalism, federalism, elections and political parties, parliamentarian versus presidentialism, as well as state regulation of political party and interest group activity (now usually discussed under the heading of corporatism or state–society relations). Most of what is called the "new institutionalism" is there, in these classic but now obviously dated accounts.

---

[30]Maurice Duverger, *Political Parties* (London: Methuen, 1954); Herman Finer, *The Theory and Practice of Modern Government* (London: Methuen, 1961); Carl Friedrich, *Constitutional Government and Democracy* (Boston: Ginn, 1950); and Karl Loewenstein, *Political Power and the Government Process* (Chicago: University of Chicago Press, 1957).

At the same time, the new institutionalism has brought some new issues into prominence.[31] These include constitution writing in countries that have recently returned to democracy; issues of centralism versus decentralization in the carrying out of public policy; the role of congresses and courts; the importance of elections, political parties, and parliaments in deciding public policy; the role of bureaucracies in implementing change; and the impact of laws and legal systems on politics and public policy. In addition, the new institutionalism has also meant in some research the emphasis on economic or "structural" matters (political economy) in determining policy outcomes.

There is both old and new in the "new institutionalism." The renewed emphasis on institutions also brings us back to the points made in the introduction and to our model of the political process. That is, in studying comparative politics, it is important to study both structure and process, both institutions and more informal aspects of policy making, and to weave both of these as well as other factors into a coherent, unified view of comparative political systems.

Implications for the Future

The criticisms and subsequent decline of the developmentalist approach, the prevailing approach in comparative politics in the 1960s, paved the way for the rise of a variety of other approaches. Dependency theory and the world systems approach, corporatism, bureaucratic-authoritarianism, political economy, state–society relations, and indigenous theories of change all emerged as alternatives to the developmentalist approach, or as amendments to it. Like developmentalism, the new approaches had their chief spokespersons, their apostles, their groupies or camp followers in the form of graduate students and young faculty, their theories, and their "bibles"—literature that was considered fundamental. The appearance of all these new approaches set comparative politics to debating as to which approach or combination of approaches was the best and most useful. More recently, rational choice theory and the new institutionalism have joined the list of comparative politics approaches.

We have also seen that within several of these approaches there are "vulgar" as well as more sophisticated versions. Some of the approaches, or at least some practitioners of them, are weighted down with heavy ideological or political baggage. Students should be careful in sorting through these various approaches as well as the separate schools of thought within them. If

---

[31]James G. March and Johan P. Olsen, *Rediscovering Institutions* (New York: Free Press, 1989); Sven Steinmo et al., *Structuring Politics: Historical Institutionalism in Comparative Analysis* (Cambridge: Cambridge University Press, 1992).

one wants to practice partisan or ideological politics, so be it. But if one wants to be accepted as a serious scholar and to have one's research and writings considered seriously, then one should try to be as balanced and neutral as possible, and not try to disguise partisanship or ideological pleading in the language of some academic approach. In short, the approaches outlined in this chapter are useful tools of analysis, but one must be exceedingly careful in utilizing them.

Among the older schools of formal legalism and developmentalism, the appearance of all these new approaches was often upsetting. The new approaches challenged familiar ideas—and persons—in the field. Most scholars of comparative politics, however, welcomed these approaches as adding diversity and new insights to scholarship. The new approaches, even though they upset the unity of the field and deprived it of a single set of "truths," were not at all a sign of sickness but rather a sign of the health of comparative politics.

Comparative politics now has a variety of approaches from which a scholar can choose. The next set of tasks, it seems to most of us who practice in the field, is to refine these approaches, separate their vulgar and dogmatic components from their more useful ones, and carry out our individual or collaborative studies employing those approaches that pragmatically offer us the greatest usefulness. At the same time, comparative politics needs to begin building bridges among these several "islands of theory." Many scholars would like to see, for example, theoretical connections made between corporatism and dependency theory, or between developmentalism and state–society relations, as well as other combinations. When such connections are made, comparative politics can begin rebuilding a more unified theory for the field as a whole, as contrasted with the present situation of a considerable variety of sometimes overlapping, sometimes competing approaches.

6

Democracy and Democratization: Transitions from Authoritarianism

During the 1970s and 1980s—and continuing into the 1990s and past the millenium—the world experienced one of the most significant, and heartening, developments of modern times: the movement of a large number of countries that had previously been governed under authoritarianism toward democracy. The transition to democracy began in Southern Europe in the mid-1970s with Portugal, Greece, and Spain; it then spread to Latin America where some 90 percent of the people could be said now to live under more or less democratic rule; East and South Asia, the Philippines, South Korea, Taiwan, Pakistan, and India undertook democratic openings or restored democratic precepts that had been previously abrogated; Eastern Europe and the former Soviet Union have undertaken transitions to democracy; and recently the concept of democracy—if not always or consistently its actual practice—has gained ground in Africa, in both the Mahgreb (North Africa) and sub-Saharan regions, and in the Islamic Middle East. The spread of democracy to so many areas in such a short period of time is quite remarkable—even heroic, if one's values lean toward democracy, pluralism, and human rights.

The vast spread of democracy, which was not predicted

by most political scientists and was not foreseen in the main comparative politics models surveyed in the previous chapter, has meant the decline and discrediting of democracy's primary alternatives. Almost no one wants to be a corporatist anymore (and certainly not in its fascistic, ideological meaning), and there is very little support for authoritarianism. At the same time, Marxism-Leninism has been discredited and undermined, as in most circles has Marxist ideology more generally. The discrediting of these other alternatives and the virtually complete triumph of democracy, which now alone among the world's great ideologies enjoys universal legitimacy, have led some scholars to assert that the history of, and competition among, ideas has ended.[1] Democracy has won, there are no acceptable or viable alternatives, and therefore the historical conflict over ideas and the proper way to organize society and polity are over. It should be noted, however, that others vigorously dispute this view.[2]

We should be careful how we define democracy. Democracy is not just the holding of an election—although that is a good first step. If democracy is defined only as holding elections, then countries as diverse as Nicaragua, El Salvador, and Russia should all be considered democracies. Democracy also requires, in addition to regular and free elections, the following functioning institutions: a strong and independent parliament, a strong and independent court system, strong political parties, strong interest groups able to get their viewpoints across, and strong grass-roots participation in government. By these criteria, the countries just named, and many others as well, are still partial democracies, incomplete democracies, democracies in the making. In addition, democracy requires tolerance, respect for different points of view, free speech—what is often called "civic culture." Hence, in addition to studying the processes of democratization, we must also recognize that there are different kinds, levels, and degrees of democracy.

In this chapter we look particularly at the transitions to democracy in Southern Europe and the developing nations; in the next chapter we examine the changes in the previously communist nations of Eastern Europe, China, and the former Soviet Union. Our focus is on the nature of the prior authoritarianism that democracy replaced, and particularly on how rising and seemingly long-standing authoritarianism shaped some of the major approaches in comparative politics. We then analyze the transitions to democracy, the causes of the transition, and the strengths and weaknesses of and prospects for democracy. Finally, we weigh the implications of these

---

[1]Francis Fukuyama, "The End of History," *The National Interest* (Summer 1989); see also Fukuyama's book, *The End of History and the Last Man* (New York: Maxwell Macmillan International, 1992).

[2]Responses are in the Summer and Fall 1989 issues of *The National Interest*. The *New York Times* also printed extensive analyses of the Fukuyama thesis and its critics, as did many other scholarly and popular magazines.

transitions to democracy and consider whether the study of transitions to democracy constitutes a new approach in its own right in comparative politics or whether it represents mainly a response to recent historical trends.

The Rise and Fall of Authoritarianism

To review: The fundamental presumption of early development theory was that economic growth would lead to social modernization, both of which would then help produce political democratization, which in turn would beget stability, moderation, and anticommunism and thus serve U.S. foreign policy interests. But in the 1960s this rosy, hopeful, and hoped-for scenario began to break down, leading eventually to a severe questioning of development theory itself. Beginning in 1962 in Argentina, in 1963 in the Dominican Republic, Ecuador, and Honduras, in 1964 in Brazil, and eventually including Peru, Bolivia, Chile, Guatemala, El Salvador, Uruguay, and virtually all of Latin America, a wave of military coups washed over the hemisphere sweeping democracy and democratic governments aside. In their stead, repressive regimes—authoritarian in character, frequent violators of human rights—took power. They outlawed democratic political parties, erased the nascent pluralism that had begun to grow up, and ruled with an iron hand. By 1977 twelve of the twenty Latin American countries were under military-authoritarian rule; in five others the line between civilian and military authority was so blurred as to be almost invisible; and for the three remaining democracies—Colombia, Costa Rica, and Venezuela—it was argued that they were really elite-directed regimes and not truly democratic.

But it was not just in Latin America where authoritarianism displaced democracy. In sub-Saharan Africa the euphoria in favor of democracy and constitutionalism that accompanied independence in the early 1960s now gave way, in country after country, to repressive military regimes. In East Asia (South Korea, Taiwan, Singapore, the Philippines) new authoritarian regimes came to power or else the rulers already in power became more authoritarian. In North Africa and the Islamic world a younger generation of nationalistic military authoritarians took power; long-established authoritarian regimes in Saudi Arabia, Kuwait, and Iran saw the opportunity to strengthen their hand further. Indonesia, Pakistan, and even India (the world's most populous democracy) for a time yielded to authoritarianism.

The causes of this shift to authoritarianism were several. First, the earlier experiments with democracy had failed to deliver very much in the way of actual goods and services. The euphoria over democracy in the early postindependence years had simply worn off. Second, many of the developing nations were suffering from economic crises (analyzed, though not entirely accurately, in O'Donnell's theory of bureaucratic-authoritarianism) which gave rise to widespread popular discontent. Third, the social mobilization of the lower-class peoples during the 1960s gave rise to class tensions and challenges to elite and governing groups. The mobilization of the lower-middle, working, and peasant classes frightened the elites, who then turned to the armed forces to help fortify their position. In addition, the armed forces often saw national crisis and fragmentation in the form of radical political groups or guerrillas emerging all around them and, fearing for their own place in society, moved to seize power to preempt national unraveling or a takeover from the left. The rise of authoritarianism in the developing world in the 1960s seemed almost universal.

But it was not just the fact of so many authoritarian regimes coming to power in so many areas in the 1960s. In addition, most of the new models emerging in comparative politics during this period served to provide explanations, rationalizations, and in some cases even justifications for authoritarian rule. Recall our discussion in the last chapter: Development theory, which was the dominant approach at the time, had posited a close correlation between modernization and democracy. But that correlation was breaking down under the wave of late 1960s military coups, and in addition, the theory of development itself was under attack and in the process of being discredited. In its place arose corporatism, bureaucratic-authoritarianism, organic statism, and dependency.

Each of these theories, even dependency theory although reluctantly or inadvertently, posited a strong, forceful, authoritative if not authoritarian state. To a degree that not even the proponents of these new approaches fully appreciated, they were responding to the rise during this period of the new wave of military-authoritarian regimes. By focusing on the elements of organicism (a unified, integrated system), corporatism (interest groups coordinated and directed by the state), the state itself as a strong, independent actor, and the bureaucratic-authoritarian features of modern governments, students of comparative politics were de facto moving away from the emphasis on democratic development that had strongly undergirded the field in the past. By explaining authoritarianism and dictatorships so thoroughly, comparative politics also offered a rationale for these forms of government. That is part of our role as comparative politics scholars: to understand and explain, neutrally and without bias, different forms of government in different parts of the world; it is part of our obligation to be objective. But one can also understand why some critics argued that by rationalizing authoritarianism as distinct from criticizing it, comparative politics may have also, inadvertently, helped legitimize it.

These approaches not only dissected and analyzed authoritarianism in new ways, but they also left the strong impression that corporatism, authoritarianism, and organic statism might be long-term, possibly even permanent systems of government. Instead of being merely a brief interruption on the presumably inevitable evolution to democracy (what developmentalism posited), the new forms of authoritarianism were now presented as alternative routes to development. Corporatism and authoritarianism were often seen as the "third way," the alternative to liberalism on the one hand and to Marxism-Leninism on the other. Franco's Spain, Salazar's Portugal, and other long-term authoritarian regimes had proved capable of stimulating economic growth and apparently also of channeling and handling the social and political forces that modernization sets loose without those forces resulting in the overthrow of authoritarianism itself. Previously, the assumption in comparative politics had been that there were only two routes to development: liberalism and communism. But the efficiency, longevity, and flexibility of some of these authoritarian and corporatist regimes led many scholars to conclude that the regimes founded on these bases—for example in Spain, Portugal, Brazil, Indonesia, and the Philippines—might go on indefinitely and also constitute a viable alternative to the other major models (democracy and communism) with which we are more familiar.

But meanwhile, the light of democracy continued to shine, however weak its glow at times in some countries. Within the authoritarian regimes or, sometimes, in exile, democratic political groups continued to exist. In addition, below the surface and often stifled from public expression by various authoritarian control mechanisms, democratic sentiment was still strong even if latent or temporarily submerged. Furthermore, those social and political changes that authoritarian modernization did in fact stimulate led over a longer term to rising societal pluralism and the desire for freedom. Finally, the international context also changed, leading to a resurgence of sentiment and support for democracy. By the mid-1970s authoritarianism had largely run its course. The result was a series of quite remarkable transitions to democracy that not only toppled or replaced a large number of authoritarian regimes but also led eventually to democratic openings in Marxist-Leninist regimes as well.

Returns to Democracy

The first returns to democracy, in a sense, occurred right after World War II. In the aftermath of the war, West Germany, Italy, and Japan all established for the first time, or reestablished, democracy, replacing long-standing authoritarianism or totalitarianism. But there were very special conditions prevailing during the transitions to democracy in these countries: All three had been defeated in war, all were occupied by Allied armies, and in all three it was the outside occupation forces that had insisted on democracy and seen to its initial establishment. Only later and as it proved workable and delivered real social and economic benefits would democracy in these countries gain definitive legitimacy.[3]

The first transitions to democracy in recent times began in the mid-1970s in Southern Europe: Greece, Portugal, and Spain.[4] Portugal led the way. On April 25, 1974, a group of disgruntled military officers staged a coup against the country's long-standing authoritarian-corporatist dictatorship. Within days, what had begun as a military movement with limited objectives turned into a full-scale social and political revolution. In succeeding months the right attempted to stage a comeback and the left sought to seize power. But popular elections were held a year after the initial coup, democracy was established, and Portuguese politics returned gradually to the center.[5]

Three months after the Portuguese revolution, the military junta ruling in Greece was forced to leave power. In power since 1967 and seeking to accomplish a permanent restructuring of Greek politics, the junta never achieved significant results or popularity. When Turkish armies invaded Cyprus on July 20, 1974, thus revealing the military miscalculations of the junta on top of all its other shortcomings, the regime was completely discredited. It fell within three days.[6]

The dictator Franco in Spain had been sick with various maladies for years. Meanwhile, Spanish society and the political culture had changed enormously toward greater openness and pluralism. When Franco finally died in November 1975, Spain was already a far different country than it had been ten years earlier. Hence, rather than serving as an example of long-term and permanent authoritarianism, Spain, like Portugal, underwent a transition to democracy. Spain's transition was facilitated by the vast social and economic changes that had occurred while Franco was still alive.[7]

---

[3]John Herz, *From Dictatorship to Democracy* (Westport, CT: Greenwood, 1982).

[4]Enrique Baloyra (ed.), *Comparing New Democracies: Transition and Consolidation in Mediterranean Europe and the Southern Cone* (Boulder, CO: Westview, 1987).

[5]Douglas Porch, *The Portuguese Armed Forces and the Revolution* (Stanford, CA: Hoover Institution Press, 1977); and Howard J. Wiarda and Iêda Siqueira Wiarda, *The Transition to Democracy in Spain and Portugal* (Washington, D.C.: University Press of America and the American Enterprise Institute for Public Policy Research, 1989).

[6]Allan Williams (ed.), *Southern Europe Transformed: Political and Economic Change in Greece, Italy, Portugal, and Spain* (London: Harper & Row, 1984); and Beate Kohler, *Political Forces in Spain, Greece, and Portugal* (London: Butterworth Scientific, 1982).

[7]John F. Coverdale, *The Political Transformation of Spain after Franco* (New York: Praeger, 1979); Samuel D. Eaton, *The Forces of Freedom in Spain, 1974–1979* (Stanford, CA: Hoover Institution Press, 1981); José Maravall, *The Transition to Democracy in Spain* (New York: St. Martin's, 1982); and Howard J. Wiarda, *Politics in Iberia: The Political Systems of Spain and Portugal* (New York: HarperCollins, 1992).

In all three of these cases, what had appeared to be a long-term or even permanent condition of authoritarianism and top-down corporatism yielded, suddenly in Portugal and Greece, gradually in Spain, to democracy. Moreover, these countries, especially Spain, served as examples—even models—for the transitions to democracy that were about to sweep Latin America.

The first Latin American country to make the transition from authoritarianism (in this case, under civilian rule) back to competitive democracy was the Dominican Republic in 1978, followed by Ecuador in 1979 and Honduras and Peru in 1980. Bolivia held a democratic election in 1982 after a long period of authoritarianism, and Argentina returned to democracy in 1983. Torn by conflict and civil war, El Salvador held constituent assembly elections in 1982 and a presidential election in 1984. That same year Panama elected a civilian president, even though the military under General Manuel Noriega remained the real power behind the throne. Uruguay, which had a long democratic tradition, also held democratic elections in 1984 after eleven years of authoritarianism. Similarly, Guatemala held constituent assembly elections in 1984 and elected a new government in 1985. And Brazil, a more prominent player on the world stage, began its transition away from authoritarianism in the late 1970s but did so gradually, returning to democracy in 1984–1985.[8]

In the next few years the number of transitions to democracy dwindled but then picked up again, and most of the holdouts also became democratic. Paraguay's longtime dictator, Alfredo Stroessner, was forced from power in 1989, paving the way for a gradual shift to democracy. In 1988 Chile's strong-arm dictator, Augusto Pinochet, held a plebiscite in which voters could indicate yes or no concerning his regime's continuance in power; to Pinochet's surprise the election signaled no, and in the next two years Chile also began a process that led back to democracy. In Marxist Nicaragua the regime was also persuaded to hold an election in 1990, one it assumed it would win, but the election proved to be a genuinely competitive one that the opposition won. Even in poverty-ridden Haiti in 1991, after several aborted efforts at democracy following the ouster of the authoritarian Duvalier family, democratic elections were held and an elected president was inaugurated. In the Western Hemisphere that left Cuba as the sole non-democratic country.

---

[8]Guillermo O'Donnell et al. (eds.), *Transitions from Authoritarian Rule* (Baltimore: Johns Hopkins University Press, 1986); James M. Malloy and Mitchell A. Seligson (eds.), *Authoritarians and Democrats: Regime Transition in Latin America* (Pittsburgh, PA: University of Pittsburgh Press, 1987); and Howard J. Wiarda, *The Democratic Revolution in Latin America: History, Politics, and U.S. Policy* (New York: A Twentieth Century Fund Book, Holmes & Meier, 1990).

As Latin America forged ahead with democracy, Asia soon had its democratic openings as well. The most dramatic turnaround occurred in the Philippines where longtime dictator Ferdinand Marcos was forced from office in 1987, paving the way for democratic elections that were won by Corazon Aquino. In both Taiwan and South Korea, regimes dominated for a long time by a single party, the civil opposition was increasingly tolerated, and the societies and politics became more open and pluralist. In Singapore, civilian prime minister Lee Kwan Yew, who had sometimes ruled arbitrarily and capriciously, gave way to a less autocratic leadership. Even in the more peripheral and less economically developed countries of Southeast Asia—Thailand, Burma, Malaysia—there were new democratic stirrings. In populous South Asia, India returned to full democracy after a brief authoritarian interlude; similarly, Pakistan restored democracy after a period of military rule.

The least progress toward democratization has occurred in sub-Saharan Africa and the Islamic world. In much of the Islamic world, both culture and a history of authoritarianism and strongman rule (political culture variables) have helped prevent the possibilities for democracy. But in North Africa—what is called the Mahgreb—there have been some openings to democracy, even though these are also Islamic nations. And in sub-Saharan Africa, despite the weakness of the socioeconomic underpinnings of democracy and a history of authoritarianism in most countries since the early years of independence, some shifts toward democracy are also occurring, most notably in Zambia, Nigeria, Tanzania, the Ivory Coast, Kenya, Angola, Botswana, Namibia, and South Africa.[9]

The sweep of democracy has thus become well-nigh universal, particularly the case if we include the transitions in the former Soviet Union and Eastern Europe and the openings in China. Currently, all of Western Europe is democratic, as is almost all of Latin America. East Asia and Eastern Europe are on their way toward democracy. Democratic stirrings (maybe more than that) are under way in sub-Saharan Africa and the Islamic world. The implications for comparative politics of this nearly global shift toward democracy are far-reaching.

Causes of the Democratic Shift

The causes of this global swing toward democracy are several, and they involve both domestic and international forces.

---

[9]Larry Diamond, Juan Linz, and Seymour Martin Lipset (eds.), *Democracy in Developing Countries* (Boulder, CO: Rienner, 1988).

Domestic Forces

Domestically, the military governments that were in power during the later 1960s and 1970s lost their popularity and, therefore, their legitimacy. Many of these military regimes had come to power with considerable popular support because the civilians whom they overthrew had often been weak, ineffectual, disorganized, and corrupt. Frequently, the armed forces intervened to correct these faults and promised to provide honest, efficient, stable government. The longer they stayed in office, however, the more the officers were seen as just as inefficient, just as disorganized, just as corrupt as the civilians they replaced. By the late 1970s most of these military regimes had been completely discredited.

A second precipitating factor was the economic downturn of the 1970s. As noted previously, Guillermo O'Donnell, in his controversial explanation of the causes of bureaucratic-authoritarianism, referred to this as the "crisis of import substitution." Whatever the exact label used, there is no doubt that the two great oil crises or "shocks" of the 1970s—in 1973 and then in 1979 when the price of oil doubled and then doubled again—coupled with a general, long-term decline in the price many Third World countries received for their raw materials and primary products, struck some severe blows to the economies and thus the prosperity of these countries. As their economies slipped into recession, support for the military regimes administering these economies also eroded. Economic hard times were soon translated into political opposition to the military regimes in power.

A third factor was social change. By the end of the 1970s many of the new or developing countries were quite different societies than they had been two or three decades earlier. They were more literate, more urban, more politically aware, and more mobilized. They were no longer quite the rural, backward, "sleepy" societies of the past. In addition, many of them had developed a small but significant entrepreneurial class, a larger middle class, an organized trade union movement, and a newly aroused peasantry. These were precisely the social forces that became arrayed against continued military rule; these movements also required greater pluralism, which translated into democracy, in the political sphere.

A fourth factor was the revival of civil and political society. In the early years of military rule harsh measures had often been taken against the democratic groups—trade unions, political parties, and the like—often associated with the preauthoritarian regimes. But by the late 1970s, in part because the military regimes had run out of gas or because they were now more lax in the enforcement of restrictive measures, civil society began to revive. In the more repressive regimes this usually took the form of secret "study groups" that really functioned like political parties, expanded activities of exile organizations that sensed the days of the dictatorship might be numbered, or the organization of initially clandestine but eventually aboveground associations that formed the nucleus of future political parties. Community groups, women's groups, revived social movements, and other newly organized forces joined the ranks of the emerging civil society. The resurrected civil society soon became a viable alternative to military rule.

A fifth and final internal factor explaining the military's departure from power is a vague and imprecise, but still important, one: the mood had changed. One aspect of this was that the military tired of governing. It knew it was hated, knew it was doing a poor job of governing, knew it was being discredited as an institution; it therefore began to plan its own withdrawal from politics. At the same time, as opposition groups sensed the weakness and hesitation of the regimes in power, they were more emboldened in their protests. It is not that the military was *driven* from power in very many of these countries; rather, the dominant pattern was that the armed forces themselves eventually shrank from power and retreated to the barracks. In some cases pushes and shoves from the civilian opposition were also involved, but in general these were evolutionary processes rather than revolutionary ones.

International Forces

At the international level, eventually complementing the local or domestic ones, important forces were also involved. First, there is no doubt that President Jimmy Carter's campaign in favor of human rights had a significant impact. President Carter is not usually thought of as being very sophisticated in the area of foreign policy, and while he was in office his human rights campaign showed only limited accomplishments. But Carter's constant references to human rights, and the translation of this into official U.S. policy, eventually had a galvanizing effect that served to undermine the legitimacy of authoritarian regimes. With their legitimacy or "right to rule" under fire, many of these regimes began to crumble.

President Ronald Reagan gave Carter's human rights campaign a broader focus on democracy. Initially opposed to Carter's stressing human rights at the expense of other U.S. interests, President Reagan eventually came to see that a strong democracy/human rights position also served his foreign policy goals. Emphasizing democracy and human rights enabled the United States to exert pressure for change and political opening in difficult countries such as Chile, Guatemala, and El Salvador; the focus on democracy also enabled the Congress, the media, and public opinion to unite behind U.S. policy. Of major importance, the Reagan focus not only helped bring down some of the most notorious right-wing tyrants—Pinochet, Marcos, Duvalier, Stroessner—but it also helped to undermine Marxist-Leninist regimes in Eastern Europe and the Soviet Union. Previously, such totalitarian systems had been considered impregnable, but now we realize how severe were the cracks and fissures in these bastions of communism. (This topic is considered in more detail in the next chapter.) Hence the sweep of democracy over the course of the 1980s came to encompass not just formerly right-wing authoritarian regimes but left-wing ones as well.

The final external factor stimulating democracy was the growing realization in the 1980s and early 1990s that democracy was the only system that worked or that people believed in. By this time, almost no one truly believed in authoritarianism (bureaucratic or otherwise), corporatism, or Marxism-Leninism. All these alternative regimes had proved ineffective, unworkable, even disastrous. Democracy therefore looked better and better. It was not that democracy was totally without faults, but in comparison with others democracy looked pretty good. As authoritarianism and Marxism-Leninism both lost their legitimacy, democracy emerged as the only viable alternative.

Issues of Democratic Transition

The task of building democracy in the wake of authoritarianism or totalitarianism is not as antiseptic or unilinear as we have so far presented it. In fact, there are many boulders and possibilities for wreckage or reversals on the road. At every step of the process difficult political choices have to be made. A study of these choices in one or several countries would make an excellent subject for comparative politics research.

The first question is, what to do about the military that is leaving power. It is ordinarily still a strong force, and it may come back into power. The military has professional interests to protect, and it cannot simply be wished away. At the same time, a new democratic government needs to be able to govern without military interference, and there may be popular pressures to try some officers for past human rights abuses. Thus many delicate political issues need to be faced. Often, as a condition of their leaving power, the armed forces have received a grant of immunity for past abuses; but what about all those citizens clamoring for justice? In addition, the new democratic regime may be convinced that the armed forces need to be reformed and restructured internally, but the military may block such interferences in what they deem their own internal affairs and threaten to oust the government if it seeks to do so. Perhaps—and contrary to our usual expectations—the newly elected civilian government may be obliged to increase the military budget, instead of directing those funds to social and economic programs, as a way of keeping the loyalty of the armed forces and of preserving democracy. There are many complex issues here regarding the military that a new democratic government needs to face very carefully.

A second question revolves around how far to extend the newly won freedom and how far to extend pluralism. After all, the armed forces had taken power in the first place in these countries often in large measure to head off a perceived leftist threat. So should the new democratic regime now extend freedom and recognition to socialist elements? To communists? To the guerrillas that the military may have been fighting all those years? To fascists or skinheads? If so, will that produce a political or military backlash from the right that threatens democracy itself? As committed democrats, the leaders of these new democracies may believe in freedom for all groups; but as practical politicians who want democracy to survive, they may have to make some compromises. On this issue, as on others, fine lines need to be drawn. The end of the cold war, on the other hand, made it much easier to welcome all groups into the political process.

A third question involves the use of social pacts. Here is the issue: The transition from authoritarianism or totalitarianism to democracy is often a very complex and difficult one with numerous possibilities for fatal mistakes. Suppose that on top of all the political issues a new democratic government must confront, it is also facing a wave of labor strikes long bottled up by the outgoing repressive regime. These strikes may be so intense, and the resulting economic disruptions so severe, that they may well undermine the economy and the democratic regime itself. Thus many new democratic governments have seen fit to work out social pacts between labor and employers to avoid such strife. Workers may get wage increases or greater benefits in return for a no-strike pledge. In this way the economy will remain productive while the government goes about its business of building democracy. Labor gives up the right to strike and business has to pay more; but the alternative may well be such violent union–employer relations that democratic rule is itself threatened.

Fourth, with the ouster or departure of the authoritarian regime, a transitional or newly installed democratic government will often feel obliged to write a new constitution. A host of controversial institutional issues are involved here that conceivably could torpedo the democratic regime. Should the country be unitary or federalist, a hot topic if there is regional or ethnic strife? Is there a predominant national religion, and should it enjoy official constitutional status, or should and can church and state be strictly separated? Should the armed forces be designated as entirely nonpolitical, or should they have some consultative or moderating role? Should vast social and economic rights be granted to workers, or should the constitution remain neutral on that subject? Should the system be parliamentary or presidential? A parliamentary system, it is often argued, is more democratic, but a presidential system may be better able to hold the often deeply divided country together. These and myriad other questions will be posed by constitution writers, and the decisions made may make or break the democratic transition.

If the transition is successful, then once a new democratic government has been installed, a new crisis often quickly sets in. Disillusionment may begin to grow if things don't change quickly enough. The population, resentful of the outgoing military regime, tends to believe that the establishment of democracy will *immediately* improve their lives. Of course, that does not usually happen; it takes time for new programs to be developed. Time, however, is not always what a democratic regime, newly installed and still uncertain of its strength, has. The result is that a democratic government has to begin to deliver quickly in the way of social or economic programs—or else! The "else" means that the government must move quickly to improve conditions or not only will it begin to lose its own supporters, but the legitimacy of democracy itself may be threatened. The government, and democracy, may be overthrown.

These and other issues are enormously important in the early stages of democratic government. Many things are hanging in the balance, including the very survivability of democracy itself. It must be remembered that in many of these countries that have recently moved away from authoritarianism, democracy is still a very tenuous and thin reed. It is not as well established as in older, more institutionalized democracies. It still lacks or may have only weak legitimacy. At this stage in a new democracy it may still be possible for the military to regain power, or for authoritarianism of another sort to seize control, or possibly for a Marxist-Leninist movement to take over. Because democracy in these countries is still only weakly institutionalized and not yet consolidated, the answers to the questions discussed here are crucial, literally life-and-death matters with regard to the survivability of the democratic regime.

Strengths and Weaknesses of Democracy

Democracy has by now been established, or reestablished, in many countries and geographic regions. Yet, it also remains precarious in quite a number of these places. In this section, therefore, we examine democracy's strengths as well as its weaknesses.

A Global Overview

To begin, we can distinguish between those countries and regions where democracy seems most well established and those where it is not. The first group of countries, where democracy is most likely to—or already has—become consolidated, is in Southern Europe: Greece, Portugal, Spain. These three are all at the higher end of the economic development scale; plus they are close to, and benefit from the proximity of, prosperous Western Europe; and, as members of the European Community, damaging sanctions (breaking of diplomatic relations, economic embargoes) would be applied against them if they deviated from the democratic path. Thus these countries are likely to remain democratic.

A second group of countries, most in South America but some in Asia, had considerable democratic and republican traditions and experience *before* the 1960s onset of military rule. Brazil, Argentina, Chile, Uruguay, the Philippines, and others may therefore be considered to be returning to the democratic fold rather than trying democracy for the first time. It is not as if they have to start from scratch. Rather, they already have strong democratic traditions and institutions that are now being resurrected. They have *interrupted* or sporadic democratic traditions and therefore, with considerable prior experience with democracy, have a leg up on the process and a strong basis for democratic continuity.

A third group is the former communist countries of Eastern Europe and the Soviet Union. On the one hand, they have very little experience with, or institutions of, democracy. On the other hand, they are geographically close to Western Europe, are in a position to take advantage of European prosperity and know-how (including on democracy), and therefore, despite their present weak institutions, may be in a better position than others to move toward democracy. However, one needs to further distinguish between Central Europe (Poland, Hungary, Slovakia, the Czech Republic) where the prospects for democracy look good, and the Balkans (Romania, Bulgaria, the former Yugoslavia) where the situation is more precarious; also, between Russia (fair prospects for democracy) and Central Asia and other areas of the former Soviet Union where the possibilities are not as bright.

The fourth group is those countries breaking out of authoritarianism and moving toward democracy really for the first time, and almost completely lacking either experience with democracy or the institutions on which democracy could be based. This category includes the poorest and least institutionalized countries of Latin America (such as Haiti), much of sub-Saharan Africa, much of the Middle East, and some of the poorer countries in Southeast Asia, as well as China. Not only do these countries and areas lack the basic institutions of democracy, but many of them are also outside the world's major trading blocs and lack the proximity to other democratic countries whose experience might help them.

That is one way to cut it, by countries and regions; another approach is to list the general strengths as well as weaknesses of the new democratic regimes. In doing so, it would be useful to keep in mind also the regional breakdown just offered to assess where these general comments apply and where not.

Strengths

The strengths of democracy in these newly democratic nations are many:

1. Other alternative models, such as bureaucratic-authoritarianism, corporatism, and Marxism-Leninism, are exhausted and no longer attractive. Thus, democracy has the field largely to itself.

2. Democracy has become stylish, "in," the wave of the future. It would be difficult for any group to resist these global trends.

3. Socioeconomic change has provided a more solid base for democracy. Most of the countries that have made a recent transition to democracy are now much more urban, literate, and affluent than they were forty years ago when the last great effort to build democracy in the developing nations was attempted. In most of these countries the socioeconomic base of older oligarchic or elitist regimes has eroded; at the same time, the growing middle class, greater moderation, and economic development have helped produce a far firmer foundation for democracy now than then.

4. Political-cultural changes have gone forward. Expanded political communications in the Third World have vastly increased the amount of information available, the level of awareness, and the proportion of the participatory population. At the same time, the expanding web of associational life (neighborhood or community groups and the like) has given people a stronger stake in society. The new culture includes rock music (including its protest lyrics), blue jeans, Coca-Cola, and—not least—democracy and the desire for freedom. These are powerful cultural currents that have now achieved global force.

5. Political and institutional development is increasing. By this we mean the growth of political parties, trade unions, farmers' groups, professional associations, and so on. In addition, governmental institutions in many of these countries have been strengthened and made more efficient. These changes have provided a stronger institutional base for democracy than ever before.

6. U.S. policy has also shifted in the direction of active support for democracy. Previously, the United States had often been ambivalent about democracy in the Third World, but under Presidents Carter and Reagan this changed quite dramatically. The United States did not always lead the charge toward democracy in the 1980s; most of these courageous democratic movements were indigenously based. But over time the United States came to see that not only ethical foreign policy concerns but hard-headed U.S. interests—stability, moderation, anticommunism—would be served by a prodemocracy stance. Hence, in many of the democratic transitions—the Dominican Republic, El Salvador, Guatemala, Honduras, the Philippines, Chile, Paraguay—U.S. policy in favor of democracy played a crucial role.

Democracy now has a far stronger base—culturally, socially, economically, politically, internationally—than it had in the early 1960s during the last noble but frustrated democratic experiment in many of these countries. Some good comparative politics studies could be developed comparing these six dimensions in one or more newly established democracies. But many of these new democracies continue to exhibit weaknesses as well, and these also need to be figured into the equation.

Weaknesses

1. The military and antidemocratic elements remain powerful. The armed forces cannot be abolished in most of these countries, nor is there a desire to do so. Rather, the military needs to be channeled into new nation-building roles, professionalized, and wrapped up in international defense obligations that discourage coups, such as the involvement of the Greek, Portuguese, and Spanish armed forces in NATO activities. New roles, as well as new avenues of communication and understanding, need to be found for the military.

2. The economies of many of these countries remain depressed, a problem compounded by large international debt. It is one of the remarkable events of the late twentieth century that so many countries undertook a transition to democracy when their economies were so depressed. The economic downturn began in the early 1980s after the second great oil shock of 1979; but even after the economies of the United States, Western Europe, and Japan began to recover, the economic situation in most of the rest of the world remained bad. Yet, even in the midst of such difficulties, most of these countries began their transitions to democracy. Recently, however, with the economic upturn of the early 1990s, many of these countries prospered and their democracies were also strengthened. But with the spread of the "Asian virus" in the late 1990s, the economic situation once again seemed precarious.

3. The newly democratic nations remain plagued by immense social problems. These include poverty, illiteracy, malnutrition, poor health care, inadequate and tainted water supplies, disease, lack of educational facilities, racial and class cleavages, ethnic strife, and immense gaps between rich and poor. The depressed and underdeveloped social conditions make it difficult for democracy to survive, let alone thrive in the long run.

4. Many traditional attitudes unconducive to democracy continue to survive. These include an admiration for authority, adherence to nonegalitarian principles, impatience with democracy, dependence on patronage rather than self-initiative, tolerance of corruption, dependence on the state, reverence for discipline and order, and a belief that fate or a god determine favorable outcomes rather than individual effort. In other words, the traditional parochial or subject political culture (as distinct from a democratic or participatory one) is still very much present in many countries.[10]

5. In many countries there are continuing institutional lags. By this we mean weak political parties, weak trade unions, weak government

---

[10]For the distinctions among these types of political cultures, see Gabriel A. Almond and Sidney Verba, *The Civic Culture Revisited* (Boston: Little, Brown, 1980).

institutions for carrying out policy, and so on. The "web of associability" that most political scientists deem necessary for democracy is still incomplete. For example, in some of the countries where I have done research, support for democracy in public opinion surveys runs to 85–90 percent of the populace. But support for political parties (*any* party) or trade unions is only at 25–30 percent. If democracy requires a solid underpinning of pluralist groups and institutions to survive, then the low support for parties and labor organizations is very troublesome regardless of the high percentage favoring democracy in the abstract.

6. Many recently democratic countries are still plagued by extremism of both the left and the right. Right-wing threats to democracy may come from the military or from extremist conservative groups; left-wing threats may come from guerrilla or terrorist groups. Frequently, the two extremes play upon and reinforce each other. Military repression thus begets greater left-wing violence, while the leftist groups seek to provoke more right-wing countermeasures that will polarize the society. The actions of one are necessary for the reaction of the other, and vice versa. Sometimes, in fact, the left and the right are in cahoots to ensure the survival of both, for without repression there is unlikely to be a serious guerrilla challenge, and without a guerrilla movement there are fewer justifications for having a military. Caught in the middle of this crossfire is democracy, which is often subverted by the strength of the two extremes. In general, however, extremism in many countries is on the decline, thus strengthening democracy.

7. The drug traffic may also serve to undermine democracy. Drugs are so pervasive in some countries, the profits so large, and the traffickers so violent that democracy may be destroyed in the process. In some countries, principally the small islands of the Caribbean, the possibility exists that the drug world will seize control and thus capture sovereignty, with all the advantages for their nefarious trade that that implies; in other countries (Colombia, for example) drug money and violence are so pervasive that, even though the drug lords are not in actual control, democracy may still be undermined and perverted.

8. Finally, the mood in various countries toward democracy may be changing. The 1980s was a period of enthusiasm for the new democratic openings; people were very happy to have democracy after many years of repression and authoritarianism. But in the 1990s, with democracy failing to deliver as much or as fast as possible, the mood (as measured by opinion surveys) has often turned sour. Democracy has failed to deliver or has proved chaotic (as in the former Soviet Union), or else people have become fed up with democracy's give-and-take or its inefficiencies. Public attitudes have become sufficiently poisoned that in *some* countries we might expect to see a

reversal away from democracy and back toward authoritarianism—but probably not a whole wave of reversions to authoritarianism.

Democracy thus has various strengths, but the new democracies in the world often exhibit severe weaknesses as well. In some countries democracy has been consolidated, in others it is hanging by a thread. Much useful research and writing could be done on the strengths and weaknesses of democracy in individual countries, comparatively between countries, and within or between various geographic regions.

Prospects and Implications

What are democracy's prospects? Actually, they look quite good in many parts of the world. One can make a strong case for democracy not just on ethical or moral grounds (democracy protects human rights) but also on pragmatic grounds: Democracy seems to be the most effective system of government for carrying out public policy, adjusting to new realities, accommodating to change, and giving the people what they want.

But democracy may also win by default. Even with all its problems, democracy looks far better than any other system of government. The British statesman Winston Churchill once said that "democracy is the worst form of government except for all the others." It is hard to make an argument for authoritarianism anymore, and Marxism-Leninism is in such disrepute (the subject of the next chapter) that almost no one wants that solution anymore either. In addition, given the severe economic and social problems of many of the newly democratic nations, the armed forces in these countries are no longer eager to step in. Why should they want power if all it will mean for them is problems, grief, and even more discredit cast on the military institution? In the absence of intense ambition or possibilities for power by these nondemocrats, democracy may well survive. Indeed, in addition to its intrinsic value, the absence presently of any viable alternative may be among the strongest arguments and set of circumstances that democracy has going for it.

Democracy is becoming better institutionalized in many of the nations that moved toward it in the last decade; the next step is the further consolidation and strengthening of democracy. Democracy may still falter in some countries, but the vast social, economic, cultural, and political changes that have occurred in most nations in the last thirty years seem to provide a stronger foundation for democracy now than previously. It seems unlikely at this stage that democracy will be overthrown in very many countries. This stronger base also leads us to conclude that democracy and authoritarianism are not just cyclical, that the present wave of popularity for democracy will not necessarily be followed by another round of authoritarianism. That may happen in the poorer and less institutionalized countries such as Haiti, but it seems unlikely to occur as a massive new wave of authoritarianism as happened in the 1960s. A convenient measure of the institutionalization and consolidation of a new democracy is if two democratic transfers of power have occurred without mishap; undoubtedly, some other measures could and should be developed as well.

In the absence of any attractive alternatives, democracy looks better and better. But not only democracy: the developmentalist approach that we analyzed in Chapter 3 also looks better. Recall that one of the chief assumptions of that literature was that as economic development, social modernization, and political development went forward, democracy would inevitably and universally follow. In the 1970s, with development efforts lagging and authoritarian regimes coming to power in so many countries, the assumptions of the developmentalist approach seemed ludicrous, and the approach was roundly criticized. But now, with development again going forward and democracy strongly ascendant, that approach is starting to look more attractive.[11] We will return to this theme in Chapter 8.

We close this chapter by grappling with the question of whether democracy—or the earlier phenomenon of bureaucratic-authoritarianism, for that matter—is really a new approach in the comparative politics field or is merely an attempt to grapple with what is presently happening in the world. The answer is, it is both, and therein lies an insight into what comparative politics as a field tries to do. There is no doubt that democracy is growing and spreading in the world, just as bureaucratic-authoritarianism seemed to be growing and spreading three decades ago. It is said that a journalist takes the first cut at history; the journalist will often be the first to report on the failures of a particular authoritarian regime and the coming of democracy. But the political scientist with a comparative politics specialization seeks to go deeper than the journalist: to examine the long-term causes of these events, to explore the patterns emerging across countries and across continents, to develop a general model of the process that applies to all or most countries, and to be able to predict what the outcome might be. I can think of no better illustration than this issue of the differences between journalists with their emphasis on immediacy and a discrete case, and comparative politics scholars with their emphasis on the *long-term, general patterns, model building*, and *predictability*.

The analysis also shows how comparative politics tends to some degree to follow the headlines—better put, how it dissects and analyzes the long-term trends in global politics. Comparative politics is, after all, concerned with

---

[11]See the essay by Howard J. Wiarda, "Political Development Reconsidered," in *Comparative Political Dynamics*, ed. Dankwart Rustow and Kenneth Erickson (New York: Harper-Collins, 1991), 32–53.

change, dynamics, and new phenomena, as it should be. But that also explains why the concepts and models used in comparative politics are always in flux—and why that is healthy, even though such frequent changes in the field are often frustrating to students who are looking for a single set of maxims. No field of scholarly inquiry can be that static and unchanging. For example, when bureaucratic-authoritarianism was in its heyday in the 1970s, it was perfectly appropriate that comparative politics should try to explain it; but after democracy became resurgent in the 1980s, it was also appropriate for comparative politics to analyze that new phenomenon.

In this way the heuristic models used in the field may come and go, or some of them may receive more attention in one epoch than another; and meanwhile the earlier "truths" become a part of our established knowledge. That is how it is and should be in the social sciences and in comparative politics: the laws and models used are not fixed for all time as in Euclidean geometry but are in flux—a dynamic, changing situation. That is, after all, how the real world is, and comparative politics both reflects and tries to comment intelligently on these changing phenomena, while always looking for regularities and patterns in the process. However, when the models we use *do* become fixed, reified, or a new orthodoxy, that is when trouble begins—as we see in the next chapter. In the book's conclusion we will be returning to these themes of the need for openness and flexibility in the models used in comparative politics.

7

The Future of Communist Regimes

While the transition from authoritarianism to democracy in numerous countries is one of the great epochal events of the late twentieth century, surely the other is the collapse of so many communist regimes. These two historic events are interrelated. While democracy undoubtedly had a subversive effect on various authoritarian regimes, it also had a destabilizing effect on Marxist-Leninist regimes. However, it took longer in the latter case. Authoritarianism, as the weaker and less complete or institutionalized of the two forms, was more vulnerable and began to crumble in the late 1970s. Totalitarian communism, stronger and more institutionalized, required another decade before it, too, began to crumble. But by the late 1980s Marxism-Leninism was also in full retreat, and the regimes established on those principles were either unraveling or undergoing profound changes, or both.

There remain, however, profound differences between the transitions from authoritarianism to democracy and the transitions from communism, perhaps to democracy but maybe to some as yet unknown system. For comparative politics purposes, we need to know the distinct starting points between these two transitions (that is, the differences between authoritarianism and totalitarianism), the nature and processes of the transitions themselves (different in the two sets of countries), and the likely outcomes or end points of the transition process. Is one group of countries more likely than the other to produce democracy? If so, why?

We pick up where we left off in the concluding comments of the previous chapter by discussing how the concepts and models developed in the field of comparative politics, if unmodified as events change and treated as permanent dogma, can not only blind us to new events in the world but can also have a major impact on foreign policy foresightedness or the lack thereof. The fact is that we in comparative politics all but completely failed to anticipate the profound changes occurring in the world of communist nations, in large part because the models we used failed to alert us to such possibilities. That blindness also led U.S. foreign policy to flounder and improvise because it, too, was caught unprepared for the depth and profundity of the changes.

Authoritarianism, Totalitarianism, and Marxism: How Our Intellectual Models Led Us Astray

Authoritarianism, which encompasses most of the world's traditional dictatorships, is fundamentally different from totalitarianism. Caesarism, sultanism, monarchism, Bonapartism, caudilloism, and military juntas are all examples of authoritarianism. Authoritarianism is generally premodern and occurs in less developed countries; its controls are usually limited to the military and political, and sometimes to a degree the social and economic arenas. Traditional authoritarianism lacks modern means of communication, the technologically conditioned terror, modern methods of thought control, and modern systems of bureaucratic organization. Without these, it cannot become truly "total." Hence, in the contemporary context authoritarianism is usually found in more traditional, emerging, less mobilized societies, which lack these modern systems of total control, whereas totalitarianism (implying total domination of all areas of life) is only really possible in a modern, developed, highly technological society, such as Hitler's Germany or Stalin's Soviet Union.

The distinguishing traits of totalitarianism are as follows:[1]

1. An official, all-encompassing ideology covering all aspects of existence and to which everyone living in the society must adhere

---

[1]This is the classic model of Carl J. Friedrich and Zbigniew Brzezinski, *Totalitarian Dictatorship and Autocracy* (New York: Praeger, 1962); see also Hannah Arendt, *The Origins of Totalitarianism* (New York: Harcourt Brace, 1951).

2. A single mass party, typically led by one person, combined with and inseparable from the governmental apparatus, and monopolizing all political activities

3. A system of terroristic police control employing modern torture and surveillance techniques

4. A technological monopoly in the hands of the party or the dictator controlling all means of mass communications, such as the press, radio, television, and motion pictures

5. A similar monopoly, under the same control, of all means of armed combat

6. A central control and direction of the entire economy, including the bureaucratic coordination of all formerly independent interest associations, typically including all group and corporate activities

In contrast, the distinguishing traits of authoritarianism, "softer" or "less total," defined systematically by Juan Linz[2] to distinguish Franco's Spain from Hitler's Germany and Mussolini's Italy, are:

1. A "mentality" (traditional Catholicism, discipline, order) rather than a full-blown ideology

2. A single party but without full-scale political mobilization

3. Leadership operating with ill-defined but often quite predictable limits

4. Limited pluralism (the church, the army) without "total" control of all groups

5. Dictatorship, but not total control over all aspects (culture, society, and the like)

6. Apathy, not mass indoctrination, as a way of keeping the population in check

The authoritarian-totalitarian distinction is a very useful one for comparative politics analysis. It enables us to distinguish clearly the more traditional forms of authoritarianism prevalent in much of the Third World from the even more nefarious totalitarianism of modern, industrialized states, of which we may have both right- (Nazi Germany) and left-wing (communist Russia) examples. It also contains a dynamic factor (modernization, industrialization, technology, communications) that enables us to see how a traditional authoritarian regime (such as the Shah's Iran or Trujillo's Dominican Republic) may evolve into a near-totalitarian one. That is, by staying in power over a long period of time and turning the country's instruments of modernization

---

[2]Juan Linz, "An Authoritarian Regime: Spain," in Erik Allardt and Yrjo Littunen (eds.), *Cleavages, Ideologies, and Party Systems* (Helsinki: Westmarck Society, X, 1964), 291–342.

(schools, media, communications, and so on) into agencies of totalitarian control, a regime may bridge the gap between authoritarianism and modern totalitarianism. We have presented authoritarianism and totalitarianism as two distinct types, but they can also be seen as constituting a continuum, with quite a number of recent authoritarian regimes seeking to use the instruments of totalitarianism and increasingly having the technological capacities to impose total control.[3]

Our main concern here, however, is with the totalitarianism phenomenon, particularly as it was practiced in the Soviet Union and Eastern Europe. We are especially interested in how this and other interpretations prevalent in the field prevented us from accurately seeing or predicting the changes, the unraveling, implosion, and collapse of these communist systems.

For a long time, the two major approaches to the study of communist regimes—Marxism and the totalitarian approach—tended to disregard the inner dynamics of these societies. Scholars ignored their internal workings, the possibilities for change within these systems, and also their vulnerabilities. The Marxist ideology leads us to think that a communist regime is the end point of the working out of the Marxist dialectical process; and once that point is reached, no further change is necessary or can even be contemplated. The dialectic, which proceeds from feudalism to capitalism to socialism, is presumed to stop with the achievement of the highest form of socialism: communism. This attitude derived both from adherence to Marxist principles on the part of many intellectuals and from the widespread belief during the Great Depression of the 1930s and World War II that socialism represented humankind's best hope. Influenced by these ideas, many Western scholars became convinced by the self-serving rationales of the Marxist-Leninist regimes themselves that they constituted the ultimate form of historical rationality. How could one talk of decline and disintegration in Marxist-Leninist regimes if the Marxist ideology posited these as the best and most progressive final conclusion of the working out of the historical dialectic?

The totalitarian model, which was the one most often used by Western political scientists, was also problematic. It suggested similarly that, once a dictatorship had fully achieved the six traits of modern totalitarianism listed earlier, no further evolution would occur. Totalitarianism was a useful model for describing the total controls of the Stalin era, but it was not as useful for describing post-Stalin changes. The totalitarian model posits that the controls are absolute and "total" in the society, which results in a very pessimistic forecast about the possibilities for change. Once the full gamut of totalitarian controls is in place in a communist regime, no further development—

---

[3]Howard J. Wiarda, *Dictatorship and Development: The Methods of Control in Trujillo's Dominican Republic* (Gainesville: University of Florida Press, 1968).

certainly no resistance—is thought possible. Adding to this static picture was the fact that, in the prevailing wisdom, there was no record of a communist system, once established, ever being overthrown; that obviously made it difficult to even contemplate the possibility of a postcommunist transition.

That is why not just scholars but also policy makers were so surprised, dumbfounded, and disbelieving when the communist regimes in Eastern Europe and the Soviet Union did in fact begin to disintegrate. It was not so much that our intelligence was faulty (although that may have been the case also) but that the basic models we use to interpret these communist regimes failed to take account of the evolutionary forces already under way. We had little literature on the subject, no "guidebooks." The models used had become reified, locked in place, ossified; they failed to take account of the dynamics within communist regimes. Both the Marxian and totalitarian models can be faulted in this regard. Only a handful of scholars recognized the changes under way in the Soviet Union and Eastern Europe that were leading away from totalitarianism and would eventually undermine these regimes. But the changes often had little effect on policy makers, and *no one* envisioned the complete collapse of these systems. This is a good illustration of how the models fashioned by comparative politics scholars, especially the totalitarianism model, can have a strong influence on policy, but also of how, if they become a fixed orthodoxy without constant attention to new factors, they can lead us to miss some of the most significant changes in the world.

Change, Vulnerability, and the Collapse of Communist Systems

By the late 1970s and early 1980s, various cracks and fissures were beginning to appear in the communist monolith. Some of these internal problems were beginning to show up in scholarly analyses and CIA intelligence data, but they were often discounted by higher-level analysts because of the powerful mind-set underlying the totalitarianism model. We propose to discuss these changes under six headings: changes in ideological underpinnings, changes in society, the growing economic crisis, the crisis of culture, the crisis of political institutions, and changes in the international system. Taken together and cumulatively, these separate problems added up to a profound systemic crisis that led eventually to the collapse of the various communist regimes.

Crisis of Ideology

The basic fact ideologically in these communist systems was that almost no one believed in Marxism-Leninism anymore. Marxism-Leninism is in any case sufficiently vague that any number of interpretations of it are possible; but if the ideology is that vague and pragmatic almost anything can—and did—go.

In any event, the ideology became softer and softer, and certainly among intellectuals it was increasingly rejected. Communist party hacks could still spout the ideology if it suited their purposes, and some of them still even believed in it, but it seldom served as a barrier to action or as a basis for decisions.

Increasingly, as the economies of the communist countries fell farther behind those of the West and the political systems proved inefficient and corrupt, Marxism-Leninism came to be seen as a cruel hoax. The once-utopian ideology appeared bankrupt. After a while, virtually no one adhered to the ideology; Marxism-Leninism came to be concentrated in such isolated outposts as Albania and North Korea, and among a dwindling handful of intellectuals—but it was all but forgotten in the Soviet Union and Eastern Europe. The legitimacy, ideological base, and sense that the communist systems represented the wave of the future had eroded.[4]

Social Change

The societal changes through which the communist countries were going by the 1970s were immense, and increasingly their stodgy ideology and political institutions were unable to keep pace. First, there was a yawning generation gap between the old, septu- and octogenarian rulers still in power and the younger generation of technocrats and bureaucrats who wanted to change the system *and* inherit their elders' cushy government positions. There was a second, perhaps even greater gap between this latter group and young people who had no interest in or use for the communist ideology and who were mainly devoted to rock music (including its protest lyrics), jeans, Coca-Cola, consumerism (in contrast to the vision of a "new," sharing and caring socialist man), and "freedom"—meaning freedom to travel to the West (prohibited under the communist regime) or even within the country.

A second social problem was ethnic discontent, which began to be a growing issue in the 1970s and literally exploded in the 1980s and 1990s. The fact is that the former Soviet Union and Eastern Europe are torn by intense ethnic, religious, and nationalistic sentiments. These groups hate each other with a passion that may go back hundreds, even thousands, of years; the hatreds will not be easily, if ever, resolved. Moreover, as these ethnic and religious enclaves began to pull apart, new minorities rose up even within these smaller units also demanding autonomy. The Soviet Union and much of Eastern Europe ran the risk of fragmenting into ever-smaller, city-state-size units.

A third problem had to do with social change. A sizable middle class had grown up in these countries; the middle class enjoyed greater affluence and wanted greater freedom. Furthermore, the working class (remember, these

---

[4]Vladimir Tismaneanu, *The Poverty of Utopia: The Crisis of Marxist Ideology in Eastern Europe* (New Brunswick, NJ: Transaction, 1988).

are supposed to be workers' paradises) was also disenchanted, impatient, and going on strike to demand change—and strikes are not supposed to happen in communist systems! The rigid, archaic political systems of the communist countries were simply not equipped to handle the social pressures thrust upon them. Since these regimes had very little capacity to bend or to respond to change, they eventually collapsed in the face of popular pressures rather than adjusting and accommodating as democratic systems can do.

Economic Crisis

At the root of the Soviet Union's and Eastern Europe's troubles were their noncompetitive, nonperforming economies. Increasingly, they were falling behind the United States, Western Europe, and Japan—and they were fated to lag even farther behind. Their agriculture was inefficient and largely ignored by the central government, their industry was old-fashioned and inefficient, and their technology was the dreariest of all, which was why they kept falling still farther back. In addition, their workforce was plagued by a host of problems ranging from drunkenness to high absenteeism and low productivity.

The Soviet Union was an advanced, First World country in terms of its military structure, but close to being a Third World country in other economic areas. Poverty, illiteracy, malnutrition, social backwardness—all problems identified with the Third World—were increasingly prevalent in the Soviet Union as well as Eastern Europe. Moreover, the conditions were getting worse rather than better, and the economic gap between the communist countries and the West was widening rather than narrowing. Something had to be done but, as with the mushrooming social problems, the communist political systems were unequal to the task of revitalizing their economies. Something would have to—and did—give.

Crisis of Culture

The crisis of culture in the communist states occurred at two levels. One involved the disaffection of the intellectuals—writers, artists, editors, journalists, academics, and cultural leaders in general—with the system. They became fed up and ashamed of their own countries, of the ideology and the political system. The cultural leaders grew increasingly disillusioned with the graft, the inefficiency, and, most important for their purposes, the lack of freedom within the system. Ultimately, they turned on it and, like Andrei Sakharov (physicist and dissident writer), led the protest and opposition movements against it.[5]

---

[5]See the special issue of *World Affairs* 150 (Winter 1987–1988), focused on "The Vulnerabilities of Communist Regimes."

The second cultural crisis occurred at the mass level. We refer here to conditions in the communist political culture experienced by the average men and women in the street: the disillusionment, the endless lines, the absence of goods of all sorts, the shoddy products, the depressed living standards, the resentments at the special privileges reserved for the communist party elites, the unwillingness to sacrifice or even work for the system, the underlying bitterness and sense of powerlessness, the truly frightening rates of alcoholism, the growing desire to emigrate or else to opt out of the system. These sentiments at the mass level created a climate in which the system either had to reform itself from within or collapse.

Political Institutions

Unfortunately, the communist system could not reform itself from within. It had no mechanisms for doing so—or even for tapping public opinion to find out how it should change. There were no competitive elections, no referenda, no public opinion surveys on serious topics. The Soviet and Eastern European communist parties, in addition, were old and tired bureaucracies; they consisted of unproductive time servers, old men who desired to hang on to their perquisites and privileges at all costs and who were incapable of reforming these systems from within. Similarly, the ministries and government agencies had become gigantic sinecure operations, resting places for party members and regime favorites who collected their salaries and other privileges but who seldom did any actual work. These are the hallmarks of a Third World bureaucracy and political system, not one aspiring to advanced or superpower status.

Soviet Prime Minister Mikhail Gorbachev tried to change these ugly features, to reform the system, while still operating within a communist framework. However, the old system was too deeply entrenched. Gorbachev faced opposition from hard-liners who thought his reforms were destroying the system (essentially correct) and from reformers who thought he was proceeding too slowly (also correct). Caught in the middle, and lacking a solid political base, Gorbachev lurched from one side to the other, appearing indecisive and ultimately failing and falling from power. The problems were so great, and the bitterness so intense, that no one leader, or even group of leaders over a longer period of time, could hope to solve the problem. Eventually, these communist regimes, like the authoritarian regimes analyzed earlier, began to totter, unravel, or implode.

International Pressures

Adding to these domestic pressures were international ones. First came President Carter's human rights campaign. The Carter campaign was directed more at right-wing regimes than left-wing ones, but eventually it had its effect on communist regimes as well. Carter's message of human rights served to undermine the legitimacy of Marxist-Leninist regimes that were gross abusers of human rights.

Ronald Reagan's defense buildup also hastened the demise of Eastern European and Soviet communism. Reagan's rhetoric in defense of freedom and democracy, his calling the Soviet Union an "evil empire," and his advancing the idea, through the "Reagan Doctrine," that communism could be turned back added further delegitimizing ingredients. Perhaps most importantly, Reagan's defense buildup during the 1980s forced the Soviets to spend more on arms, reinforced the conclusion that technologically and economically the Soviets could not keep up with the West, and drove home to Soviet citizens the realization that they had a "Cadillac defense system and a dinosaur economy."[6] This pressure policy undoubtedly hastened the undoing of communist states.

Finally, the examples of Japan, Western Europe, and the Newly Industrialized Countries (NICs) played an important role. The prosperity of Japan and Western Europe offered vivid examples to the Soviets of how successful these areas had become, as contrasted with their own backwardness and shabbiness. Also tipping the balance was the experience of such NICs as South Korea, Taiwan, Hong Kong, Singapore, Mexico, Brazil, Argentina, and Venezuela. These examples demonstrated to the Soviets that the future of the Third World lay not in such underdeveloped and strife-torn Soviet-sponsored, Marxist-Leninist basket cases as Cuba, Ethiopia, Angola, Mozambique, Afghanistan, and Vietnam—and not in socialism—but in the newly prosperous NICs, which used capitalism, export-led growth, and the creation of Western markets to develop at unprecedented rates.[7]

Patterns of Postcommunist Change

The pressures just described, beginning in the late 1970s in such countries as Poland, Czechoslovakia, Hungary, and the Soviet Union, continued to build during the 1980s. Popular discontent began to rise, more cracks and fissures began to appear in these once monolithically totalitarian regimes, alienation grew, and the signs of a regime unraveling began to appear unmistakably.

---

[6]The analysis, language, and assessment of the Reagan presidency in this light come from former Arkansas governor and Democratic President Bill Clinton, in *The Washington Post*, October 17, 1991, A4.

[7]Once when we were participating together in a conference in Singapore, Soviet expert Jerry Hough made national headlines by stating that Singapore had actually won the cold war. By this he meant that NICs such as Singapore had demonstrated to the Soviet Union that capitalism was the wave of the future in the Third World, not socialism. Naturally, it was flattering to small Singapore to be told that it had determined the cold war.

Such leaders as Lech Walesa (Poland) and Mikhail Gorbachev (Soviet Union) tried to exploit these new openings politically while also holding their nations together and taking them in new and altered directions. These were tight-wire acts that ran the threat of the wire snapping, the artist losing his balance and falling off, or the entire tent coming down about their heads.

Our purpose here is not to trace the several national histories of these regimes in any detail; that can be done by following the specialized literature on Russia and Eastern Europe. Rather, our purpose is to suggest the patterns, parallels, and/or contrasts that may exist in these individual national experiences, and to compare these with other areas, to further genuinely *comparative* analysis.

The first comparison—virtually unexplored territory—is between the Russian and Eastern European experiences and the transitions to democracy in Southern Europe, Latin America, and East Asia. The Southern European comparisons are probably most instructive since Southern Europe (Greece, Portugal, Spain) and Eastern Europe (including Russia) are at roughly comparable levels of development, are both a part of Europe and therefore share certain common traditions, and yet both Southern and Eastern Europe have long been considered to exist at the margins or periphery of Europe.

As a hypothesis—really, a series of hypotheses—Southern Europe would seem to have better possibilities for successfully making the transition from authoritarianism to democracy than does Russia or some Eastern European nations in making the transition from communism to democracy.[8] All these propositions need to be tested empirically (which is what comparative politics scholars do), but let us here at least state the dimensions of the issue and the paths along which future research could be directed:

1. The political culture of Southern Europe had already shifted to support of democracy at the time in the mid-1970s when the political transition began; Eastern Europe lacked this long preparation time and the groundswell of change in attitudes that had occurred in Spain, Portugal, and Greece.

2. Greece, Spain, and Portugal all had considerable prior democratic traditions and institutions on which to reconstruct democracy; those features were either lacking or not so strong in Eastern Europe, which had to build democracy from scratch.

3. Spain and Portugal, and to a lesser extent Greece, bridged the transition to democracy during a time of relative economic growth and prosperity, which helped ease the transition process; Eastern Europe undertook its transition during hard economic times.

---

[8]For a general discussion, see Howard J. Wiarda, "Transitions to Democracy in Comparative Perspective," *PAWSS Perspectives* 1 (December 1990): 25–31.

4. In its transition Southern Europe received major financial and political support from the United States and the European Community; it is not certain whether Eastern Europe or Russia will continue to enjoy the advantages of such strong international support.

5. At the time the transition began, civil society (trade unions, political parties, interest groups of various sorts) seemed to be considerably more developed in Southern Europe than in most of Eastern Europe.

6. In Southern Europe social and economic welfare and "safety net" features were also, compared to Eastern Europe, already quite well developed and in place at the time the often disruptive transitions began.

7. In Southern Europe the social pacts between labor, employers, and government enabled the *political* transition to be carried out successfully without disruptive labor strife (Portugal was a major exception); in Eastern Europe economic, social, cultural, and political transformations are occurring all at once rather than in sequence, overloading the circuits and creating the potential in some countries for major systems upheaval.

8. The Southern European nations (except possibly Spain) either had less ethnic or nationality strife or had largely solved these problems earlier in their histories. In contrast, ethnic strife threatens to tear some Eastern European nations and some of the new republics of the former Soviet Union apart, and to undermine their possibilities for successful transition to democracy. Many scholars see ethnic nationalism not just in Eastern Europe and Russia but in the Middle East, Southeast Asia, and sub-Saharan Africa as one of the next major subject areas in comparative politics.

9. While Southern Europe often had autarkic, inefficient, or quasi-mercantilist markets and economies, at least they had markets. In contrast, Russia and much of Eastern Europe (Hungary, the Czech Republic, and Poland excepted) had virtually no experience at all with markets or a modern economy. This difference (without a functioning economy it's all but impossible to have a functioning democracy) may have been the most important.

These factors suggest that the transitions to democracy in Southern Europe will prove to have been smoother, easier, and more successful than is likely to be the case for Eastern Europe and Russia. Future research will have to confirm or disprove these hypotheses.

A second approach (in addition to the Southern/Eastern Europe comparison) is to compare the quite distinct experiences of the various formerly Marxist-Leninist regimes themselves. Six categories of regimes may be identified, although some subgroups may also be discerned.

1. *Russia.* The U.S.S.R. (now Russia) is *sui generis*, unique, because of its immense size, large population, vast resources, and long-standing

great-power status. None of the other communist or formerly communist countries (except possibly China—more on that later) has these distinctive features. Thus, while we want to facilitate and encourage comparison, we must also recognize that on several dimensions Russia is distinct, a category all by itself. Both economically and politically, Russia's transition looks very precarious.

2. *The Commonwealth of Independent States (CIS)*. Today's Russia is only one (the biggest) part of the former Soviet Union; other areas (Georgia, the Ukraine, Bylorus, the Trans-Caucuses, Central Asia) have broken away to form independent states. Many of these are less developed economically and less well institutionalized than Russia; their democratic prospects, therefore, are even more precarious.

3. *Central Europe*. This category includes Poland, Slovakia, the Czech Republic, and Hungary. These are the countries that, it is hypothesized, have the best possibilities for successfully making the postcommunist transition. They are comparatively well developed, have a better infrastructure, have fewer ethnic divisions, and are closer to and in a position to benefit from the powerful German economy and from broader European prosperity; also, their political culture is less fractious and divisive.

4. *Southeastern Europe*. This area, commonly referred to as the Balkans, includes Romania, Bulgaria, the former Yugoslavia, and Albania. The possibilities here for a successful democratic transition are less bright. These are comparatively less developed countries economically; they have weak political infrastructure; they are torn by severe ethnic, religious, and political conflict; they are farther from the main centers of European prosperity; their communist *apparatchik* and secret police have not been entirely eliminated; and their political culture is deeply divided and fractious.

5. *Third World countries that have abandoned Marxism-Leninism*. Examples include Angola, Ethiopia, Mozambique, and Nicaragua. The problems for most of these countries are that they are so poor, have so few developed institutions, have so few resources, are so deeply divided politically, and are so far from the main centers of economic prosperity that no matter what they do, or what *systems* (Marxism, democracy) they opt for, they will still be poor and backward. Successful transitions to democracy *may* occur in these countries but they will be very difficult processes.

6. *Marxist-Leninist countries that have not begun a transition to democracy*. This category includes China, North Korea, Vietnam, and Cuba. Of these four, North Korea and Cuba remain isolated and inward looking, and have not yet begun the transition to either free markets or democracy. In contrast, China and Vietnam have in part abandoned Marxism in the economic sphere even while retaining a Marxist-Leninist system of political controls.

However, both countries are changing, and it will be interesting to see whether greater economic freedom also produces greater political freedom.

Utilizing these categories, at least three types of comparisons may thus be suggested: comparisons among countries within one of the given categories; comparisons among countries in two or more categories; and comparisons among noncommunist countries in Asia, Latin America, or Southern Europe undergoing comparable transitions.

Policy Reforms

At the macro level, most of the Marxist-Leninist regimes (actual or former) surveyed here are going through major changes. They are making fundamental *systemic* decisions: whether they will be socialist or capitalist, authoritarian or democratic, or some combination of these. Even while engaging in these major, wrenching, system-transforming debates, however, they are also being called on by their populations to solve pressing, immediate social and economic issues. The question is, Can these countries, while deciding the major systems debates, also provide the basic goods and services for which their peoples are clamoring? And how do these two levels interrelate? The issues, we have already seen, are very difficult and complex; at this stage no one is certain if both levels of problems—macro and micro—can be resolved at once.

Social Policy

Under their old communist regimes, leaders in the former Soviet Union and Eastern Europe would sometimes grudgingly admit that their peoples did not, by Western standards, enjoy complete political freedom and liberty. But, they would counter, these are only "bourgeois freedoms"; real freedom comes in the form of economic and social progress for the masses. And by these standards, they would argue, Marxism-Leninism has done very well.

However, now that the old communist leadership has been ousted and we are gaining access to archives and information previously unavailable, we are learning more facts about these regimes. The truth is that many of the supposed social programs and accomplishments of these regimes were a cruel hoax. In education, housing, and health care—those policy areas in which Marxist-Leninist regimes had staked their claim to major progress—most of these countries were steadily falling farther behind rather than moving ahead. True, there were minimum levels of education for most people; few people starved to death; health care provided the basics; and there were relatively few homeless people. Above the barest minimum standards, however, Marxist-Leninist regimes failed to deliver; and in fact the condition of their people, their standard of living, and life expectancy have all been in decline.[9] Moreover, in many areas things have gotten *worse* since the collapse of communism.

The housing shortage is acute in both Russia and Eastern Europe. Families must double, triple, or quadruple up in small rooms; the waiting time for apartments often stretches into years; the existing housing stock is of generally shoddy construction and deteriorating; and there are few alternative sources of housing. Medical care had also slipped badly, particularly in rural areas often characterized by poverty, malnutrition, and declining life expectancy; but even in the cities hospitals are woefully overcrowded; medicine and trained personnel are frequently in short supply; and there are severe lags in technology and equipment.

The food situation was often similarly bleak: lagging production, backward agriculture, poor distribution, severe shortages—except for the communist party elite. Virtually all goods—clothes, food, hardware—were often unavailable, in short supply, or of poor quality. Now that many of the economic restrictions of the former communist regimes have been abolished, foods and other goods are available but prices are high, beyond the reach of most people. Similarly, the once-vaunted educational systems had also slipped backward under communism with rising illiteracy, shortages of educational materials, and a lack of the computer and technological equipment that holds the key to the future. A decade after communism's fall, the educational systems are still often in decline.

Evidence has poured in that the high literacy, housing, and health care figures that the Soviets and East European communist regimes presented to the outside world were "cooked." They were made up, exaggerated, or deliberately falsified. The statistics were often invented so as to make the communist countries look better, both to their own people and to the outside world. By now, however, with Russia and Eastern Europe opening up to foreign visitors, the depressed conditions in many areas are visible for all to see. Many areas, particularly in rural regions of Russia and Eastern Europe, are closer to Third World living standards than to the prosperity of the West.

The communist regimes also claimed that in their supposed "workers' paradise" there was no pollution, no nuclear contamination, no environmental degradation. But the reality is that there are many areas of Russia and Eastern Europe that are unlivable, environmental disaster areas. Much of the vegetation is dead or dying; the buildings are caked in poisonous soot; runoff from chemical and nuclear facilities mingles with the water supply; and the people—sometimes neglected by their own governments—are afflicted with severe lung diseases and cancers. Because of poor or nonexistent quality

---

[9]Nicholas Eberstadt, "Health, Nutrition and Literacy under Communism," *Journal of Economic Growth* 2 (Second Quarter 1987): 11–22.

controls, bad planning, and shoddy building materials, dozens of Chernobyl-like nuclear disasters, where the reactor melts down and explodes, spreading nuclear pollutants for hundreds of miles, may be waiting to happen. In addition, Russian and many East European smokestacks are still pouring pollutants into the air in unregulated and irresponsible ways. It is pure myth that these Marxist-Leninist regimes were uniquely environmentally sensitive; indeed, their records on environmental issues were far worse than in the West.

Meanwhile, the social indicators that point to grave problems in Russia and some areas of Eastern Europe are way up: wife and child beating, alcoholism, crime, antisocial behavior, and, perhaps not paradoxically, church attendance. At the same time, life expectancy in Russia and Southeast Europe has fallen dramatically from seventy-two to about fifty-five years—as compared to nearly eighty in the developed Western nations and Japan. Clearly, these countries have a long way to go to solve their many social problems. And the difficult social circumstances also make the establishment of democracy and a functioning economy that much more difficult.

Economic Policy

It is now all but universally agreed that Marxist-Leninist economic systems are incapable of producing sustained growth in the modern world. Marxism-Leninism may be a useful system of establishing political control in countries in the early stages of development (China, Vietnam, the Soviet Union), but as a system of economic organization it is woefully inadequate—and as countries modernize and need to adapt to new technologies and overall globalization, the situation only gets worse. Marxist-Leninist systems cannot consistently produce goods and services, they cannot distribute goods efficiently, they have no way of determining prices and wages rationally, they lead to shortages and inefficiencies as well as corruption, they have no way of telling what their own people want, and they are notoriously unable to adapt to new demands and technologies. Belatedly realizing these shortcomings, the former Marxist-Leninist regimes of Russia, Eastern Europe, and the Commonwealth of Independent States (CIS) have rushed to embrace capitalism. At the same time, the few remaining Marxist-Leninist countries such as China and Vietnam have sought to instigate capitalist reforms even while retaining autocratic, Marxist-Leninist political controls. But we need to know what form this "capitalism" has taken, how complete are the changes, and whether it is possible to have free markets in the economic sphere but not political freedom.

The issues are as much political as economic. On the economic front, Russia, the CIS, and much of Eastern Europe lack the capital, the investment, the physical plant, the skills, the entrepreneurship, the technology, the banking system, the stock markets, the financial institutions, the know-how, and the overall infrastructure to make a market system work. Only a market mechanism has the capacity to adjust productivity, set wages, determine prices, mobilize capital, and adjust rapidly to make a modern economy function. These are the basics; of course, once you have the basics in place, you also need an efficient, democratic government to play a strong regulatory role and to provide for social welfare and equity issues. The problem is that Russia, the CIS, and much of Eastern Europe, a decade after the fall of communism, still do not have these basics in place, so their regulatory and welfare roles also lag. Making the transition from Marxism-Leninism to a successful market economy thus involves a host of thorny issues. It is much more complicated than either the countries involved or those who have sought to assist them thought, and the transitions in all these countries are still not complete.

The economic issues are one thing, the political processes involved another. The problem is that two rationalities are involved, both logical and at the same time directly contradictory. On the economic side, everyone agrees that the former or still existing communist countries need to introduce market reforms and downsize and privatize their inefficient, bloated, often corrupt state industries. But from a political point of view, that is far less obvious. That is why economic reform, if it occurs too fast or too completely, could be the Achilles' heel of the transition process. A lot of powerful people in Russia, the CIS, and Eastern Europe have a strong stake in things as they are. The stakes include jobs, patronage, perquisites, spoils, access to wealth and money, and political power and support. Reducing or eliminating the state sector, which is rational and reasonable in economic terms, would upset all that and undermine the basis of the leaders' political support. Hence, for many presidents, party officials, government bureaucrats, farm and factory managers, and regional or local officials, thoroughgoing economic reform is the last thing they want since it undermines the basis of their patronage support and, hence, of their power.

The situation is parallel to that in Latin America and other developing nations, similarly under pressure to privatize and reduce the state sector. The difference is that, whereas in many developing nations, the state sector may be only 30 to 40 percent of GNP, in Russia, the CIS, and Eastern Europe the state monopolized 80 to 90 percent of GNP. Hence, in Latin America and other developing areas not only is the problem of state downsizing, difficult though it is, smaller and more manageable than it is in the former communist countries but also Latin America and these other developing nations (South Korea, Taiwan, Indonesia, and so on) already had a small but potent private sector on which they could build. The former communist countries, in contrast, had almost no preexisting private sector and, therefore, must start from scratch. For these ex-Marxist-Leninist regimes, the stakes (a *huge* public sector) are higher; the private sector base almost nonexistent; and the risks to political leaders whose base of support and power lies in all those public sector patronage positions, far greater. Not surprisingly, the pace of economic reform and state downsizing in the former communist countries has been slower than expected and may, in some countries, prove unsuccessful. Economic rationality in these countries often runs head-on into equally powerful political rationality.

Another problem is the type of capitalism that is emerging in the former communist countries. It is called "robber baron capitalism" and is reminiscent of early exploitive capitalism in the United States and other countries. Almost nowhere in Russia, the CIS, or Eastern Europe does one find small entrepreneurs opening up hardware stores and other small businesses, putting people to work, paying salaries, benefitting the economy, and eking out a small profit. Rather, capitalism mainly takes the form of present or former communist party officials, government officials, and other insiders, using their contacts and privileged position within the system, to sell off former state-owned properties (80 to 90 percent of the economy), to gain enormously advantageous government contracts, or to reap the profits for themselves of so-called "privatization." This is not a free market system that any of us would recognize; instead, this is rip-off capitalism in which a handful of individuals are becoming enormously rich through their special access to government wealth and favors but are creating few jobs and not benefiting the economy as a whole.

This is a harsh condemnation; we need, therefore, to distinguish carefully between countries. Russia fits this "model" as do other countries of the former Soviet Union. The Balkan countries, Romania and Bulgaria, also fit this model. Poland, Slovakia (formerly part of Czechoslovakia, now independent), and Slovenia (formerly part of Yugoslavia, now independent) are more of a mix: part robber-baron capitalism and part entrepreneurial capitalism closer to the West. The Czech Republic and Hungary tip the other way: mainly an emerging Western-style capitalism but with worrisome remnants of the robber style. Of course, *all* these economies are now a mix of old communist ways and newer capitalistic ones but, as indicated, in varying degrees. Moreover, the trends seem to be toward entrepreneurialism and more open-market systems but slowly and with great agony as jobs in the old statist economy shrink but before new ones in the private sector are created.

Given these conditions, the questions become, How much should the United States and Western Europe assist or invest in Russia, the CIS, or Eastern Europe if they know a sizable share of the investment funds will be lost or squandered on patronage deals? What is the capacity of these countries to use the aid and investment in useful, constructive ways? Can the Western nations assist the formerly communist nations in this difficult transition period, or must they reform themselves first and then, with a stronger base to build on, look to outside assistance? The answers, if you are an investor, are, You try to distinguish between countries as above, looking for good opportunities rather than being stuck with bad ones; you want to get in on the ground floor so that, if things work out well, you have a head start;

and you look for guarantees from the Treasury Department or the international lending agencies (World Bank, International Monetary Fund) that will protect your investment. And if you are a Western foreign policy or government official, you may want to invest in Russia and the other formerly communist countries even if the economic prospects are not good because of overriding political and strategic considerations: an economically distressed, politically unstable Russia, Ukraine, or Bylorus, with thousands of nuclear weapons, could be dangerous.

Political Change

In some aspects the formerly communist regimes of Russia, the CIS, and Eastern Europe are facing the same issues of political transition as are the countries analyzed in the previous chapter that evolved from right-wing authoritarianism. Should they be federal or unitary systems? Should they be presidential systems, parliamentary systems, or some combination of both? How much freedom should be allowed to dissident groups? How much to former or present communists who want to turn the clock back to older, repressive, but what are widely thought of as stable, more settled ways? Should there be an established religion or complete freedom for all groups? How big a role should the state play in the economy? In social issues? How much autonomy can be allowed to ethnic or nationality enclaves who may push for complete independence? On almost all these fundamental issues, the formerly communist countries now in transition must start at a far more basic, less settled level than did the countries of Southern Europe when *they* bridged the transition to democracy.

None of these are easy issues and some of them have the potential to derail the possibilities for successful democratic transitions, as for example on the issue of federalism versus unitarism. In the United States, Australia, and other well-established federal systems, the issue between central and state or regional power—always a dynamic relationship—has been largely settled in the sense that no state or region wants to break up the Union, as in the American Civil War. But in countries such as the former Soviet Union, the former Yugoslavia, and the former Czechoslovakia (the use of the word "former" gives the point away), where ethnic, religious, nationality, and regional tensions and conflicts abound—and frequently all of these combined—and where the long-simmering tensions have produced rebellion, civil war, and powerful separatist movements, these are hot, burning issues. Much is at stake, including the very survivability of the nation itself. In the previous decade the former Soviet Union has split up into separate nations consisting of Russia and the various entities of the Commonwealth of Independent States, and in many of these the process of ethnic and national disintegration may well continue. The former Yugoslavia has also split up into at least four independent nations, at least two of which are wracked by conflict and civil war. The former Czechoslovakia has peacefully (but not without anger) divided into the separate states of the Czech Republic and Slovakia. In many of these, as well as in countries not yet mentioned such as Romania, Hungary, and the Ukraine, there are other separatist movements that have not succeeded in splitting the country but are nevertheless divisive and make successful transitions to democracy difficult.

Since Marxism-Leninism, on one side of the political spectrum, and authoritarianism, on the other, have largely lost their legitimacy, democracy is the only acceptable form of government. But in many of the formerly communist regimes, "democracy" sometimes takes strange forms and its institutions are not yet well institutionalized. Democracy is often seen as a patronage system or as a means of using public office or access for private gain. As a result, political parties remain weak; pluralism is only in its early stages; and government agencies serve more to benefit those who work in them and those willing to pay to gain special favors than the general public. Russia, the CIS, and Eastern Europe have now all had elections that could be called democratic but the institutional infrastructure of democracy is still quite weak.

Below these institutional issues may be an even deeper problem: changing the values and political culture of these formerly communist countries. Some of their institutions are now formally democratic but what about fundamental underlying attitudes? Have Russia, the CIS, and Eastern Europe developed the "civic culture" (see Chapter 4) that is the only basis on which democracy can survive? Have they yet acquired the sense of tolerance, the respect for other opinions, the willingness to give as well as take, the basic trust, the sense of responsible government and loyal opposition, the widespread respect for human rights, the willingness to listen and take advice as well as give it out—in short, all the elements of a "political culture" of democracy? Often the nastiness, divisiveness, and personal character of the debates, to say nothing of high levels of corruption, brutishness, and orchestrated political violence, leave observers with the sense that basic attitudes have only marginally changed since the fall of communism. Recall that in Southern Europe the underlying society and political culture had changed even while the old regimes were still in power; but in Russia, the CIS, and Eastern Europe the fall of communism was abrupt and is still undergoing a slow transformation. And until the political culture changes, which may require two or three generations, changes in institutions are likely to remain quite superficial.

Toward the Future

The collapse of Marxism-Leninism and the disintegration of the communist systems of the Soviet Union and Eastern Europe constitute one of the epochal changes of the late twentieth century. These transformations have ended the cold war, fundamentally altered the face of the globe, ushered in some truly pathbreaking events, and forced the United States as well as other nations to rethink virtually every previous assumption of foreign policy. They have also undermined Marxism-Leninism as a possible alternative political system. Comparative politics at one time suggested "three worlds of development": a First World of modern, industrial, democratic nations; a Second World of industrialized communist nations; and a Third World of developing nations. But now the Second World is dead and gone, and so comparative politics must rethink its categories as well.

Communism may be dead as an ideology and form of political system, but in most of the former communist countries democracy is not yet well established. Their transitions are not yet completed; their new democratic regimes, not yet consolidated. So far, democracy and free markets appear to be the only options open but these newer systems are only weakly established and not yet well institutionalized. In Russia, the CIS, and Eastern Europe many necessary structural reforms have yet to be made—of the educational systems, of agriculture, of government institutions, of finances, of political attitudes, and so on—before democracy can be said to be effectively functioning.

Once again, the contrast with Southern Europe is striking. In Greece, Portugal, and Spain, no one doubted that, once authoritarianism ended, democracy would be the preferred option and outcome. No other alternative was possible, certainly not one with the legitimacy and popular support to govern. But in the formerly communist countries the outcome may be less certain. Any one of a number of possibilities remain. In countries lacking established democratic institutions, with little or no experience in democratic government, absent democratic political culture, and with immense social and economic problems, a variety of outcomes is possible. Uncertain and sometimes violent political conditions can produce a wide range of types of regimes.

Hence, in the formerly communist countries of Russia, the CIS, and Eastern Europe, what can we expect? The answer is not clear, which in itself is worrisome. Five distinct possibilities as well as various combinations of them seem possible. First is a successful transition to Western-style democracy and integration into European economic and political organizations. Though not without continuing problems, the Czech Republic, Slovakia, Hungary, Poland, Slovenia, and the Baltic Republics (Estonia, Latvia, Lithuania) seem likely to continue moving in this direction. A second option is the *formal* adoption of democratic procedures but only limited implementation of genuine democracy: Russia, Romania, Bulgaria, Bylorus, and the Ukraine may fall into this category. A third option is a reversion to full-scale communism: no country has yet gone this route although some have elected "reform" communist governments, and in many countries the nostalgia for the stability and certainty, especially of jobs and wages under communism, is strong.

A fourth possibility is a new authoritarian regime, different from the old communism but with the army, secret police, and old communist party apparatus and bureaucracy continuing to rule in an authoritarian fashion. Most of the states that were once a part of the Soviet Union but are now loosely organized as the Commonwealth of Independent States fall in this category.

Fifth and finally is the possibility for national breakdown, disintegration, civil war, and/or such widespread violence that effective government is impossible: Serbia, Bosnia, much of the former Yugoslavia, and Chechnya (a part of Russia) are the major candidates in this category. Keep in mind there could also be a succession from one to another or an alternation between these several types of regimes.

The outcome as regards the formerly communist countries is thus far less certain and predictable than it was in Southern Europe. In Russia, the CIS, and Eastern Europe there are still major *system* issues that need to be decided. The often unsettled conditions make predictions harder; moreover, the predominance of the totalitarianism and Marxist models for a long time made it difficult for scholars of comparative politics to see the changes occurring in these Marxist-Leninist regimes or to construct new models to help us understand the processes of transition. The result is that comparative politics lacks both a model of postcommunist change and a set of categories to help us understand the often mixed, frequently turbulent, crazy-quilt patterns and halfway houses (between communism and democracy) that are emerging. There is obviously room for a great deal of research yet on these postcommunist transitions.

8

The Developing Nations: What Works in Development— and What Doesn't

In the late 1950s and early 1960s the developing nations made their big splash onto the world stage. Latin America had become independent from Spain and Portugal in the 1820s, a handful of countries had gained independence after World War I, and India and Pakistan as well as parts of North Africa and the Middle East had become independent following World War II. But by 1960 a host of countries in Africa, Asia, the South Pacific, the Middle East, and the Caribbean had become newly independent. As an indicator of these changes the United Nations swelled to a membership of over 150 nations, and power began gradually to pass from the major countries represented in the UN's Security Council (the United States, Russia, China, France, Great Britain) to the more democratic (one nation, one vote) General Assembly. The sudden proliferation of so many new nations marked a turning point in world history; the emergence of scores of new political entities also broadened enormously the universe of comparative politics.

In Bandung, Indonesia, in 1956, Prime Minister Sukarno, Gamel Abdul Nasser of Egypt, and many other leaders from these new and largely non-Western nations got together to plan a common strategy. This was the beginning of the nonaligned movement or what we commonly call the "Third World." The leadership of this movement and the countries they represented actually had few things in common (China and Yugoslavia were also members), but most of them did share common histories of poverty, backwardness, and colonialism; a desire for socialism or maybe central planning; and a hope that, by remaining neutral and playing the then two great superpowers, the United States and the Soviet Union, off against each other, they could preserve their independence and reap assistance from the major powers for themselves. Thus was born not only the post–World War II tripartite organization of the world's nations into First World (developed capitalist states), Second World (developed communist states), and Third World (developing states) but also a fundamental feature of the cold war, with both the United States and the Soviet Union competing for influence in numerous, often marginal Third World nations.

Now this structure of the post–World War II world has collapsed or is changing very rapidly. The former Soviet Union, Eastern Europe, China, and other previously communist nations are undergoing fundamental transformations. In addition, the Third World has learned, or is beginning to learn, that in the modern global economy socialism and central state planning do not work very well; some kind of free market is necessary. But more than these epochal changes, it may be that, in the absence of a viable Second World or communist threat, the very concept of a Third World independent from and playing the other two "worlds" off against each other has lost all meaning. What can it possibly mean to be "nonaligned" these days? With the Soviet Union having collapsed, who is there left to play the United States off against? In this chapter, therefore, we examine not only what has changed in the Third World's strategy of development but also where the Third World now fits in the organization of world power.

The Theory of Development

In the 1950s, when the early academic literature on development was written, Western economists had almost no experience in the developing nations and almost no literature on which to build. Whatever had been written about these Third World areas that were now, suddenly, independent nations was mainly by cultural anthropologists and a handful of journalists. Political scientists had not spent much time in these formerly colonial territories, nor did economists have a sure handle on how to stimulate development there. In the absence of either experience or prior literature, economists fell back on the models of development that they did know: the United States and Western Europe.

Most of the economists who wrote about development in those early days—John Kenneth Galbraith, Raúl Prebisch, Paul Rosenstein-Rodan, Albert Hirschman, Robert Heilbroner, Everett Hagen, W. W. Rostow, Lincoln Gordon—were Keynesians, brought up on the politics and economics of Franklin Delano Roosevelt's New Deal, who believed in strong state intervention in the economy.[1] Their beliefs were backed by the leading European economists and sociologists such as Gunnar Myrdal.[2] Some of these economists were socialists, but most were social democrats who were often more strongly committed to central planning than to free market mechanisms.

During the 1950s, when Dwight Eisenhower was president and a conservative economic policy still reigned, most of these Keynesian economists were located in universities where they wrote the first articles and books on what was called "development economics." In fact, since a lot of the early literature was written at Harvard and MIT, this emerging body of literature came to be known as the "Charles River School," after the river that flows by both campuses and out into Boston Harbor. But when John F. Kennedy was elected president in 1960, many of these academic economists from the Cambridge, Massachusetts, area went with him to Washington where they filled influential government posts in the new administration and helped design such programs aimed at the Third World as the Alliance for Progress, the Peace Corps, and the Agency for International Development. All these programs were based on the assumptions of a leading role for the state in promoting development, central planning, a "balance" between private and public ownership, and a guiding, directing function for a plethora of new state regulatory agencies. The private sector, entrepreneurship, and markets received almost no attention either in the literature on development or in the main programs of the Kennedy administration.[3]

These emphases of the development economists corresponded closely with the preferences of leaders in the developing nations. For one thing, many of the early leaders of the new nations were themselves socialists (Sukarno, Nasser, Nkrumah, Kenyatta) or social democrats, having been trained in many cases at the London School of Economics (LSE) or perhaps the Sorbonne in Paris. At the ideological level, therefore, they mostly agreed with or went beyond their American advisers.[4]

---

[1] A useful collection on the major figures in development is Gerald M. Meier and Dudley Seers (eds.), *Pioneers in Development* (Oxford: Oxford University Press, 1985).

[2] Gunnar Myrdal, *Asian Drama: An Inquiry into the Poverty of Nations* (New York: Random House, 1972).

[3] An exception is Peter Nehemkis, *Latin America* (New York: Knopf, 1964).

[4] Paul Sigmund (ed.), *The Ideology of the Developing Nations* (New York: Praeger, 1972).

But these political leaders in the emerging nations often had a second, political agenda that the well-meaning Americans who advised them seldom understood: that more power, resources, and economic control concentrated in the hands of the central state vastly increased these leaders' political power. It gave them greater patronage, sinecure positions, levers of authority, and hard cash that could be used for graft, the rewarding of friends, or the paying off of enemies. Often unbeknownst to the sometimes naive American academics who helped design and rationalized these Third World development programs, the money was used not always for development but too often for these essentially graft, patronage, and political functions.

Expanding state size was the main cause of the massive political corruption that came, unfortunately, to be endemic in many Third World countries. That was not, of course, the purpose that the foreign economists had in mind when they designed these programs, but it was one of the unintended consequences. Moreover, the longer these early independence leaders stayed in power, the higher the level of graft and corruption required to keep them there. It is an unfortunate fact of life, regardless of ideological or political preferences, that the amount of corruption was directly proportional to the size of the state sector. As the size of the state increased, so did the amount of graft. Eventually, the corruption reached such a level that it largely squeezed out what was left of the private sector, bankrupted many Third World economies, discredited the state and its leaders, and led to the situations of mass starvation, incredible inefficiency, national disintegration, and widespread violence that are prevalent in some of these countries today.

The theory of development advanced by these early scholars joined by most Third World leaders was state-led economic growth. It paid very little attention to markets, entrepreneurship, or private business. Rather, it was the state that was to lead economic development, channel the resources, make decisions on investment and consumption, set prices and wages, and centrally plan the economy. In most Western nations, including the United States, we now recognize that such strict central economic control and so many programs run by the central government do not work very well and are neither efficient nor productive; imagine, then, how inefficient and downright disastrous such programs would be in countries lacking the institutions to carry them out effectively.

In addition, in part because the theory was fashioned mainly by economists, it had an economic determinist foundation of undergirding assumptions that proved to be quite wrong. The theory assumed that economics was the driving force in development. It also assumed that social change—a rising middle class, responsible trade unions, trickle-down benefits to the poor, greater societal pluralism, moderation and resistance to extremist appeals, a better-informed and participatory citizenry—would all result from economic development. Importantly for our purposes, it further assumed that democratization and stable governments would, inevitably and universally—regardless of cultural and historical differences—follow from economic development. All we needed to do, therefore, was prime the pumps, provide foreign aid, and stimulate investment; democracy would seemingly be the automatic result of the economic engine of change. But of course the actual practice of development proved to be far different, more complex, and disappointing than the theory.

The Practice of Development

Recall that in the 1950s when the early literature on development was published, we had very little actual experience with the developing nations. There was no literature on the subject, so scholars largely fell back on the experiences they knew: the United States and Western Europe. This helps explain why, in the absence of experience or much empirical data, the models of development presented tended to be highly abstract, very theoretical, and without solid grounding in actual Third World realities.

But now, over forty years later, we have abundant experience with development. Our models need no longer be so abstract and theoretical, we can now ground them in reality and experience instead of abstractions. The fact is that we now more or less know what works and what doesn't work in development.

Where, then, did early development theory go wrong? The question is particularly poignant because to most of us, as Americans, it seems so reasonable. All we need do is provide the economic wherewithal and some advice, and democracy and pluralism will presumably flower. The question may be especially difficult for Americans because, after all, so much of the model was based on our own experience. That complicates matters because when we say the theory of development went wrong, we are also saying that maybe the American or, more broadly, Western experience of development doesn't work in, or has little or no relevance to, the Third World. That is a heretical proposition that flies in the face of the widespread U.S. belief not only that our institutions are the best there are but that we have a duty and an obligation to export them to less favored lands.

In fact, this belief contains elements of truth: Some of our institutions and practices are useful, workable, and transferable in somewhat modified form to the developing nations, and others are not. We need, therefore, to sort out what is valuable, universal, and exportable in the American experience and what is not. Clearly, many aspects of the U.S.-inspired development theory are not workable abroad—although some aspects of it are.

Here are some of the key dilemmas in the U.S.-based development theory. First, we believed that by pouring in assistance the money would trickle down to the poor and the middle class, but in many Third World countries the funds were monopolized by the elites in control of the government and never reached the poor. Second, development theory assumed that a larger middle class would be a bastion of democracy and stability, but in many developing countries the emerging middle classes aped upper-class ways, disdained those who worked with their hands, and turned to the military to protect their interests from the lower classes. Rather than democracy, authoritarianism was the result. Third, we assumed that nonpolitical labor unions could be created that would be assimilated into the existing system, but in fact in many developing nations unions turned out to be highly political and often revolutionary.

The list of wrong, misleading, or only partially correct assumptions in development theory goes on. Fourth, developmentalism assumed that the leaders in these countries were public spirited and desirous of benefiting their people, but in too many cases the leadership proved greedy, selfish, and rapacious; instead of serving the public interest, its main goal was to serve its own private interests—or those of its family, cronies, clan, community, or tribe. Fifth, development theory assumed that a professional, apolitical military could be created, but instead, the middle-class officer corps shared the ambitions and fears of the middle class more generally and often intervened to snuff out democratic movements and to frustrate the desires of peasants and workers. Sixth, development theory assumed a commitment to national development on the part of Third World bureaucracies and to carrying out effective public policies, but instead, supposedly public policy too often actually served to line the pockets of the bureaucrats and their friends.

The most egregious mistake of development theory, however, was that it completely ignored political and cultural variables. It assumed that economic development would automatically generate social change (pluralism, a larger middle class, and so on), which would automatically produce political democratization. Furthermore, these processes were thought to be universal; once the great engine of industrialization got started, nothing could stop it and no local culture could resist it. But democratization does not just happen as a result of some inevitable process: it requires hard work, skilled political leaders, party organizers, well-run public programs, well-organized political groups, and so on. There is nothing *inevitable* about democracy; rather, democracy has to be *built*; it is an independent variable and not just dependent on economic factors. Obviously, economic development helps to stimulate social change and can serve to make democracy more secure—although, as we saw in Chapter 6, the recent great wave of transitions from authoritarianism back to democracy came at a time of economic recession, not prosperity, in most of the Third World. In short, democracy has to be seen as something worth working and fighting for and not just as the inevitable by-product of economic growth.

Related was the issue of culture, which development theory largely ignored. It assumed that economic development would produce a leveling of culture, a homogenization, in which cultural differences would become less apparent and less important. Hence, the theory paid very little attention to historical, regional, religious, or cultural differences. It assumed that what worked in the United States would also work in Latin America, that what worked in Latin America would also work in Africa, and so on. But culture, like politics, is an independent variable, not a dependent one. It is preposterous to think that religious beliefs, legal systems, history, value patterns, and traditional ways of doing things do not have an impact on development, or that they are erased and disappear as development proceeds. Japan is the clearest example: a country that has achieved phenomenal economic growth but that has also preserved its own culture. Its culture stresses harmony and consensus in social relations rather than the conflict of American-style pluralism; culture also helps explain the chumminess of Japanese business–government relations and the continuity and stability of its political system. The Japan case and numerous others illustrate that culture and development exist in a dynamic relationship: culture shapes the path and peculiarities of development, while development in turn also has a long-range effect on culture. In either case, culture, like politics, cannot be ignored as it was in the early development theory.

We could easily extend this list to include virtually every assumption of development theory.[5] All proved wrong or, at best, only partially correct. What went wrong? How could our theories lead us so far astray?

There are several key (and lots of small) reasons, most of which are interrelated and which flow from the previous points. First, prior to 1960, virtually none of the early theorists of development had ever actually spent much time in a developing nation; they often held an antiseptic, even romantic view of development, untainted by the hard political realities of actually living in the Third World. Second, the models they used derived from the American and European experiences and had very limited relevance for Third World nations with different histories and cultures. And that leads to the third main explanation: They ignored crucial political, cultural, and regional variables, and instead assumed that once the great motor force of economic development began, the outcomes socially and politically in all countries would be the same. But, of course, development does not occur that way, and it is wrong and misleading to think so. In fact, culture has been a filter of development, a way of keeping some Western ideas out and allowing others in, a factor in forcing development either to adapt to local conditions or to produce failures and

---

[5]Devastating critiques may be found in two volumes edited by Claudio Veliz: *Obstacles to Changes in Latin America* (London: Oxford University Press, 1965) and *The Politics of Conformity in Latin America* (London: Oxford University Press, 1967).

unintended consequences. The ignoring of these factors by development theory doomed both the overall model and many specific programs to failure.[6]

Some countries, however, did begin to develop. They developed far faster economically and socially than they did politically. Beginning in the 1960s quite a number of Third World countries began to grow economically. Their per capita incomes increased by 2, 3, or 4 percent or even higher per year, industrialization went forward, and affluence began to increase. In addition, social changes took place, the middle class increased in size, trade unions were organized, literacy and urbanization increased, peasants began to mobilize, and so on. But these changes, while often impressive, did not lead to any inevitable, let alone universal, situations of pluralism, secularism, or the fading of traditional culture and behavior as the theory suggested. Nor, as we have seen, did they lead necessarily to democracy.

While the economic direction in most developing countries in the 1960s and 1970s was slowly upward, toward increased economic development, some other countries (mostly in East Asia but elsewhere as well) experienced truly phenomenal growth—rates of 5, 6, or 7 percent per year. At the same time, other countries remained mired in poverty, without improvement. All three of these patterns—the spectacular growers, the slow growers, and the true disaster areas—command our attention in the next section. But note again that in none of the three patterns was economic development correlated automatically or necessarily with the growth of democracy.

Cases and Patterns of Development

We often use the terms *Third World* or *developing nations* to designate a certain group of countries that have been poor and that have recently begun the development process. But these terms gloss over the enormous variations that exist within the Third World. The differences among these countries are in fact growing wider—so wide that a single designation is no longer applicable to them. Later in the chapter, on this and other grounds, we suggest that the term *Third World* has outlived its usefulness.

East Asia: The NICs

Newly Industrialized Countries (NICs) is a term invented by the World Bank. It is used to designate those countries, mostly concentrated in East Asia but

---

[6]A. H. Somjee, *Parallels and Actuals of Political Development* (London: Macmillan, 1986); and Howard J. Wiarda, *Ethnocentrism in Foreign Policy: Can We Understand the Third World?* (Washington, D.C.: American Enterprise Institute for Public Policy Research, 1985).

not exclusively so, that have undergone exceedingly rapid economic growth in the last forty years. In fact, their growth has been nothing short of phenomenal. Industrialization, GNP, and per capita income have often shot up exceedingly rapidly. These countries are the true wonders of the developing world.

The most successful NICs have been South Korea, the Republic of China (Taiwan), Hong Kong, and Singapore. The first two countries, although small in size and resources, became economic giants, matching and in some areas surpassing even the miraculous growth rates of Japan. The latter two countries are manufacturing and trading/commercial centers.

Their formula has been export-led growth. They have skillfully exploited external markets, principally in the United States, and they have been smart and flexible enough to shift products and exports as the markets change. They now export clothing, plastics, wood products, steel, manufactured goods, and high-technology items, as well as many other products. These countries have an educated, hard-working labor force, and they are disciplined and well organized. They utilize open markets but they also employ state assistance. They value education and skills highly. Their social systems are orderly yet accommodative; their political systems, while not always fully democratic, have similarly accommodated themselves to change and to the new requirements of greater democratization and human rights observance. Political order and stability have given them the internal peace necessary to develop their economies. They have enacted vast social programs to assist their citizens in living longer, more creative, more productive lives. Some of these East Asian economies have also experienced recession but, since they have the basics right (stability, education, a work ethic, discipline, organization, greater political freedom), few doubt that they will soon recover.

So what is the key factor in explaining the growth of the East Asian "tigers"? Is it the structural institutions (business–government cooperation) that these nations have put in place to encourage development, or is it the work ethic of their common Confucian culture? The answer is, some of both. No doubt the institutions put in place to encourage growth, such as government assistance to beginning industries, planning, careful market research, cartels, and strong state ministries and bureaucracies, had a strong impact on growth. But remember this story also: Once, while riding on a plane between Singapore and the Philippines, the author sat next to a gentleman of Chinese background, married to a Filipina, who also had business connections in the Philippines. We conversed for a time about his life and business, and then I asked him to explain to me why Taiwan, Hong Kong, and Singapore had done so well while the Philippines had not. My companion thought, looked around to make sure no one was listening (the passengers were mostly Filipinos), and then whispered, "They're not Chinese!" This response was not only a reflection of his own prejudices but probably a widespread Asian belief in the importance of Confucian cultural factors (hard work, belief in education, strong family values, initiative) as well.

However, it is not just in Asia where we find examples of successful NICs, successful development. In Latin America, Brazil, Chile, Colombia, Venezuela, Mexico, and Argentina have also achieved some phenomenal growth rates. These are all quite large countries, with sizable internal markets, substantial natural resources, and, increasingly, the political stability and democratic institutions on which economic growth can be built. All have taken significant steps recently to move away from the state-directed, import substitution, mercantilist policies of the past, toward more open-market economies. All have evolved toward pluralism and greater human rights observance, and all have expanded social programs to provide for the poorest of their citizens.

Nor is it only the tigers of East Asia that have done well. Other countries of that area, historically mired in poverty, are now also beginning to develop. Burma, Thailand, Malaysia, the Philippines, and Indonesia have all begun to pick themselves up. All of these in the past have tied themselves to the great motor force of Asian development: Japan; now China has emerged as a major Asian, and global, economic power as well. All have used the formula that is becoming increasingly associated with economic growth: more open markets, export-oriented growth, political stability, encouragement of entrepreneurial spirit, allowance for social change and provision for social programs, and increasing openness to democracy.[7] Let us see how these features are working in other areas of the globe.

Oil-Exporting States

The oil-exporting states of the Middle East, which suddenly became wealthy because of their vast petroleum, occupy a special place in our catalog: they don't fit. On the one hand, such states as Saudi Arabia, Kuwait, Bharain, Dubai, and Abu Dabi are enormously wealthy in per capita terms—right up there with the wealthiest nations in the world (see Table 1.1). On the other hand, their social development (education, social programs, pluralism, egalitarianism) and, even more so, their political development (numbers of civic groups and interest associations, institutionalization, and, above all, democratization) lag way behind other developed nations. They also lag behind many other developing nations, who are much poorer economically than the oil-exporting nations but are sometimes more advanced socially and politically.

These oil-exporting nations are basically sheikdoms or sultanships that have undergone some limited modernization but whose social and political systems are still mainly traditional, often anachronistic. They are exceptional cases. As alternative future scenarios, one could expect that continued eco-

---

[7]Thomas W. Robinson (ed.), *Democracy and Development in East Asia* (Washington, D.C.: American Enterprise Institute for Public Policy Research, 1991).

nomic prosperity would give rise over time to greater demands for social and political development, or else that the regimes in these countries would be obliged to use more absolute or totalitarian controls to stay in power while their populations become increasingly restless. As we have seen in numerous other cases, such authoritarian regimes cannot hold in check forever the social and political forces that modernization sets loose.

The oil-exporting countries thus constitute exceptions—so far—to the rules of development we have observed.

Latin America

Latin America has long been a kind of laboratory, or experiment station, for U.S. efforts to encourage reform and development in the Third World. When we speak of "developing nations," it is usually Latin America (and a few others—Egypt, India, Indonesia) that we have in mind.

Latin America has long been committed to a statist model of development. Depending on the country, the state in Latin America may generate anywhere from 30 to 70 percent of GNP. That means that Latin America has considerably less state ownership than the present or former communist countries, but considerably more than the United States or most capitalist countries. Indeed, it is useful to think of the differences between communism and capitalism as forming a continuum, not a simple two-part categorization (see Figure 8.1).

What we are suggesting is that, in addition to the capitalist and communist economies with which we are more familiar, there is a third category that we can call statist or mercantilist. Statist economies are intermediary between capitalism and communism. Typically in statist economies, the state will own

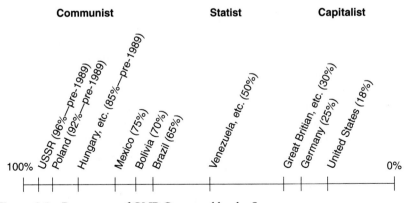

Figure 8.1   Percentage of GNP Generated by the State

and generate at least a third, maybe a half, perhaps even three-quarters as in Mexico, of the GNP. The state will usually own or monopolize the oil, petrochemical, steel, communications, transportation, and insurance industries as well as all utilities, banking, liquor, and gambling; it will also hold considerable interest in other economic sectors. In addition to its actual ownership, the state will usually be heavily involved in central planning; will often itself (rather than the market) set price, wage, and production levels; and will tightly regulate that part of the economy that is still privately owned.

Several lessons follow from this description of statist economies—which are not very much different from the lessons learned about communist countries. First, they are very inefficient because, in the absence of market incentives, there is very little reason to be streamlined or efficient. Second, they tend to be quite corrupt because corruption is often the only way to make the system work. Third, they tend to be top-down bureaucracies bloated with excess red tape, because efficiency is not rewarded and there is no reason to process work speedily. Fourth, they tend to become gigantic sinecure, patronage, or spoils agencies because, in the absence of efficiency as a criteria of appointment, that is how friends, cronies, allies, and family members are rewarded. Fifth, they breed a dependence on government (as distinct from entrepreneurship) because the state is virtually the only source of employment and because it is *the* source of contracts, licenses, and permits.

The list could go on, but enough has been said to indicate that these systems have not historically been very efficient economically in stimulating growth and that the statist regimes of Latin America and elsewhere, like their communist counterparts, have been very poor performers as compared with the East Asian NICs. Mexico and Venezuela have done well in the past because they almost literally float on oil (and thus have features comparable to the Middle Eastern oil-exporting nations), and Brazil is so big and resource-rich that it continues to grow even in the face of a statist regime ("Brazil develops at night," it is said, "while the government sleeps"). But when such factors as richness of resources are held constant, most statist regimes have performed very poorly. Many of these countries, especially Chile, Argentina, and now Brazil and Mexico, have recognized the debilitating effects of statism and have begun to move away from it.

In addition, a close connection may be made between countries that have statist economies and authoritarianism politically. When the state exercises so much power and control economically in terms of employment, licenses, contracts, monopoly, patronage, regulation, and so on, it is a very short step to political control. The connections are twofold: direct, in the form of control over individual employment possibilities, because the state is by far the country's largest employer and one does not criticize, let alone rebel against, the government that is paying one's wages; and indirect, in the form of all those licensing and regulatory procedures that can be used to hamstring political as well as economic activities. In short, developing nations that are heavily statist economically tend also to be authoritarian politically.

When Latin America began its impressive transitions to democracy in the late 1970s and early 1980s, it initially did so without changing its economic substructure. It made a political transition to democracy but not an economic one. As the inefficiency and bankruptcy of the statist model became increasingly apparent, as the successes of the East Asian NICs highlighted Latin America's deficiencies, and as the United States and the international lending agencies began to exert pressure, the Latin American countries began to change. They realized they would have to liberalize and free up their economies. In a time of declining foreign assistance, they could no longer rely on outside aid, nor could they blame all their internal problems on outside forces—as in dependency theory. After all, the successful East Asian NICs had been just as dependent on outside markets and capital as had Latin America, but East Asia had turned these conditions to advantage while Latin America remained mired in poverty. Beginning in the late 1980s, however, all the Latin American countries were sending trade missions to Asia to learn how the Asians had achieved such phenomenal development. Latin America was forced to become serious about development. It began to introduce privatization and free markets in the economic sphere just as it had earlier reintroduced political freedom and democratization.

A variety of reforms ensued in all the Latin American countries—though some were more successful than others. The Latin American countries moved to streamline their bloated bureaucracies, to open their markets to competition, to remove the various layers of red tape that hamper business dealings, to emphasize exports, to privatize state-owned enterprises, to reduce the size of their public sector, and in general to free up their economies. The pace of change was often exasperatingly slow because it is hard to find buyers for inefficient public industries or to actually fire people from public sector jobs. Sometimes they would fire thousands of public workers while the International Monetary Fund (IMF), whose loans were contingent on serious structural reform, was watching, and then hire thousands back when they thought the IMF wasn't looking.

Nevertheless, the reforms in some nations have been impressive. Inefficiency has been reduced, the economies of the area have been partially privatized, more open market systems are being established, new investment is coming in, and economic growth has been stimulated. The most successful economies have been Chile and Argentina, although Brazil, Colombia, Mexico, and Venezuela are also showing improvement. These are all, again, the larger and resource-rich countries. Some of the smaller nations are also doing reasonably well and beginning to pull slowly out of the depression conditions of the 1980s—what is referred to in Latin America as the "lost decade." But quite a number of others, who have few resources and have not reformed their economies, are still locked in their historic poverty and in fact are slipping backward.

Latin America, along with East Asia, thus provides us with the clearest-cut case of the need for structural as well as cultural, social, and political reform in order to achieve development. The correlation is not exact or 1:1, but it is not far from that mark. Those countries that have democratized and moved toward open, free markets are doing very well. Those countries that have not freed up their economies are not doing well, nor are they likely to until the necessary reforms are made.

India

India is the world's most populous democracy and, next to China, the second most populous country in the world. It has become *the* regional power in South Asia, including the possession of nuclear weapons. What happens in India, therefore, has immense consequences for the rest of the developing world.

India is a case par excellence of a country governed in the past by a small elite educated at the London School of Economics (LSE) and determined to follow a socialist/state planning model of development. India not only fashioned many of its political institutions after its former colonial master, Great Britain, it took its economic model from the LSE as well. For a long time the Indian elite rested comfortably in the belief that it had all the right answers, which included a (sometimes vaguely) socialist economy and centralized state planning.

But in recent years the political elite has been shaken in its beliefs. The Congress party, which had governed India for most of its independence period since 1947, has seen its near-monopoly on political office broken at the polls; in addition, the central planning system has not been working very well. Central planning can work in a small, homogeneous country such as Denmark, but in large, chaotic, ethnically diverse India a single set of guidelines emanating from New Delhi cannot possibly take into account all the local contingencies.

Hence, at the political level India has moved toward greater pluralism, and economically it is also changing. While still clinging in some quarters to socialism as a goal, the Indian elite has also recognized the need to make the public bureaucracy more efficient, to streamline and rationalize the economy, to open the country to outside investments and freer trade, to allow private markets to operate, and to liberalize the system. It is allowing greater economic freedom, encouraging entrepreneurship, and permitting the business skills of its people to flourish. At the same time, as in Latin America, there is a certain reluctance by the state to let go, to relax government controls because of the fear that change may get out of hand. Thus, again as in Latin America, the changes so far have been often piecemeal, limited, cautious. But if India truly wishes to be more prosperous, then it will likely have to go farther toward reform and economic liberalization. The main question is, as in Latin America, whether the elites are willing to possibly upset their own applecarts by making the changes necessary.

China

China is the world's most populous country with 1.2 billion people. It is also one of the world's last remaining Marxist-Leninist states—along with North Korea, Vietnam, and Cuba. At the same time, China is trying desperately to develop economically. So the key question: can China succeed in developing economically without fundamentally changing its communist and often repressive political system as well?

The Chinese formula so far has been to maintain a Marxist-Leninist system of *political* controls, while allowing in some areas a considerable degree of economic freedom. Thus, eastern coastal cities like Shanghai as well as areas in the south near the commercial city of Hong Kong enjoy considerable degrees of economic freedom and autonomy, while in much of the central, northern, and western areas of China communist controls are still in place. But can you have economic freedom in some of these areas without that inevitably translating into a demand for political freedom as well that would undermine the very basis of communist rule?

It is not an easy question to answer. The Marxist-Leninist rulers of China believe they can allow enough economic freedom to raise the country's prosperity, but without that leading to political upheaval. To that end, they have also allowed somewhat greater political, religious, and cultural freedom in the increasingly trendy capital city of Beijing as a way of providing young people and a rising middle class with a political escape valve, while also keeping tight controls over other areas of the country. Meanwhile, Western countries are betting on just the opposite scenario: that greater trade and contacts with China and rising prosperity will eventually result in greater political freedoms and human rights.

While China is a huge country in terms of size, resources, and especially population, it is still exceedingly poor, with a per capita income of only $600 to $700 per year, a very small middle class, and therefore a small market for imported products. While China is beginning to modernize, it is still about 80 percent rural; and if it industrializes and goes through roughly the same changes that other, earlier industrializers did, the majority of that rural population (really a *billion* people) will be moving to the cities in the next generation or two. No country ever has experienced that kind of urbanization, with its likely attendant problems of housing, education, health care, water supplies, electricity, sanitation, crime, delinquency, social breakdown, and so forth.

The Chinese leadership is gambling that it can maintain stability and control in the face of these mammoth changes. But what if it cannot or does not? What if neither of the two options mentioned earlier, a continuation of Marxism-Leninism or a gradual evolution to democracy, work out? To these two earlier scenarios for China, we need therefore to add a third one: the possibility of fragmentation, social unraveling, ungovernability, and breakdown.

The Middle East

The Middle East has long been divided between rich and poor Islamic states, as well as between Arab states and Israel. The wealthier oil-producing states (Saudi Arabia, Kuwait, the Persian Gulf emirates) have already been discussed; here we focus on the poorer states: Iraq, Iran, Syria, Jordan, Egypt, Tunisia, Libya, and Algeria. It may be noted that there is enormous diversity among these countries and that they do not always get along very well; recall that one of the key reasons for Iraq's invasion of Kuwait in 1990 was Iraqi resentment of the far richer Kuwaitis.

There is great variety among these states but some common features as well. Since the ouster of their traditional monarchies (Jordan's King Abdullah is the sole monarch left), most of them have been committed to an Arab, or Baathist, form of socialism. Several of them (Iraq, Iran, Syria, Libya) have not done altogether badly under this kind of regime because they have considerable oil reserves that enable them to generate some economic benefits no matter how inefficient they are. Egypt is able to subsidize its inefficient economy through immense U.S. and Saudi assistance programs; similarly, Jordan is propped up by the United States, the wealthier Arab states, and Israel. Algeria and Tunisia receive benefits chiefly from the fact that they lie close to prosperous Western Europe. None of these regimes is very efficient, nor could any of them be even remotely described as democracies (although a limited democratic opening may have occurred in Tunisia).

The pattern here is clear. In the political realm all these regimes remain top-down and authoritarian, although several of them have experienced a degree of political opening. Economically, some have done reasonably well lately not because they are efficient or self-sufficient but because of oil, foreign subsidies, or proximity to wealth that rubs off on them. At the same time, these remain poor countries and with immense social gaps between rich and poor. Hence, these countries are not very good illustrations of what works in development and what doesn't. Oil alone or foreign aid alone do not make for a successful economy or society. Their "Arab socialism" has not been very successful and has served as a legitimizer for some rather authoritarian, even miserable, regimes. None of them have successfully made a transition to democracy or even shown much sign of wanting to do so; nor have any of them begun seriously to streamline, privatize, and open up their economies. These are examples not of how to achieve democratic development but of how *not* to do it.

Depressed Areas

About forty countries in the world have not done and are not doing very well either economically or politically. (See Chapter 1, Table 1.1.) Most of these countries are in sub-Saharan Africa, but some are located in Asia (Bangladesh, for example), and others are in Latin and South America (Haiti, Nicaragua, Bolivia, Guyana, Suriname). These are among the world's poorest countries. Even worse, they show few signs of being able to improve their situations. That is why we label them "depressed areas."

The problem with most of these countries is that they lack basic economic resources: they have no oil, no valuable minerals, and seldom even decent agricultural land. Nor do they have the organization and institutional infrastructure, either economic or political, to carry out a sustained development effort. Virtually none of them have undertaken a transition to democracy, nor do they have the social and economic base to sustain democracy successfully should it be tried. The difficulty for these countries is that their poverty and underdevelopment are so great that probably no systemic change—presumably toward democracy and more open markets—can help them, and certainly not in the short run. They will remain poor and backward whether they have socialism or capitalism, democracy or authoritarianism.

Having said that, we must also note that there *are* some positive steps these poor countries could take. The benefits would probably be marginal for a time, but at least there would be benefits—and they might conceivably lead to better things. First, almost everyone agrees by now that the socialism many countries followed in the early decades of independence has not been productive; eliminating that system and the institutions that go with it would probably be a useful first step. Second, reducing the size of the public sector would help immensely, since we now recognize the close relationship between the size of the public sector and the level of corruption. A smaller state sector simply gives the regime and its bureaucrats fewer opportunities to steal; if private entrepreneurship could simultaneously be encouraged, that would also be helpful. Third, many of these unfortunate countries are governed by exceedingly brutal, corrupt, and rapacious dictators; getting rid of them could not help but improve the situation—unless the successor was equally bad, in which case nothing would have been lost.

Some success stories do exist, however, in this otherwise bleak picture from which lessons can be drawn. The Ivory Coast, while not democratic by

American standards, has allowed some considerable degree of freedom; and in the economic sphere its longtime president, Felix Houphouet-Boigny, provided both stability and an openness to free-market activity that was unique on the African continent. The Ivory Coast remained a poor country, but it was certainly better off than its neighbors; and the fact that the regime allowed, in the absence of a developed capitalist infrastructure, informal and low-level (street vendor) markets to operate gave it an economic vitality that most of the newly independent countries lacked.[8] Other depressed countries in Africa, Asia, the Middle East, and Latin America may also be slowly edging their way toward somewhat greater prosperity.

Eastern Europe

Eastern Europe was discussed in the previous chapter, but brief mention should be made of it here to round out our discussion of development.

All of the Eastern European countries under Soviet control and a Marxist-Leninist economy were depressed, but some were worse off than others. Those that had the most Stalinist totalitarian regimes and the most tightly controlled economies—Bulgaria, Romania, and Albania—remained the most economically depressed and the most backward. East Germany was also Stalinist, but it had considerable resources—and now, unity with the prosperous West in a united Germany. Others—Poland and the Czech Republic—allowed a somewhat greater degree of economic freedom and activity, and they were not as bad off; these countries currently also have good prospects for democracy and economic growth. The one country—Hungary—that allowed the greatest degree of economic freedom and capitalism even while functioning within a communist regime was also the best off economically of the Eastern European countries in terms of living standard and was best able to take advantage of the new freedoms and economic opportunities once the Marxist-Leninist regime collapsed in 1989. In contrast, the former Yugoslavia has split apart along ethnic, nationality, and religious lines: some areas (Slovenia, Croatia) are doing better politically and economically, while others (Serbia, Bosnia-Herzogovinia, Kosovo, Moldavia) have been torn by conflict and their futures are uncertain.

Thus, the pattern that we have been observing—that freer and democratic political systems and less statist, more open-market economies are the best indicators of developmental success—holds in these former communist countries of Eastern Europe as well as in the developing nations.

---

[8]Hernando de Soto, *The Other Path: The Invisible Revolution in the Third World* (New York: Harper & Row, 1989).

New Trading Blocs

Although the theme of new global trading blocs is a bit outside traditional comparative politics, it does have a bearing on the subject particularly as it relates to regional groupings, the developed and developing nations, and the political-economic models these countries are using.

The fact is that much of the world has now organized itself into trading blocs. The first, most important, and most long-standing is the European Economic Community (EEC), now the European Union (EU). It includes most of the countries of Western Europe; to a still uncertain extent, many of the countries of Eastern Europe will likely be included within it. Quite a number of developing nations also have special arrangements to buy and sell with the EU without cumbersome tariff restrictions. The EU has reduced tariffs among member countries and these others, is developing a common currency, has already developed numerous common regulations and quality controls among the member countries, and is to an extent erasing Europe's old national boundaries and even the concept of national sovereignty itself. For example, citizens of the member countries can now travel quite freely throughout the area without passports; at the same time, police in hot pursuit in one country can chase suspects across the border in another. The EU has developed central institutions in Brussels, Belgium, and Strasbourg, France, as well as other countries; it is the most developed of the several common markets; and it seems likely to proceed even further toward both economic and political (common foreign and defense policies) as the twenty-first century proceeds.

A second and less well-known trading bloc has formed in the Asia/Pacific Rim region. There the driving force has been mainly Japan but China and India are also jockeying for leadership roles. The so-called Asian tigers—South Korea, Taiwan, Hong Kong (now part of China), and Singapore—have shown miracle growth rates, and the developing economies of Indonesia, Malaysia, Thailand, and the Philippines have been stimulated by internal reforms as well as the power of their neighbors' economies. The Asian bloc is newer and less institutionalized than the European one; in addition and often in competition with each other, the Asian nations are all trying to increase their exports to other areas as well as defending bloc interests.

The third major trading bloc (North American Free Trade Association, or NAFTA) includes the United States, Canada, and Mexico. The United States has plans to include other Latin American nations in this bloc, but those plans suffered a setback when the Congress denied fast-track negotiating authority to the president. Meanwhile, impatient at the U.S. delays and eager to pursue their own agendas, some of the major South American countries (Argentina, Brazil, and others) formed their own free trade association, MERCOSUR (literally, Southern Market), which lowered tariffs, significantly expanded trade among the member countries, and began negotiating separately with the EU and Asia. But the power of the U.S. economy is such that, with or without an expanded NAFTA, it will remain the dominant economic power in the Western Hemisphere.

But note also the striking patterns. First, all three of these superblocs are primarily market oriented; there is no longer a socialist bloc. Second, a scramble is under way among almost all developing nations to achieve cover under one or another of the three umbrellas; those who are not a part of one or more of the blocs are likely to be left out in the economic wilderness: unprotected, vulnerable, and without markets for their goods. Third and particularly among the larger, more powerful economies (the United States, Japan, Germany, China, and others), an effort is being made both to integrate neighboring economies into a free trade bloc and to remain free to trade with other nations and blocs outside of one's own area. Thus, regional trade agreements are being formed at the same time that global trade is also increasing; the most dynamic economies try to increase their markets in *all* these areas.

What Works in Development

Economic development is generally taken to mean economic growth. Growth is sought to achieve better living standards and higher well-being for the people of the country. Economic growth and higher living standards also increase the prestige and power standing of the country involved. Economic growth is usually measured in terms of increases in the gross national product (GNP). However, since it cannot be called real growth if population increases mean larger numbers of people continuing to live in grinding poverty, growth is usually measured in GNP per capita. That is, not only must the GNP go up, but average income per person must also increase. Hence, an essential element of development is to increase investment, and thereby productivity, at a rate greater than that of the population growth. In this effort both agricultural development and industrialization will typically be involved.

Less developed countries (LDCs) are not the only areas where the study of economic growth is relevant. As we see in the next chapter, the study of economic development enables us to understand both where the already developed nations have come from and what is likely to be their future trajectory. It also enables us to examine how such recently developed countries as Brazil or South Korea achieved their impressive growth records. Furthermore, these principles of economic growth are relevant to the problems of structural reforms and development in the formerly communist countries of the Soviet Union and Eastern Europe. The ex-communist countries may serve as illustrations of the limits to the growth that can be achieved by capital investment in the absence of real structural reform.

Since World War II, the onset of the cold war, and especially the surge of new, developing nations onto the world scene, economists and others have been debating what strategies or model can best achieve development. What policies should be employed to stimulate development, and what should be the role of the state or government in the process? A leading early theory, that of W. W. Rostow, which, because of Rostow's positions in the State Department and the White House, also was incorporated into U.S. foreign aid policy, saw development in terms of linear stages that would be approximately the same in all nations. This theory focused on the fundamental need for investment, regardless of cultural traditions or political institutions, to generate increased productivity and output.

A second theory, identified most closely with economist W. Arthur Lewis, focused on the need for structural change in the Third World. Lewis's discussion of economic growth was more subtle than the "stages" thesis; it involved an analysis of the transition from an agricultural to an industrial economy and the ways in which the country's main institutions of both government and economics needed to be restructured to facilitate those transformations. However, this theory was seldom embedded in actual policy, as Rostow's was.

Dependency was a third theory. As analyzed by its leading early spokesman Raúl Prebish, who headed the United Nations' Economic Commission for Latin America, it argued that Latin America (and other developing areas) was underdeveloped because it was too heavily dependent on outside markets and called for a protectionist, import substitution policy. This strategy demanded central planning and state-led development rather than reliance on open markets.

The current consensus in development theory may be termed neoclassical. It emerges from the experience of the last forty years as recounted in the previous discussion, and not from theory. It suggests that development is markedly faster and more sustainable if fundamental reliance is placed on markets for the allocation of goods and services, and not on an all-powerful government.[9] Some central planning, coordination, and resource allocation by the state may still be necessary, but not at the expense of primary reliance on open markets. Socialism has been shown to be woefully inefficient and not conducive to development, and so have the excessively statist economies of Latin America. Hence, governments should focus on areas that are not well handled by the market, such as infrastructure (roads, communications), education, macroeconomic policy, social welfare, the environment and other externalities, and a legal system or policy framework that permit markets to operate and ensure optimum incentives to economic activity.

---

[9]See, for example, Peter L. Berger, *The Capitalist Revolution: Fifty Propositions about Prosperity, Equality, and Liberty* (New York: Basic Books, 1986); Michael Novak, *The Spirit of Democratic Capitalism* (New York: Simon & Schuster, 1982); and Howard J. Wiarda (ed.), *The Relations between Democracy, Development, and Security: Implications for Policy* (New York: Global Economic Action Institute, 1988).

This approach considers openness to international markets (both imports and exports) as essential to discipline domestic prices, end the antiexport bias of the older import substitution model, and provide markets for new areas of production. Hard work, organization, and discipline are also necessary. Political stability, effective leadership, and democratic government over a considerable period of time enormously facilitate capital investment and hence growth. Political stability is best achieved, we now know, not by either Marxism-Leninism (witness Eastern Europe) or authoritarianism but by democracy, which entails respect for elections, human rights, pluralism, and freedom. Stability is also best achieved through the provision of adequate levels of social services, education, and social justice for the nation's citizens. Without social justice and a stable political order achieved through democracy, all the best-laid plans for economic growth—as both the communist and authoritarian regimes found out—can go astray. Of course, there will still be questions about what precise percentage of scarce resources should go into investment and what into social programs; those questions can only be resolved in a democratic political process, as they should be. Also useful in terms of stimulating economic growth are programs to control excessive population growth.

There we have it: an agenda for development. After forty years of experience the consensus on what works in development is widespread:

- Hard work, discipline, organization
- Free, open markets
- Democracy and human rights
- Stability and internal security
- Widespread literacy and good public education at all levels
- Social programs and modernization
- Efficient and honest public administration
- Intelligent, rational, but limited state planning systems
- An effective legal system
- Family planning

These are the sine qua non for development. With these features development in the emerging countries is feasible and highly likely; without them, or most of them, development is highly unlikely.

Implications for U.S. Policy

In the past, U.S. assistance programs directed toward the developing nations have not always been based on this formula. Instead, foreign aid, influenced by Rostow, has been based on the "stages" theory. If only we can invest enough capital, Rostow argued, economic development will occur, and social modernization and political development will automatically follow. But in the past they did not follow; Rostow got the cart before the horse. It is not enough merely to encourage investment and economic growth; rather, stable, effective, democratic political institutions and programs that promote education, equity, and social justice are also necessary. The agenda must then be well balanced to include political and social reforms as well as economic ones. There is nothing automatic or inevitable (as Rostow assumed) about investment automatically or inevitably producing economic development, because if the government and bureaucracy are corrupt, greedy, and mainly interested in lining their own pockets (as in the Philippines under Marcos or Indonesia under Suharto), growth will benefit the few rather than the many and will not help the country in long-range terms.

The issue becomes even more complicated. A strong argument can be made that in the early stages of development, a country needs a strong, stable (not necessarily democratic) government to stimulate growth, overcome the weight of traditional practices, and get the process of self-sustained growth started. That was the strategy of the successful Asian tigers (Hong Kong, Singapore, South Korea, Taiwan) in their early stages of development. But even if the government at this stage is nondemocratic, it must be honest, efficient, and dedicated to national growth, not just private enrichment. Moreover, as economic development goes forward, it gives rise to new social groups (trade unions, businessmen, middle class) that must be politically accommodated and incorporated into the system if growth is to continue. In other words, even a development strategy that starts under nondemocratic leadership soon requires a more open and democratic system to manage the new pressures and pluralism to which development itself gives rise. Furthermore, in the present context, the pressures of global lending agencies, the media, the international community, and neighboring countries all but force a developing nation to take a democratic route.

None of this was acknowledged in the U.S. foreign aid program where, under Rostow's influence, the emphasis was on economic assistance and large construction projects, and not on democracy or social justice. Political, social, and cultural variables in achieving development were largely ignored. Moreover, the Rostow model and U.S. aid tended also to emphasize central planning and the role of the state in development, not the role of open markets and private entrepreneurship. U.S. development assistance in the early days thus ignored the need to direct its funds toward effective democratic governments and often favored authoritarian and dictatorial regimes whose records in stimulating national development were often weak. Many of these early foreign aid programs ended in failure.

The U.S. foreign assistance program in developing nations has gone through several incarnations since the 1960s. First came the emphasis on large infrastructure projects (dams, power companies, highways) and agrarian reform. But the infrastructure projects mainly benefitted the elite groups in the society, and agrarian reform, under governments controlled by these same elites, was never carried out seriously. Next came the emphasis in the 1970s on "basic human needs"—feeding the poorest of the poor—but that program, however laudable in design, was woefully inadequate to meet the need and ignored long-term development projects. Republican administrations emphasized private business while the Democrats championed "sustainable development."[10]

None of these programs provided the balanced, comprehensive program that the developing nations truly needed. Look back at the list on page 162: from this list and the accompanying analysis, it is clear that successful development requires political, economic, social, and cultural- psychological transformations all at once. Attacking one problem in isolation from the others will not work. Economic development cannot be achieved unless you have a political system committed to it; you also need the right social programs and a value system or political culture supportive of modernization. But most aid programs have concentrated on economic to the exclusion of political and cultural factors, which helps explain why so many of them have been failures. A successful development program has to be comprehensive in scope and take *all* relevant factors into account.

The Transformation of the World

Is the model that seems most successful in the developing countries also appropriate in the formerly communist world? Can open markets and political democracy be made to work in previously Marxist-Leninist regimes? The answer is, No one knows for sure. We hope and tend to assume so, and much of our aid to Russia and Eastern Europe is based on the assumption of a successful transition to democracy and free markets. Certainly the formerly communist states themselves also tend to think so and are putting lots of their eggs in the free-market basket. But the outcome remains uncertain, and large obstacles stand in the way. Marx and Lenin tried to show us how capitalism would give way to socialism, but when we set sail on the reverse course—from socialism to capitalism—we are sailing into uncharted waters. And there

---

[10]For AID's own view, see its publications: *Economic Growth and the Third World: A Report on the AID Private Enterprise Initiative* (Washington, D.C.: U.S. AID, 1987); *AID Policy Paper: Private Enterprise Development* (Washington, D.C.: U.S. AID, 1985); and *Development and the National Interest: U.S. Economic Assistance into the 21st Century* (Washington, D.C.: U.S. AID, 1989).

are no maps and no models. No one has ever gone this route before. So the issue of whether a transition from communism to capitalism is possible or feasible remains a big unknown.

In comparative politics, a number of scholars have tried to use the models of transitions to democracy in Southern Europe (Greece, Portugal, Spain) and applied them to postcommunist Eastern Europe. But Southern Europe already had some democratic traditions and institutions on which to build, the economies of the area were considerably more developed than Eastern Europe, vast social and cultural changes had already occurred in Southern Europe before the onset of democratization, and—most important—the Southern European economies already had market systems in place to help facilitate both political and economic transitions. Eastern Europe not only lacked the institutions of either political democracy or open markets, but it also had to undertake all of these changes—political, economic, social, cultural—at once and without a base on which to build. Many scholars now believe that the Southern European model is *not* appropriate for Eastern Europe, which must begin their transitions from scratch, and that it will be necessary to develop entirely new models to explain these postcommunist transitions. But that is a daunting task since, until recently, there had never been a case—and therefore no road maps—of a former communist country returning to democracy and free markets.

Nevertheless, it is significant that these large *system* transformations are changing the face of the globe. In the 1970s and 1980s many previously authoritarian and right-wing regimes undertook the transition to democracy. Then, beginning in 1989 Eastern Europe and the former Soviet Union began their transitions *both* to democracy and to more open-market systems. Not only did these involve some stupendous changes in the countries affected, but it also meant, for comparative politics, new and particularly significant transformations to study and, related, the need for new models and new approaches to help us understand these remarkable events. In systems terms, it also meant the discrediting and disappearance of many authoritarian as well as Marxist-Leninist regimes. The result at the turn of the century was that only democracy in the political sphere and some form of open markets in the economic enjoyed widespread legitimacy, although countries would and could differ considerably over the precise forms that these could take. But the great systems debate of the past appeared to be over: democracy and free markets had won and there were no other serious challengers.

These changes also implied the need for new classifications and new nomenclature in comparative politics. The First World of industrialized, democratic nations remained standing but, of course, it consisted of a great variety of countries (Japan, Germany, the United States) with quite different economic and political systems. Meanwhile, the Second World of developed communist states had disappeared, replaced by a variety of transitional regimes seeking mainly to emulate the First World. And the Third World was divided between those countries making it into the level of modern nations and those lagging behind, not only still mired in extreme poverty and underdevelopment but also unable any longer to try to play off the First World against the Second World.

It is, therefore, clear that the terms used for the past forty-five years (the era of the cold war) to categorize the world's political systems no longer have much basis in reality. The cold war is over and the world (or much of it) has changed. Comparative politics badly needs a new set of definitions and categories to describe and help us analyze these newer economic and political realities.

The end of the cold war and the new thrust toward globalization also suggest a return in attention to the politics and economics of the developed nations. It is to these main currents and the future of the First World that we turn next.

9

The Future
of the
Developed
Nations

This chapter is more speculative than the preceding
ones. Any time one ventures
into the area of futurology, one
necessarily has to be somewhat
speculative; that is the nature of
futurology. Hence, this chapter
falls in the realm of crystal-ball
gazing but, hopefully, *informed*
crystal-ball gazing.

Just because the analysis is
future oriented does not mean
that it is equivalent to astrology
or palm reading. Nor is it the
case that the opinion of any
given person in the street about
these subjects is as good as any
other's. That is the beauty of
the comparative politics
methodology and approach: it
enables one to think analytically
and systematically, not only
about the past and present but
also about the future. Such
future thinking has to be firmly
grounded in trend analysis,
tendency statements, and developmentalist perspectives. Just as
we can say some things about
the developing nations based on
the prior experiences of the
already developed ones, we can
also say some things about the
future of developed nations
based on an analysis of recent
and current comparative trends.
We need to couch such predictions in tendency statements ("it
looks as though," "it appears
likely," "the tendency is toward
such-and-such"), rather than as
definitive predictions. It may

still turn out that our crystal ball is no better than that of the uninformed. But what comparative politics does do is enable us to make *informed* judgments about the future rather than uninformed ones, and that gives us an enormous advantage over the opinion of that proverbial person in the street.

In this chapter our analysis turns to the high-income, already developed nations. We have talked a great deal about the developing countries and the current or former communist countries and what they may be developing toward, but here our attention turns to what the World Bank calls the "industrial market economies." We are particularly concerned with the countries at the higher reaches of that category since they, presumably, represent the future. A glance back at Table 1.1 will provide some further socioeconomic background on these countries. Although we will not discuss any one of them in any detail, the countries we will be referring to (in ascending order of wealth per capita) are South Korea, Portugal, Greece, Spain, New Zealand, Ireland, Israel, the United Kingdom, Australia, Italy, Canada, Finland, Hong Kong, Sweden, Netherlands, Belgium, France, Austria, United States, Germany, Denmark, Singapore, Norway, Japan, and Switzerland.

Patterns of Success

It should be immediately obvious that some geographic and cultural areas are particularly strongly represented in this list: Western Europe, North America, and the British Commonwealth (Australia, New Zealand). Japan, Hong Kong, Singapore, and South Korea are the only Asian countries that have so far made it into this select company—although the Republic of China (Taiwan) is fast closing the gap. Israel, Kuwait, and the United Arab Emirates are the only Middle Eastern countries on the high-income list. Note that not a single country from Africa, Latin America, or South Asia is included on the list.

The second striking feature is that most of these—with the exceptions already noted—are Western countries. That is, these are all countries that are directly part of the European, Western heritage, or are offshoots of that Western heritage (Canada, the United States, Iceland, New Zealand, Australia). The only non-Western countries on the list are Japan, the NICs of East Asia, Israel, a Western country located in the Middle East, and two Persian Gulf oil kingdoms. Whatever our position in the current debate over studying Western culture versus multiculturalism, the facts are that, so far at least, the Western countries must be considered not only the most developed in an economic sense but also the most successful, by most criteria, sociologically and politically as well. Is this success of the Western countries purely coincidental? Is it due to institutional developments in the

West? Or is there something in the Western sociocultural tradition that helps explain it?

The answers to these questions are important, have recently been the subject of major studies,[1] and have profound implications for the developing countries. First, the West was blessed by geography and climate with good soils, most of the important natural resources, abundant rainfall, and moderate temperatures that helped limit disease while also providing for a sufficient growing season. Second, the countries of the West developed extensive trade, commerce, and open markets before anyone else and on a level that enabled them to break the bonds of earlier feudalism. Third, the West industrialized before anyone else and was able to sustain industrialization for a long period. Fourth, the West developed stable, effective, growth-oriented, and eventually democratic institutions that not only stimulated modernization but also enabled the Western countries to manage and adjust to change better than other areas. And fifth (and most important, in the view of increasing numbers of scholars), the Western nations developed such cultural and behavioral attributes as entrepreneurship, an emphasis on education, hard work and discipline, tolerance, and democratic participation earlier and more thoroughly than other nations.

Another striking commonality is that all these countries are democracies. Not a single exception. They represent different types and forms of democracies, to be sure, but they are all democracies. Not a single Marxist-Leninist or authoritarian or totalitarian country is on the list. Again, the question must be asked, Is this coincidence, or is there a correlation between democracy and development? We certainly think so, and the previous chapter indicated that the correlation is valid for the developing countries as well as the developed ones. The obvious lesson to be learned is this: successful countries tend to be also democratic countries.

There are other common sociological features among all the developed countries. All have good educational systems and high literacy rates—above 90 percent. All are predominantly urban. All have significant manufacturing/industrial bases, as well as sizable and growing service sectors. All have reduced the income gap between rich and poor, and now are predominantly middle-class societies. All have high life expectancy—about seventy-five years. All these countries have turned a demographic corner, so that population has stabilized or grows only modestly. At the same time, all have advanced social programs and could be called "welfare states."

Economically, all these countries have reached a stage of high mass consumption. They have *pockets of poverty* but not a society-wide *culture of poverty*,

---

[1]David Landes, *The Wealth and Poverty of Nations* (New York: Norton, 1998).

as is the case in the developing nations. All are entering what might be called a postindustrial or more technological era, where their old, "rusty" industries (coal, steel) are in relative decline and new high-tech and service industries are on the rise. All have become, or are becoming, affluent, consumer-oriented societies. All are capitalistic or have achieved a workable balance between open markets and central state planning, ownership, and regulation.

Most of these countries have sizable internal markets, sufficiently numerous in terms of purchasers to support a strong industrial and manufacturing base. But several of them—Denmark, Luxembourg, Switzerland—have very few resources and are so small that they cannot support large-scale industry. How, then, did they become so affluent? And if they could make it to the top ranks of the world's richest countries, why can't other small, resource-poor countries in the (former) Third World do the same?

The question is an intriguing one for comparative politics. How did these small (in terms of markets) and resource-lacking (no oil or iron deposits) countries do it, and why can't others emulate their successes? Why can't we convert El Salvador, or Botswana, or Bangladesh into tropical Switzerlands? What is the key (or keys) to Switzerland's, Denmark's, or Luxembourg's success if it is not resources or size? Is it structural factors that could, presumably, be transferred to these poorer nations? Is it cultural factors—the Western tradition—which would be far harder to transfer? Or is it fortuitous: the fact that Switzerland, Denmark, and Luxembourg happen to be located in Western Europe and therefore that the wealth of their larger neighbors—Germany, France, Britain, Italy—rubs off on them and enables them to be prosperous, too? It is hard to arrive at final, definitive answers to these questions, but they are the kind of big issues that comparative politics ought to explore.[2]

New Trends

The countries we are dealing with here are all modern societies. They all have their persistent problems, to be sure, but on the indices by which we commonly measure modernization they rank at or near the top of the list. If they are already modern societies, the question then becomes, What will follow modernity? What is the next step or stage? What are the new currents? It is here that, even using trend analysis, we enter the realm of speculation. What kind of future developments are we likely to see?

2A provocative discussion may be found in Mancur Olson, *The Rise and Decline of Nations* (New Haven, CT: Yale University Press, 1982).

The End of Ideology

For the last thirty years scholars have been debating the end of ideology.[3] That is, have the intensive ideological debates of earlier in the twentieth century over communism, fascism, and democracy now faded or died out? The consensus is that, yes, they have faded, but the level of decline may vary over time and from country to country. And, of course, new issues are always arising to replace the earlier ideological debates.

Fascism was the first to collapse; almost no one calls him- or herself a fascist anymore. Nor does fascism have much public support. It is not a threat anywhere—although the term may still be used as a label of disopprobrium toward persons or movements or countries that we may wish to castigate. For example, there are xenophobic or extreme nationalist political parties in Western Europe and Australia whose bile is mainly directed against immigrants, but these are minority, often single-issue, parties and could not be considered fascist in the 1930s and totalitarian sense of that word. Fascism as an ideology and full-fledged political movement is all but dead.

More recently, communism has also collapsed and, with it, the ideology based on Marxism-Leninism has also been discredited. The nearly total failure of communism in the Soviet Union and Eastern Europe has seen to that. Outside of a few fringe groups, or in some countries where loyalty to the communist party has residual effects akin to belonging to a religion or being a member of a large "family," almost no one believes in the communist ideology anymore. Electoral support for communist parties in most countries is down, often dramatically so; and in many countries communist leaders are running away from their own former ideology, calling themselves "social democrats" or perhaps "reform communists." Hence, the two great radical, alternative ideologies of the twentieth century, fascism on the right and communism on the left, have both been discredited and have rapidly diminishing popular support.

That leaves democracy as the only viable alternative. The ideological argument is over; democracy has emerged triumphant, overwhelmingly so. That triumph is what led political scientist Francis Fukuyama to write his famous essay (later, book) entitled "The End of History."[4] It is not, obviously, that history per se is actually over but that in the great German philosopher Hegel's notion of the conflict between and working out of ideas in history, democracy has clearly come out on top. There is no current competition.

---

[3]See especially Daniel Bell, *The Coming of Post-Industrial Society* (New York: Basic Books, 1973).

[4]Francis Fukuyama, "The End of History," *The National Interest* (Summer 1989); also his book, *The End of History and the Last Man* (New York: Macmillan, 1992).

Thus, at least in the more developed nations, we have entered an era in which political ideology at the level of national systems of politics will not be as important as in the past. Democracy is presently the only system of government that enjoys near-universal legitimacy and support.

The victory of the democratic idea, however, does not mean an end to all political or even ideological conflict. Note that it is in the developed nations where ideological competition is mainly ending, but not yet in the developing ones. And even in the developed nations, political differences over specific issues—or over the kind and degree of democratization—will continue to occur. In both developed and developing nations there will surely be new and different ideas, programs, and agendas around which people will rally. But in terms of the great systems debates of the 1920s, 1930s, and even later—among fascism, communism, and democracy—that ideological debate is now over. Fascism and communism have been discredited; democracy has emerged triumphant. Moreover, the political movements and parties based on those ideologies in many countries are breaking up or losing support as well. We will have future political conflict and differences, to be sure, but not centered on the old ideological conflicts of the past.

The Decline of Political Parties

In most of the comparative politics literature, political parties are assumed to be essential institutions in a modern polity. Political parties are thought to perform the essential interest articulation and aggregation functions. They articulate issues, write party platforms, set forth an agenda, bring various interests together to support certain candidates, recruit members and leaders, and help provide the personnel and cadres that can staff a government. Since political parties are thought to be a hallmark of a developed political regime, developing nations are urged—if they want to be considered modern—to strengthen their party systems.

But this is now thought to be an idealized, unrealistic, and out-of-date vision of the role of political parties. In fact, political parties are in decline in many already developed countries—and not just in the United States. As the great ideologies of the past have declined, so have the organized movements—the parties—based on them. There are almost no real fascist parties anymore, and the communist parties in most countries are in decline. However, many of the moderate and centrist parties in the advanced nations are in disarray or decline as well. Consider the United States: Do the parties still really perform the functions that the literature ascribes to political parties? Is it the parties who articulate issues, or is it other agencies like interest groups, think tanks, political action committees (PACs), or the media? The parties write platforms, but does anyone ever read them? Do the parties really set forth an agenda that brings various groups together, or are they just temporary conglomerates of interests? Do the parties recruit members and leaders? Do they really aggregate interests? Are the parties a help or a hindrance to effective governance?

Posing the questions in such a challenging and straightforward way helps us see how few of—or how inadequately—the functions that the literature says parties ought to perform are in fact being performed. The parties in many developed nations are simply not doing their jobs. Or else, the functions traditionally ascribed to political parties are being performed by other kinds of organizations: lobbies, bureaucracies, legislatures, PACs, citizens' or neighborhood groups, ethnic and professional associations, television, and the like. Take this acid test: If you are in trouble and need something, would you go first to your political party? How often do people turn to a political party anymore to resolve complex issues?

Political parties are in decline in many areas of the globe. They no longer command fierce loyalty. A person who describes him- or herself as a devoted partisan of one party or another is often thought of as an oddball. The parties—all parties—are often seen as irrelevant. There are other avenues to power—the nature of which we will explore in a moment. Even in France or Italy, which have historically had stronger parties than the United States, the idea of the party as a primary, almost familial organization (for socializing, drinking, friendship, and the like) is fading. In country after country, political parties seem to be becoming less important, no longer an agency of intense loyalty or commitment. Public opinion polls show political parties to be among the least respected institutions.

While the parties are declining in importance, however, they are not about to disappear. Instead, their functions are becoming more circumscribed, as other institutions take over the roles they once performed. The parties are still the agencies that put up candidates and participate in elections. They present platforms and, in a parliamentary system, help run the government. Parties are still important players in the electoral arena. But that is only one arena among several in the modern polity. We will need to discuss what the other arenas consist of; meanwhile, the important interest articulation and aggregation functions once thought to be the specialized preserve of political parties are increasingly being performed by other agencies.

The Decline of Farm and Union Groups; the Dominance of Business

As social change occurs and as societies become more pluralistic and multi-class, new interest groups tend to appear. These include various business groups, middle-class associations, and trade unions. But once all these groups appear, the process does not end. Political scientists over the last forty years have tended to view pluralism as the end point of political evolution, as if a certain form of pluralism were inevitable and fixed in place.[5] But of course social change continues to occur. Some of the older interest groups tend to fade in importance, and new ones rise. These changes force a reassessment not only of the relative balance of power among interest groups but also of the role and importance of these groups.

The most obvious case is that of farmers. In the United States farmers now constitute less than 3 percent of the population, as compared with 30 percent fifty years ago. The farm voice, once powerful among politicians, has faded in importance. At the local and state level in some rural areas (Kansas, Nebraska) farmer influence is still important, but not at the national level. The numbers are simply not sufficient for politicians to pay much attention to farmers or farm organizations. The decline of the farm influence has occurred in other industrialized democracies as well. As these countries—Japan, Germany, the Scandinavian nations, Switzerland, Holland, Belgium, Great Britain—have become more urban and manufacturing oriented, their farmers have declined in numbers and hence in political influence. In more rural countries such as France, Italy, and Spain, farm groups still have some political clout, but even there their influence is waning.

A more controversial subject is the decline of workers' groups or trade unions. The issue is controversial because workers' movements were the subject—even the heroic figures—of Marx's famous analysis, and because the subject of worker-led socialism or social democracy remains attractive as an ideology in some circles. Two things have happened with regard to the power of trade unions. First, the nature of production has changed in all the industrialized nations, away from the old manufacturing, assembly, craft, and industrial unions, and toward more high-tech industry and services. Given the differences in salary between the United States and Mexico, for example (a minimum of $5–$6 per hour in the United States versus about 60 cents in Mexico), and given also that about 80 percent of the costs of producing textiles and clothing is in the cost of labor, it is hard to conceive of the United States having a large textile industry twenty years from now. Most of it will go "offshore" to Mexico, Central America, and the Caribbean. But that is happening in other areas as well: German optical equipment will be made by Polish workers, the Mercedes automobile will be assembled by Turkish workers, Japan will "farm out" its manufacturing to Thailand or Burma. In virtually all the developed countries the same trends are apparent: less manufacturing and heavy industry, more service and technology industries, immigrant labor and the farming out of manufacturing,

---

[5]The classic statement is by Robert Dahl, *Who Governs?* (New Haven, CT: Yale University Press, 1961).

and therefore fewer unionized workers. With the decline of these traditional industries in the advanced societies comes also the decline of the unions associated with them: the garment workers' union, the auto workers' union, the steel workers' union, and so on.

It is not just that manufacturing has shifted; there has also been in most of the industrialized nations an absolute decline in the organized workforce and hence in the political power of the trade unions. Part of the problem is the perception in many countries that unions are old, tired, and out-of-date, or that the leadership is corrupt or that it is tied to passé political ideologies. Part of the problem is that as the United States and other industrialized nations move increasingly toward high-tech, service industries, and greater professionalization of much of the workforce, workers are less inclined to join unions. Or, if they do, they join professional associations or associations of public sector employees, which are quite different (better educated, less militant) than the traditional unions. Third, when the economies of industrialized nations are mired in long-term recession or stagflation (as in much of Europe in the 1980s and 1990s), workers are so eager to get and hold on to scarce jobs that they may be frightened and/or unwilling to organize unions.

Unions, like political parties, will not disappear. But they are in decline in terms of absolute numbers, percentage of the workforce organized (down to about 8 percent in the United States), and political influence. Moreover, as the nature of the economies and society continue to change in the industrialized nations, these trends will likely continue. We make no value judgments about these trends; our purpose here is simply to point out the phenomena occurring and to suggest that this has major implications for our understanding of pluralism and interest group politics, and therefore also for comparative politics.

While organized labor has been in decline in most countries in recent years, big business has been thriving. That is now reflected in the growing political power of business. Business provides the jobs, the production, and therefore the prosperity that every country and government wants. Without a climate conducive for business, no economy nowadays can attract or keep the investment that is so necessary. Part of business's new clout stems from globalization: if business is not made to feel welcome in one country, it will transfer its jobs and productivity to others, leaving the first country in the lurch. Part of business's new influence is also due to the triumph of neoliberalism globally, which implies few restrictions on business activity. At present, therefore, business is largely in the saddle and driving the global economy; unions have been tamed and are in decline; and even governments are lagging behind as business forges ahead, trying to maintain some, often limited, regulatory role while big business is the main economic force.

Postmodernity

In his 1960 book *The Stages of Economic Growth*,[6] W. W. Rostow saw the United States and other highly developed, industrialized nations as entering after World War II an age of high mass consumption and social welfare. That was, in his view, the highest stage in the development process. But, once again, history does not stand still, and we are now in a new age of computers, advanced communications, globalization, and high technology. Scholar and former national security adviser (under Jimmy Carter) Zbigniew Brzezinski coined the term "the Technetronic Society" to describe these new phenomena and their social and political implications.[7] Now, with the collapse of the Soviet Union, we are in a post–cold war era—the "end of history," as Francis Fukuyama called it—which requires a reconsideration of all our earlier foreign policy assumptions.[8] These combinations of factors—high mass consumption, social welfare, computers, advanced communications, high technology, globalization, an end to the cold war, and the triumph of democracy —help us define what the postmodern era will be all about.

What are the implications of these changes for comparative politics? We have already analyzed a number of the agencies and institutions—ideology, political parties, farm groups, and trade unions—that are currently in decline and likely to continue to decline in the foreseeable future. But what are the new groups, institutions, and practices that will be ascendant or that will replace the institutions and issues described here as fading?

Postmodern Issues

Postmodernity has brought a host of new issues to the fore that have in many cases replaced the issues of the past. Whereas in the past, public policy tended to focus on such bread-and-butter issues as labor or industrial relations, social welfare, and the state's role in the economy, now the trend in many developed nations is toward lifestyle issues. The old issues are still important in many respects and are considered later in the chapter, but recently it has been the newer lifestyle issues that have commanded attention.

Lifestyle issues are a product to a considerable degree of rising affluence in the developed countries. Many of the old bread-and-butter issues stimulated by earlier industrialization and urbanization have been solved or at least are

---

[6]W. W. Rostow, *The Stages of Economic Growth* (Cambridge: Cambridge University Press, 1960).

[7]Zbigniew Brzezinski, *Between Two Ages: America's Role in the Technetronic Age* (New York: Penguin, 1976).

[8]Fukuyama, "End of History."

not so troublesome in the developed nations, and they can now turn their attention to the new postmodern or lifestyle issues. Other reasons for the increasing attention to lifestyle issues are the end of the cold war and thus the decline of international tensions, and the decline of ideological passions that were largely the product of industrialization and the social problems it engendered.

In virtually all the developed, industrialized nations (except the United States), religion is in decline. Japan as well as most of Western Europe have become thoroughly secularized countries. Religion is important to only 10 to 15 percent of the population, but for most people religion has ceased to be a crucial issue. They may consider themselves still religious in a vague cultural sense (Northern Europe is mainly Protestant; Southern Europe, mainly Catholic), but they seldom attend religious services or have any contact with organized religion. The decline of religion in many developed nations (not, incidentally, in developing nations where religion seems to be experiencing a revival) has given rise to a widespread search for values, to a "politics of identity," and to the effort frequently to substitute lifestyle changes, expressive individualism, or group identity (ethnic, racial, nationality) for the older religious values.

In addition, and in part a reflection of religion's decline, a variety of new lifestyle issues have gained prominence. These include drugs, pollution, the environment, divorce, abortion, sexual freedom and orientation, and personal choice and freedom—including freedom to travel, body piercing, the right to break parental bonds, and so forth. Immigration may fit in this category as well, although it is a product mainly of economic considerations. In turn, a number of these lifestyle issues force governments to deal with new public policy issues such as AIDS, drug legalization, needle exchanges, street people and homelessness, new requirements in health care, and so on.

In most developed countries, the older issues of wages, welfare, the management of the economy, and so on, are still present, although rising affluence has often rendered them less critical. In the meantime, and a product of that same rising affluence, a variety of new lifestyle issues have come to prominence. We would expect these trends to continue into the future.

Corporatism and Corporatist Structures

Earlier we made a distinction between the traditional corporatism (based on clans, tribes, and neomedieval sociopolitical organizations) found in many developing nations and the modern corporatism or "neocorporatism" found in virtually all advanced industrial nations. Whereas in our previous discussion we emphasized the corporatism of the developing countries, here we need to stress the modern type.

The rising influence of corporatist institutions and practices in modern industrialized nations is directly related to the decline of political parties and trade unions. As corporatist influences have become stronger, political parties and labor groups have become weaker. We need to understand the connections between these two phenomena.

The modern state, it is often said, consists of multiple, overlapping "iron triangles." The "triangle" image refers to the interconnections between legislative committees or subcommittees, executive branch bureaucratic or regulatory agencies, and organized interest groups.[9] The "iron" refers to the fact that these connections are very close and that they tend to exclude other groups and interests (including sometimes the general public!) from the process. (See Figure 9.1.)

This system of corporatist or iron triangle representation is quite different from traditional interest group lobbying, with which we are more familiar.[10] For one thing, the relations of these groups to the state have now become so intimate that the interest group representatives are no longer independent actors but often a part of the state itself and inseparable from it. In some countries (for example, Portugal under Salazar) such interest group representation was highly formalized, with the major groups having direct representation in the legislature or other representative or decision-making bodies: the wine growers had six seats in the Corporative Chamber; the

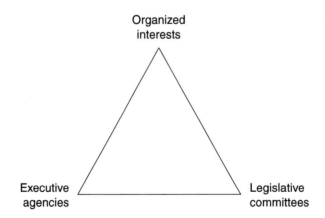

Figure 9.1   The Iron Triangle

[9]Theodore Lowi, *The End of Liberalism* (New York: Norton, 1969).

[10]On corporatism in the modern state, see Philippe C. Schmitter and Gerhard Lehmbruch (eds.), *Trends toward Corporatist Intermediation* (Beverly Hills, CA: Sage, 1979); Suzanne Berger, *Organizing Interests in Western Europe* (New York: Cambridge University Press, 1981); Martin O. Heisler (ed.), *Politics in Europe: Structures and Processes in Some Postindustrial Democracies* (New York: McKay, 1974); and Howard J. Wiarda, *Corporatism and Comparative Politics* (New York: Sharpe, 1996).

Church, six; the armed forces, eight; and so forth. At the opposite extreme is the United States, where these relations are very informal, with the interest groups meeting with congressmen or regulatory officials informally to help hammer out legislation or executive orders. Most other developed, industrialized countries fall in between these two extremes—there are not formally designated seats for these interest groups in the legislature (these are reserved for political party personnel), but rather a certain number of seats on regulatory boards, in government agencies, and in policy-making offices are "reserved" for interest group representatives. Corporatism is not an either/or matter, then; rather, it represents a continuum (see Figure 9.2).

Modern-day corporatism should not be thought of as nefarious influence peddling, as interest group lobbying is frequently viewed in the United States. Rather, corporatism is an integral, consultative feature of the modern state. The modern state is a bureaucratic state, often a technocratic state, a state that requires regular consultation between its vast regulatory boards and the groups they regulate. Decisions cannot and should not be made in the dark without the groups affected having a say. The best way to ensure that this consultation takes place on a regular, timely, and more or less formal basis is to incorporate the groups affected into the regulatory or decision-making process. The United States, which has less corporatism than any other modern state, is frequently criticized for allowing these discussions to take place too informally, in the dark corridors of the Capitol, late at night, and with little public oversight. It would be better, the argument goes, to allow such interest group representation to operate in the sunlight, above board, at a public and formal level where accountability and responsibility can be maintained. There can be various degrees of such corporatism, as Figure 9.2 indicates, and also varying degrees of distinction between the public or governmental agencies and private interests. In Japan,

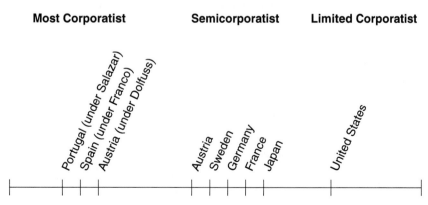

Figure 9.2 Corporatism: A Spectrum of Countries

for example, the line between public and private is nearly invisible in some sectors of the economy; in the United States the public and private spheres are still kept separate, although in recent years a considerable blurring of the public/private distinction has occurred.[11]

Corporatism usually implies limits on the number of groups that can participate in the political process. For example, in some political systems only one trade union organization and one business confederation may be authorized by the government to bargain for their members and to have representation on state regulatory boards. Others may be excluded, meaning some groups will have a monopoly, or perhaps oligopoly, of power. Such authorizations/exclusions may be done on a more or less democratic basis or on an authoritarian basis, thus defining the different forms that corporatism may take. If a regime is corporatist, it cannot have the plethora of diverse, free-wheeling, almost anarchic interest groups present in the United States. A trade-off occurs: In return for access to and representation in the political system, a group must give up some of its freedom to operate independently. That is probably the price to pay in a developed, bureaucratic political system.

The emergence of corporatism in so many modern polities may thus come at the cost of some democracy. That may also be the cost of modernity. In fact, in many countries a corporatist structure of institutions has grown up alongside and parallel to the democratic institutions. On the one side are the institutions of democracy: public opinion, elections, political parties, and parliament. On the other side are the institutions of corporatism: large-scale and quasi-monopolistic interest groups, state regulatory agencies, and bureaucracies. These two sets of institutions often coexist within the same polity; sometimes they cooperate, sometimes they overlap, and often they compete. Thus, a democratic regime may simultaneously be a corporatist regime, and vice versa. A hallmark of the modern polity is that it is likely to be both democratic and corporatist. And for developing countries the question is, Can they progress from the earlier forms of traditional caste, tribe, or medieval corporatism to the updated, modern form of neocorporatism described here?[12]

Bureaucratization/State Downsizing

The modern state is not just a corporatist state; it is also a bureaucratic state.[13] The two go hand in hand: as interest groups have grown in size and

---

[11]Howard J. Wiarda, "The Latin Americanization of the United States," *The New Scholar* 7 (1978): 51-86.

[12]See Howard J. Wiarda, *Politics in Iberia: The Political Systems of Spain and Portugal* (New York: Little, Brown/HarperCollins, 1992).

[13]Michael Crozier, *The Bureaucratic Phenomenon* (Chicago: University of Chicago Press, 1964).

complexity and been increasingly incorporated into the structure of the modern state, the size and complexity of the bureaucracy have grown as well. The increasing differentiation and rationalization of society means that bureaucracy must become more differentiated and rationalized too. Bigness in one area (interest group and representational activity) breeds bigness in the other (bureaucracy). The growth of social welfare programs and of the state's role in the economy are further factors in explaining modern bureaucracy.

The growth of such large-scale bureaucracies is in many ways lamentable, for we all know that such bigness breeds inefficiencies, red tape, increased paperwork, delays, and probably corruption. It also often breeds favoritism. Unfortunately, there is not much we can do about such bigness or its accompanying bureaucratization. More people globally, fewer open spaces, the absence of available and unexplored frontiers, crowding, urbanization, complexity, rationalization—all give rise to increased bureaucratization. We may not like it, but big bureaucracy is a hallmark of the modern era and state, and is probably inevitable. Moreover, in many countries the civil service takes pride in providing honest, efficient, capable service to the public.

Actually, many people like such bigness or have a strong stake in it: not necessarily bigness per se, but the fact that their jobs, livelihood, and careers are tied to public service and hence to the big budgets and big bureaucratic agencies that support such services. Teachers, federal, state, and municipal workers, social workers, planners, environmentalists, housing specialists, managers and administrators, and many others all work for the state in varying capacities and at varying levels. They depend on government employment, their families depend on that government paycheck, and their entire working lives may be spent in the employ of government. In the United States the percentage of persons who work for the government is relatively small—about 25 to 30 percent—but it has been growing rapidly. In Europe or Latin America, however, the percentage may reach 50 to 60 percent of the gainfully employed workforce—or higher. In some countries the state is virtually the only employer, particularly of educated persons. These facts give the modern state and its public bureaucracy vast political and economic power.

Along with the growth of the public sector has come the growth of public sector unions. In many countries the teachers' union or civil servants' unions are among the most powerful interests in the country. Such public sector unions are increasingly replacing the craft, manufacturing, and industrial unions of the past. They are influential because in the modern state the services they perform are so essential. A shutdown of schools by the teachers' union and of municipal services (garbage, electricity, telephone) by the municipal workers' unions cannot be tolerated in a modern, complex, interdependent society. In addition, such unions of public sector employees are often part of the corporatist structure of the modern state: they are part of and incorporated into the state rather than being separate from it. Their size, power, and strategic location inside the government mean that politicians are unwilling to take them on in a conflict.

Such bigness and bureaucracy almost inevitably give rise to waste, inefficiency, and corruption. The bureaucracy may come to serve patronage functions—jobs in return for a favor—rather than the efficient management of public affairs for which it was intended. Political parties or interest groups may carve out a special niche in the bureaucracy for themselves from which they reward their friends and clientele. Whole agencies or ministries may be coopted or even captured by the groups they are designed to regulate. Or the bureaucracy, or some parts of it, may come to serve as a giant sinecure agency: a place for time servers or for the employment of people who show up only to collect their paychecks. The government becomes a kind of giant employment agency.

Presently there is a worldwide campaign under way to reduce the size of these often bloated public bureaucracies, streamline them, decentralize them, make them more efficient, and privatize the functions many of them once performed (state-owned airlines, steel industries, and the like). We may want to wish these efforts well, but we ought to remain skeptical of what can actually be achieved in many cases. Even Ronald Reagan, the most conservative American president in the last seventy years, could not, despite a good deal of rhetoric to the contrary, reduce the size of the federal bureaucracy. In fact, under Reagan the Washington bureaucracy continued to grow. Other leaders in Britain, France, Russia, and other countries are facing similar difficulties in reducing the size of their public bureaucracies or trying to decentralize. Despite well-publicized efforts to sell state-owned enterprises back to the private sector and to reduce overall the size of the public bureaucracy, the number of state employees usually continues to grow. Those laid off are frequently hired back by other agencies, transferred or reorganized rather than fired, or put back on the public payroll when the overseers (World Bank or IMF) are not looking. Decentralization and privatization have often provided not greater efficiency but a breakdown or decline in social services. We may hope these streamlining and privatizing efforts work, even while doubting that all that much will come of them.

In the comparative politics literature, there has been considerable discussion of this state downsizing and even whether the state will "wither away." Not only are the pressures to streamline, reduce, and privatize great; but it is also argued that, with the cold war over, countries will not need such large foreign policy and defense agencies and furthermore that, with economic integration, policy making will be mainly handled by transnational agencies (such as the EU) and not by sovereign nations. Even national sovereignty itself is said to be at bay. But so far the figures do not bear out many of these predictions. Streamlining, privatization, and decentralization are occurring in many developed countries, but state size and importance have not as yet been reduced.

In the meantime, bureaucracy has also grown at the international and transnational levels. Here we have in mind the United Nations and its mushrooming functional organizations (for health, education, welfare, and so on), various regional organizations (the Organization for African Unity, the Organization of American States), as well as myriad international agencies dealing with global population, human rights, the environment, hunger, and so on. Particularly important has been the steady, now mushrooming growth of the agencies of European integration located in Brussels, Strasbourg, and other cities, a phenomenon almost entirely unknown in the United States. In effect, a core of experienced and skillful international European bureaucrats has incrementally wrested important responsibility, decision making, and even some degree of control over defense and foreign affairs as well as economic and social policy away from national officials located in London, Paris, and Berlin. As Europe moves toward further integration, the role of these international agencies will surely increase still more. It will be interesting to see if the European model of integration—and the vast international bureaucracy that goes with it—will become the model for the North American and Asian integration networks presently coming into existence.

Changing Public Policy

In the modern state, public policy is similarly undergoing a transformation. Society is changing, society's problems are changing, and therefore public policy is changing as well.

First, none of the advanced nations we are discussing have to deal with the problems of poverty to anywhere near the degree that the developing nations do. The latter must often face societywide poverty, an entire culture of poverty, whereas the advanced nations are dealing with only pockets of poverty. Such "pockets" may still amount to 5 to 10 percent of the population, but that is a far cry from the 80 to 90 percent poverty rates in the developing nations. Having only pockets of poverty changes the way advanced nations think about poverty (almost a residual problem rather than a stark or immediate one), the allocation of resources to deal with poverty (increasingly less), and the priorities of public policy.

Second and as mentioned earlier, public policy in the advanced nations increasingly deals with lifestyle issues: pollution, drugs, the environment, human rights, global warming, and so on. In contrast, many developing countries are so poor that they cannot devote many of their scarce resources to these kinds of issues. In this sense, lifestyle issues may be seen as the province of richer, more affluent countries, not of poor ones. In fact, the poorer countries are so eager for capital and investment that they sometimes advertise in Western newspapers: "Give us your polluting and environmentally dangerous industries if you [the richer countries] don't want them or if you regulate them out of business, because we are so desperate for jobs that we will take anything." As development proceeds, therefore, a basic needs policy (food, clothing, housing, water), characteristic of the poor nations, tends to yield (though not completely) to the lifestyle issues of the more affluent countries.

Third, people in more developed nations have longer life expectancies, and their age curves are weighted more toward older people. In many developing nations the average age of the population may be under fifteen years, but in the modern ones it may be thirty or older. Countries that have older populations have different public policy needs than those with younger populations, focusing on old-age insurance, retirement plans such as social security, and health care programs such as Medicare. New issues tend to arise in these affluent and older societies because older people vote more than do younger people, and they tend to vote in a concentrated fashion for the issues of concern to them. At the same time, the question of whether the younger generation workforce will be sufficiently large and willing to continue paying to support the retirement programs of their elders becomes a major issue.

Fourth, and related, is the shift in advanced countries toward a large service sector. We have already touched on this subject in discussing the changing nature of trade unions. In the postmodern societies traditional industries and manufacturing (coal mining, steel, textiles, machine tools, others) tend to go into decline: it is simply cheaper to import such products than to produce them domestically. Or else, as in the case of Western Europe and increasingly the United States, they are produced domestically but with cheap immigrant labor. More and more, however, the postmodern economy focuses on the service sector: computers, education, information processing, telecommunications, research, health care, and so on. This focus requires a better-educated and more skilled citizenry than is needed in a developing nation where unskilled labor is used in the initial stages of the more traditional industries. This shift to services and high tech also implies a need for different public policies (greater emphasis on higher education, on research and development, on computer skills, on worker retraining) than those in a nation in an earlier stage of development.

Fifth, in both underdeveloped and developed societies questions concerning the distribution or redistribution of power and resources continue to come to the fore. In some senses, both ideology and class conflict of the traditional sort (workers versus capitalists) tend to decline in advanced societies; but new sources of conflict, including new forms of class conflict, often reassert themselves. As a society moves from the traditional manufacturing industries to high tech and services, for example, a greater premium is placed on education and computer skills. But what about those—still roughly half the population—who lack such skills and are unable or unwilling to acquire them? Are they condemned to be gas station attendants (there are fewer of those nowadays) or fast-food dispensers on a permanent basis? Tax reform, welfare reform, and who should pay also continue to be divisive issues in developed countries.

Many developed countries are increasingly dividing between the professional and the working classes, with the key determining factor being education. In the United States about half of seventeen- to twenty-one-year-olds now attend college, and a college education has become the key to "making it" in American society. Education provides access to the better jobs and higher salaries, and it is by now a better determinant of class standing than family name or social status. This split into a basically two-class society based on education is evident even in the early grades where students are grouped into college-bound and non-college-bound sections. The system is great for the college-bound but often stifling and demeaning for those who are not. In Europe and Japan the entrance exams that determine admission into the better secondary schools and the universities serve essentially the same functions as the American system of "grouping." The result, again, is a two-class society divided between the educated and higher-paid professional middle class, and the less well-educated and lower-paid working class, whose jobs also tend to be far less stable. Thus new class complications tend to replace the older ones, with immense implications for public policy.

These shifts in public policy making, recall, are occurring and often being fought out in a context of increased suspicion of "big government," demands for greater accountability and responsibility on the part of public officials, demands for privatization, and insistence on no new taxes. Globally, and not just in the United States, there is a demand for new programs in the areas of housing, health care, and welfare, but a considerable reluctance to pay for them. Politicians and public agencies are thus caught in a bind: Demands by and expectations of citizens for public services keep rising, the nature of public policy must shift to reflect the changing nature of society in the postindustrial age, and yet a fewer number of taxpayers is willing to pick up the tab. These issues provide abundant opportunities for further study on a variety of fronts: comparative welfare policies, comparative health care policies, and comparative studies of how different political systems cope both with new demands and with shifting priorities.[14]

Let us take the current debate in many of the developed countries over economic development and welfare policy. Currently neoliberalism, with its doctrine of open markets, state downsizing, and privatization, has emerged triumphant in the economic sphere; and, based on this conception, the

---

[14]Arnold J. Heidenheimer et al., *Comparative Public Policy: Policies of Social Choice in Europe and America* (New York: St. Martin's, 1975).

United States and the British economies have been the best performers among the developed countries. In Continental Europe, in contrast, while they acknowledge the superior ability of neoliberalism to create jobs and stimulate growth, they are reluctant to make the tradeoffs necessary for reducing state size and, especially, giving up cradle-to-grave welfare programs. The result is a vigorous debate in many developed countries over the future course of public policy. On the one side are the Americans and British who have been stimulating growth while also cutting back on social programs; on the other are the French and the Scandinavian countries who have opted to retain their beloved welfare systems but at the cost of slower economic growth. In between are the Dutch and the Germans who have tried to devise a formula that encourages business and entrepreneurship while also taxing them heavily to maintain social programs. These three models of how to balance the need for economic growth against the demands for social welfare help provide a road map of the current public policy debate in many developed countries.

Ungovernability?

Modern political systems are called on to satisfy an ever larger number of demands. In modern polities people are no longer illiterate and uninvolved; rather, they are educated, mobilized, and aroused to defend their interests. They demand education, housing, medical care, social welfare, environmentally sound programs, a flourishing economy, jobs, social security, zoning, drug treatment, rent control, highways, bridges, snow removal, parks, open space, wetlands protection, efficient government, and so on—the list of expectations and demands is lengthy and constantly growing. The question is: Can government cope with all the new and multiple demands that have been thrust upon it?

In comparative politics this question has given rise to a considerable literature on what is called "ungovernability."[15] We all know what it means to govern effectively, but what happens when a political system is so overloaded with demands that it is unable to handle them all? When the burden of governance and of satisfying so many expectations becomes so great that a political system can't respond? When it begins to lose legitimacy and unravel? When it almost literally implodes, as the Soviet Union did in 1989 to 1991?

---

[15]Michael Crozier, Samuel P. Huntington, and Joji Watanuki, *The Crisis of Democracy Report on the Governability of Democracies to the Trilateral Commission* (New York: New York University Press, 1975).

The possibility of ungovernability and breakdown has become a major issue in quite a number of the advanced nations. At least four dimensions or variations of the problem may be identified.

The first of these is that government may actually go bankrupt. Of course, at one level, no sovereign state can actually go bankrupt because it can always print more money to satisfy its domestic creditors; international creditors, however, are another matter. But such cranking up of the treasury's or central bank's printing press will cause inflation, which may also be unacceptable. Suppose we have a country such as Poland or Russia in which demands and expectations keep rising, there is little investment, the population is unwilling to pay more taxes, and the country threatens to go belly-up? Austerity would have to be imposed, jobs lost, and government programs dramatically cut back. But what if the public service labor organizations, the teachers' unions, police officers and firefighters, and government employees generally refuse to accept such cuts? Government services would have to be cut back in a time of still-rising expectations, but the groups affected would refuse to accept the rollbacks and the citizens would not pay more taxes. A gridlock would develop; the government would be paralyzed. That is one dimension of ungovernability.

A second form of ungovernability involves ethnic strife that becomes so violent that it tears the country apart. Lebanon in the 1980s is an example, as are Ethiopia and the Congo in recent times, Yugoslavia in 1991 and continuing to today, and perhaps Russia in the future, as it continues to break apart. Ethnic strife is not confined to the developing nations; strong separatist movements also exist in Spain (the Basques), France (Normandy and Brittany), and Great Britain (Wales, Scotland, and Northern Ireland). These can be, as in Northern Ireland and in Spain, very bloody conflicts. They can also be long and protracted; the bloodshed may go on for a decade or more. In Yugoslavia's case the ethnic conflict goes back to the founding of the country and was only submerged but not blotted out by communist rule.

A third form of ungovernability is political or ideological conflict that becomes so intense that it produces conditions of endemic civil war, usually with on-again, off-again actual fighting. In El Salvador, for example, the three worlds of development that coexist within the country—feudal, capitalist, and socialist—are so far apart, and the gaps among them so wide and unbridgeable, that it produced a civil war that raged for nearly two decades. Spain also had a major civil war in the 1930s, Greece in the 1940s, and Portugal fell into nationwide political and civil strife in the 1970s. A number of countries in Eastern Europe, including Russia, are deeply divided by both ethnic and political/ideological strife.

A fourth type of "overloaded" and therefore ungovernable political system is one in which the interest group battle becomes so intense and nasty that no reasonable compromise or political solution seems possible. The primary example is the United States with its incredible plethora of interest groups (fifty thousand in Washington, D.C., alone) and its increasingly divisive policy struggle. The result of the oftentimes incredible kaleidoscope of American interest group struggles is no longer effective policy but, more likely, conflict and deadlock. Indeed, paralysis, sclerosis, and immobilization have come to characterize many areas of domestic and foreign policy making in the United States.[16] The debate over policy issues becomes so intense, with so many groups lined up on both sides, that effective policy is stymied and the entire system becomes paralyzed and prone to breakdown. The result of such rancorous discussion is constant conflict, indecisiveness, creeping paralysis, and the inability of the political system to function effectively. In the modern political system this kind of gridlock is probably the most likely form of ungovernability.

Global Political Economy

What is the new global political economy going to be like in the future? And where do the more advanced nations fit into this new global scheme of relations?

First, the new global political economy will be characterized by even more complex interdependence than in the past. In the wake of the Soviet Union's demise, for example, Mexico may well become the most important country in the world from a U.S. foreign policy point of view. The United States and Mexico are interdependent on so many fronts—water resources, pollution, investment, oil, labor supplies, trade, drugs, tourism, diplomacy, natural gas, immigration, manufacturing—that it is no longer possible to separate foreign policy from domestic policy and politics. Rather, what is required is a new language (complex interdependence) to deal with the multiple levels at which the United States and Mexico interact.[17]

But it is not just the United States and Mexico and other nations to our south that exist in a new relationship of complex interdependence. Across the Mediterranean, the nations of Europe and North Africa (the Maghreb) are similarly involved in new relationships that involve migration, pollution of the Mediterranean, trade, investment, labor supplies, oil, diplomacy, and so on—almost the same agenda of issues that makes the United States and Mexico interdependent. In the wake of communism's fall, Western Europe and Eastern Europe are similarly drawing closer together in more complex

---

[16]Howard J. Wiarda, *Foreign Policy without Illusion: How Foreign Policy Works and Fails to Work in the United States* (New York: HarperCollins/Scott Foresman, 1990).

[17]Robert O. Keohane and Joseph S. Nye, *Power and Interdependence* (Glenview, IL: Scott Foresman, 1989).

ways. In Asia, Japan, China, India, and Australia are also becoming more interdependent, both with one another and with other, smaller countries of South and Southeast Asia. To replace the outdated and simplistic terms of the past, we desperately need a whole new vocabulary and set of categories to describe and analyze these complex patterns of interdependence.

A second theme is the rise of international trading blocks: North America, Europe, Asia. We discussed this issue in Chapter 8 with reference to the developing nations, but we now need to look at it from the point of the already developed countries. For example, the United States wants to forge trade links with Canada and Latin America (Mexico first and foremost) because it wishes to maintain access to various raw materials—especially petroleum—of which the Western Hemisphere has abundant supplies. That is also a way of stabilizing the historically volatile Latin American area. Moreover, Canada and Latin America are logical economic partners for the United States during the next stage of international relations, which will surely concentrate more on economic interrelationships. Access to large and growing regional markets and joint production efforts that combine U.S. capital and technology with Latin America's resources and labor force will be a key to maintaining U.S. global competitiveness.[18] The European Union (EU) and Japan are forging similar kinds of relationships with their neighbors: Japan with the large Asia–Pacific area and the EU with Eastern Europe, Russia, North Africa, and many developing areas.

While the world of the future will undoubtedly be strongly shaped by the three major trading blocs, these same nations—both the large bloc leaders (the United States, Germany, Japan) and the countries with which they are linked—are also seeking, so far as is feasible, to maintain a system of free trade. They want to protect their interests under the umbrella of their respective blocs while also maintaining what is called "GATT compatibility." GATT stands for the General Agreement on Tariffs and Trade; it is an instrument for maintaining trade on a global level. Thus, while at one level the major economic powers are seeking to organize their own regional trading blocs, at another they are trying to maintain a global regime of free, or at least fair, trade.

A third theme, related to the first two, is the progressive erasing of national borders and even, to some degree, of sovereignty. In the United States we think of this as involving our borders with Canada and Mexico; the flow of people, dollars, goods, and services across these borders is phenomenal. The borders have not been erased, but they are becoming more and more permeable.[19]

---

[18]See the research report prepared at the National Defense University, War Gaming Center, "Refining U.S. Interests in Latin America" (Washington, D.C.: NDU, 1991).

[19]Eugenia Georges, *The Making of a Transnational Community* (New York: Columbia University Press, 1990).

In Western Europe, with the progressive development of the Common Market, the process of erasing borders is even further along. There are, or are about to be, common EU passports, a common currency, common trade policies in dealing with the outside world, no tariff barriers between member nations, and so on. There are virtually no passport or border controls between EU countries. In addition, the power of the Common Market bureaucrats located in Brussels is growing, is often greater than that of political leaders in individual countries, and implies potentially a far greater loss of national sovereignty than anything even talked about as yet in the negotiations over a North American free trade area. The next steps in the Brussels bureaucrats' agenda include a common European foreign and defense policy; that implies some common political structures as well. These further steps toward a common European political or even military entity will doubtless be opposed by some interests in the several member countries who want to retain national control over their own foreign and defense policy (most prominently in Great Britain, which is not yet convinced fully to join Europe economically, let alone in foreign policy), and some compromises will be necessary. Nevertheless, in the long run, the march toward the erasing of borders likely will proceed—certainly in Europe, probably in North America, and maybe in other areas as well.

Finally, there are out-of-area issues that need to be discussed. The world is undoubtedly dividing into trading blocs, but what about the countries and regions that lie outside those blocs? We saw in the last chapter that those countries are scrambling to find "cover," in one bloc or another, but the bloc leaders also have a powerful say in these matters. Europe, and especially Germany, is taking the lead in dealing with Eastern Europe and perhaps with Russia; Europe is also reaching out to Africa and the Caribbean to include some of those nations under a more expanded Lomé convention. The United States will serve as the center for a Western Hemisphere trade bloc, and Japan and perhaps China will do the same in Asia.

While such trade blocs are undoubtedly coming into existence, one should distinguish between them and at the same time not concentrate on the blocs to the exclusion of other trade patterns. The EU is the most tightly knit bloc, and will undoubtedly be a major force in the future. But the United States and Japan are both *global* economic powers whose influence will not be limited to any one region. Japan, for example, trades more with the Western Hemisphere (primarily with the United States) than with Asia; and the United States trades more with Japan, Taiwan, South Korea, and Europe than with all of Latin America. The key for such economic superpowers as the United States, Japan, and Germany, and for many middle-level powers, will be to trade on a global basis while also securing special access and protection within their own respective regions.

International Politics: The Post–Cold War Era

International politics and comparative politics are separate fields within political science, but they are also interrelated. Hence, I conclude this chapter by examining the post–cold war international environment and some of the implications of these vast changes for comparative politics studies.

First, we need to emphasize that the cold war as we have known it is definitely over. The recent disintegration of the Soviet Union means that the superpower conflict that many of us grew up with and that shaped so many of our policies and assumptions is gone. The United States emerged triumphant from the cold war and is the world's only military, economic, and political superpower. Other countries (Japan, Germany) also wield economic power, but only the United States has all the ingredients of world power status: military, diplomatic, strategic, and economic. The end of the cold war forces us to reexamine virtually every one of the foreign policy assumptions contained in the textbooks: Who is our enemy? What are our foreign policy goals? What is the purpose of international politics? Who will police unstable or unruly areas? And so on.

Second, the world of the future will be much more heavily dominated by economic or political-economic issues than the world of the past. In previous years political, diplomatic, and especially strategic issues have been paramount, but now economic issues will be more important: international trade, banking, commerce, lending, resources, labor supplies, and so on. This shift from strategic to economic issues also means that the countries that are powerful in an economic sense—Japan, the United States, Germany—will be even more powerful in the future. It also means that scholars of comparative politics should get as solid a grounding in international economics as they do in international politics.

Third, with the collapse of the Soviet Union, the United States not only has emerged as dominant among nations in the world but will probably remain so until well into the twenty-first century. A considerable number of books have been written recently about the presumed decline (known as the "declinist" literature) of the United States,[20] but we need to be very careful in assessing and evaluating this supposed decline. No one doubts that the United States has some severe problems; moreover, on a global scale the U.S. share of *world* GNP has declined. This is a quite natural process having to do mainly with the incredible recovery of Japan, Germany, and the rest of Europe after World War II; the emergence of a variety of NICs (Brazil, India,

---

[20]See especially Paul Kennedy, *The Rise and Fall of the Great Powers* (New York: Random House, 1987).

Venezuela, and the like) onto the world stage as intermediary economic powers; the rise of the oil-exporting countries and their new wealth; and the generalized greater prosperity in much of the Third World. Note, however, that while all these other countries were recovering and/or growing, the U.S. economy also continued to grow, not shrink—often at a faster rate than other developed countries. Therefore, when we talk about the U.S. "decline," we are really talking about its *relative* decline. There has been no diminishment of U.S. GNP; indeed, it has often shown impressive growth. What has changed is the *percentage* of the U.S. share of the total world GNP, relative to other nations. That means the United States has not lost any absolute power, only that others have gained comparatively. Hence, it is premature at best to say the United States is a declining power; instead, U.S. dominance will last well into the next century, and within the foreseeable future there will be no serious challenges.

A fourth, and closely related, trend, given the collapse of the Soviet Union and the end of the cold war, is the lessened potential for global war. At present, such a superpower confrontation seems highly unlikely, since one of the superpowers has unraveled and no longer has the capability to carry out a full-scale international war. On the "Doomsday Clock" that the Bulletin of Atomic Scientists has been using to chart the potential for nuclear war, the hands have been turned back to the "earliest," or least-likelihood-of-war, time since the cold war began forty-five years ago. With the lessened likelihood of full-scale, major-power confrontation, most countries will be free to focus more on domestic policy and not so much on foreign policy.

Other, newer conflicts and wars may develop. However, these would most likely be at lower or regional levels and not have the potential to engulf the entire world. For example, we may see conflicts between regional powers such as that between Iran and Iraq in the 1980s; we may see border skirmishes between the two Koreas or some South American countries; we will likely see greater ethnic conflict in Eastern Europe, Africa, and Russia; we may see occasional U.S. police actions such as that against General Manuel Noriega of Panama or against the drug lords of Central and South America; and we will probably see irredentist conflicts revolving around old nationality and/or territorial claims in the Balkans and Central Europe. Nevertheless, none of these seem likely to expand into generalized war, nor are nuclear weapons likely to be used. The post–cold war era may not always be a peaceful and happy time, but at least the potential for nuclear holocaust has been greatly reduced.

Finally, the end of the cold war suggests a greater importance for international organizations such as the United Nations (UN), the Organization of American States (OAS), and the Organization of African Unity (OAU). It is not necessarily that independent states will cede much sovereignty to these international bodies. Instead, as the United States did in the Gulf War with Iraq in 1991, the major powers have learned that it is often useful and advantageous to proceed multilaterally through an international agency such as the UN as well as bilaterally or unilaterally. Governments or states remain, for the most part, the prime actors in international affairs, but on some issues and in some cases multilateral initiatives, or else initiatives that combine multilateral and unilateral approaches, may be preferred. In addition, the growth of international perceptions and even law in such areas as human rights and democratization will make it very difficult for a single country to resist international pressures. Growing interdependence among nations also means that some issues (acid rain, global warming) cannot be addressed by one nation alone but must be dealt with internationally. Such approaches that combine the multilateral and the unilateral are very complicated undertakings, and they require elaborate planning and diplomacy—as did the U.S. effort in this regard in the Gulf War and in Bosnia. But they may come increasingly to represent the wave of the future in international conflicts.

All of these futurology subjects provide ample room for additional research and a more refined, specific, and detailed exposition. They provide the grist for numerous future comparative politics studies.

10

Frontiers of Research in Comparative Politics

Comparative politics is a dynamic field. The entire globe is our research terrain, and things are constantly changing, in flux. There are always new issues, new approaches, new political movements, and even new countries to explore and explain. To most of us in the field, these changes and the dynamism engendered are what make the subject matter of comparative politics so interesting.

In this chapter we examine some of these new issues. The topics explored include women in politics, drug policy, immigration, regionalism and decentralization, gay rights, and pollution and the environment. Our purpose is not to exhaustively examine these subjects (which cannot be done in one short chapter) but to introduce them and to offer some preliminary comments concerning the dimensions of these issues and the approach of diverse countries or regions to them, to show how comparative politics can increase our understanding and analysis of them. Hopefully, the discussion will stimulate other scholars and students to explore the issues more fully and in a variety of national contexts.

Women in Politics

The comparative study of women in politics is a subject

of growing interest in the field.[1] On the one hand, women are playing an increasingly important political role in many countries; on the other, the place, position, and political influence of women varies greatly from country to country and region to region. That is precisely the kind of issue that comparative politics seeks to explore, involving change and new dynamics (women in politics) but also variation among countries and regions.

To begin, let us make some distinctions. First, the movement to involve more women in politics has been stronger in the developed countries than in the developing nations. Second, it has been stronger in the Western countries: North America (the United States, Canada), Western Europe, and the countries that are offshoots of Western civilization (Australia, New Zealand). In contrast, Japan, South Korea, Taiwan, Hong Kong, and Singapore—the developed and emerging market economies of Asia—have so far lagged behind in terms of women in politics, although that is now changing. Third, women in the developing areas have similarly lagged behind women in the developed nations, although (1) that is also changing and (2) there are major differences between the roles and position of women in Africa, Latin America, and the Middle East (Islamic Society).

If we examine the number of women at cabinet level in the developed, Western countries (Table 10.1), some interesting comparisons emerge. Sweden and Norway are the only countries in which women hold almost as many ministerial posts as men do. Note that the top four countries are all in Scandinavia: Sweden, Norway, Finland, and Denmark. They are followed by the Netherlands, the United States and Austria, Canada, and Ireland, and so on down the chart.

In general, the lower one goes in the socioeconomic scale the smaller the percentage of women in high government posts. Note that in Table 10.1, the wealthiest Western countries tend to be at the top, while the poorest countries (Slovakia, Portugal, Bulgaria, Russia) tend to have the fewest women cabinet members. Countries that are Southern European and predominantly Catholic also tend to rank behind countries that are Northern European and predominantly Protestant.

These figures of the number of women at cabinet level are largely reflective of the number of women who began their careers in parliament and at the local government level. Here we focus on parliament because the figures

---

[1]Among the better comparative studies of women in politics are Jane S. Jaquette, *Women and Democracy* (Baltimore: Johns Hopkins University Press, 1998); Jaquette, *Women in Developing Countries* (New York: Haworth, 1983); Ann M. Pescatello, *Power and Pawn: Women in Latin America* (Westport, CT: Greenwood, 1976); Susan Bourque, *Learning about Women* (Ann Arbor: University of Michigan Press, 1989).

Table 10.1   Proportion of Women in National Cabinet Posts as Percentage of Total Cabinet Seats in 1995: Top 20 Countries, plus Russia

Source: Washington Post (September 20, 1997), A16.

are readily available. (See Table 10.2.) Once again, Sweden and Norway lead the way with approximately 40 percent of the parliament composed of women. The Scandinavian countries are followed by the Netherlands, Germany, Spain, and Britain. Among the industrialized countries, the United States, Italy, and France occupy the lower end of the scale, while Japan again falls at the bottom. One conclusion that could be drawn from these tables is that the Scandinavian countries have so many women cabinet ministers because they have such a large pool of women members of parliament from which to choose these ministers. It is striking that those countries that have relatively few women members of parliament also tend to have few women cabinet members. In other words, training and experience for women at the local government and parliamentary levels is crucial in being selected for higher-level cabinet-level positions.

However, even in the progressive Scandinavian countries, women tend to get what are called the "soft" cabinet positions of health minister, education

Table 10.2 Women in Parliament

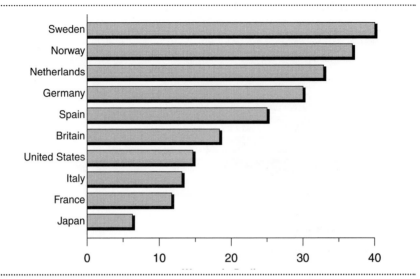

Source: Inter-Parliamentary Union.

minister, social affairs minister, and culture minister. The "hard" portfolios (foreign affairs, finance, defense, and justice) are still largely monopolized by men—although that is now changing. Only in Finland have women, at one time or another, held every type of cabinet position. And women prime ministers are, so far, quite rare: Britain and Norway.

Now let us turn to the developing countries. Table 10.3 provides the figures on the proportion of women in national cabinet positions in the top-ranking Latin American, Asian, and African countries. In Latin America, the relatively prosperous, former British colonies of Barbados and Trinidad and Tobago top the list followed by Guatemala, Haiti, and Mexico. One would expect the more developed Latin American countries of Argentina, Brazil, Chile, and Uruguay to be at or close to the top of the list, but they are not and so we have some anomolies here.

In both Asia and Africa it is similarly striking how many of the top-ranked countries were former British colonies, including Seychelles, Sri Lanka, Bangladesh, India, and Pakistan in Asia, and Gambia, Tanzania, Uganda, Ghana, and South Africa. Our data, therefore, reveal three possible hypotheses for further exploration: one, that the percentage of women in politics is related to levels of economic development; two, that the percentage of women in politics is related to religious differences (Protestant versus Catholic or Christian versus Islamic); and three, that there was something

Table 10.3   Proportion of Women in National Cabinet Positions as Percentage of Total Cabinet Seats in 1955: Top Developing Countries

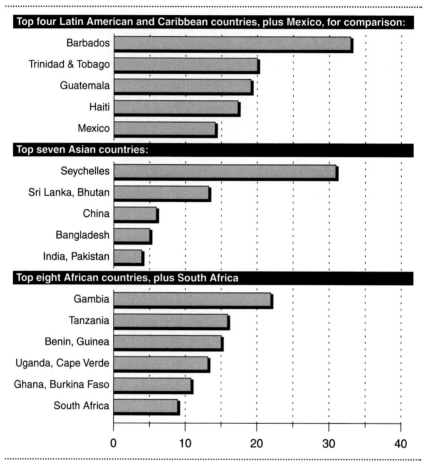

Source: Washington Post (September 20, 1997), A16.

about British colonialism in Latin America, Africa, and Asia (greater emphasis on equality or on the education of women, perhaps) that has enabled women in the former British colonies to rise to higher levels politically than women under other former colonial regimes. It is not our purpose here to fully answer these questions but to raise them in a provocative way and urge that students explore them in greater detail.

There are cultural factors and differences that need to be taken into account as well. In all developing areas (Africa, Asia, Latin America, the Middle East) one can find major cultural, religious, and social barriers to women's greater involvement in politics. In Asia and Latin America, however, well-educated women are increasingly occupying professional positions (including in politics), while less well-educated women are increasingly finding work outside the home in manufacturing and service industries. However, as the earlier tables show, in both Asia and Latin America a glass ceiling still blocks access for women to high-level political and governmental positions. In both Africa and the Middle East, strong cultural, religious, and social barriers, as well as underdevelopment and lack of jobs, still frequently block most women from participation in the gainfully employed workforce, which in turn also contributes to a lack of political influence.

All of these are, of course, preliminary findings and speculation; the subject of women in politics viewed from a comparative perspective clearly calls out for more detailed and thorough analysis.

Comparative Drug Policy

Drugs, almost everyone agrees, are a scourge and a menace.[2] Not just in the United States but in Western Europe as well, and increasingly in other countries, drugs are poisoning our youth, adding to social and health problems, and leading to increased crime and violence. At the same time the profits from drug growing, transport, and dealing are enormous. Farmers in the producing countries can get as much as twenty times more from growing drugs as from growing more traditional crops; the production and shipment of drugs have turned some of the narcotraffickers into multimillionaires who may in their own countries also operate like patronage politicians bestowing benefits on their neighbors in return for loyalty and service. At the same time, military officers and bureaucrats in the sending countries often supplement their meager salaries by assisting or winking at the traffickers, and governments in those countries often benefit as well, as drugs become their major export crop and increase GNP, yet corrupt their courts, legislatures, and police.

Drugs are a complex problem and there are no easy solutions. The United States tried initially to stem the use of drugs on the consumer side but found its efforts to administer drug tests randomly to key sectors of the population (teachers, airline pilots, truckers, and train engineers) stymied by constitutional guarantees and the opposition of these groups' unions. Frustrated in its efforts on the domestic side, the United States turned to the international or production side and instigated the "war on drugs" in

---

[2]For some background on drugs and drug policy, see Rensselaer Lee, *The White Labyrinth* (New Brunswick, NJ: Transaction, 1989); Scott B. MacDonald, *Mountain High, White Avalanche* (New York: Praeger, 1989).

an effort to interdict and cut off the flow into the U.S. But that proved no more successful than the earlier effort. President George Bush sought to implement a balanced approach that combined education, interdiction, public affairs advertising, rehabilitation, and a focus on money laundering. That approach made a modest dent in the drug program for a time, but by the mid-1990s drug use was again up along with the crime and violence associated with it.

Western Europe is in general more tolerant than is the United States on drug use; at the same time, that policy is made easier by the fact Europe does not have the same levels of crime and violence associated with drugs as does the United States The most tolerant of the European countries is the Netherlands, followed by Switzerland (which provides free needles to drug users to prevent the spread of disease) and the Scandinavian countries. In Holland, cannibas (marijuana), though officially illegal, may be openly bought and sold in small quantities, usually on the street or in "coffee shops." The logic of the Dutch experiment is that, if drugs are cheap and openly sold, the criminal and violence elements associated with drugs are removed; that by tolerating the retail trade in cannibas, young people are kept away from dealers who might lure them into more dangerous drug use; and furthermore that this way the government can raise revenues by taxing the open drug transactions, without looking too closely at the source of supply. In Holland, even the use of hard drugs is usually not prosecuted.

Neither France nor Germany nor Britain nor other European countries have so far been willing to go so far toward legalizing or tolerating drugs as the Dutch. Their policy has been generally to tolerate individual, low-level drug use as long as it does not cause a disturbance or get out of hand, but to crack down hard on the criminal or violent aspects of drugs. The U.S. government has been strongly critical of the Dutch approach. And, while some advocates in the United States have been urging a similar decriminalization of drugs, public opinion surveys tell us that less than 10 percent of the population is willing to follow that route. With such a low percentage of the public supporting decriminalization, American politicians have been unwilling to consider this option.

Americans tend to see the drug issue in moral and religious terms (drug use is wrong and sinful and, therefore, must remain illegal), and not in the purely pragmatic terms of price and criminal statistics which is how most Europeans view it. In addition, the United States is a quite different society and culture as compared with Western Europe, having significantly higher levels of violence and criminality more generally which are then exacerbated by the drug problem. So the solutions will likely have to be different as well. A third variant among industrial countries is Japan where, because of close-knit families and Confucian-style social obligations, drug use, though rising, is considerably lower than it is in either the United States or Western Europe.

Drug policy is a very complex issue having to do with the relations be-tween producing and consuming countries, the economics of the drug trade, levels of social and economic development, and a host of other factors. At the same time, it is clear that distinct countries and regions have very differ-ent attitudes toward drugs and drug use, have different societies and cultures in which the drug issue is played out, and also have different government at-titudes and policies concerning drugs. So here again we have both a fascinat-ing, challenging, and controversial issue and the very "stuff" of comparative politics: drug policy (which we will call the dependent variable) and then a host of factors—social, cultural, economic, political, religious, interna-tional—that must be included in any explanation of the policy and that varies enormously from country to country. It is another area of the field that cries out for further, more detailed analysis.

Immigration

Globalization, we saw in the last chapter, is an issue that affects all countries. When we think of globalization, we usually think of increased trade in goods, services, and materials, as well as culture and ideas. But globalization has also been a factor in the increased drug trade considered above, in immigration (traffic of people and labor rather than goods), and in the environment and pollution considered below. All these new trends and new issues are either products of globalization or were accelerated by it.

Immigration is another one of those hot, complex, front-burner issues, like drugs.[3] Immigration affects many countries, not just the United States. The general pattern is this: people go from poorer, low-wage, fewer-benefits countries toward wealthier, higher-wage, greater-benefits countries. More-over, we need to think that immigration affects not just the receiving coun-tries, in the form of more people as well as, usually, pressures on housing, schools, utilities, social services, health care systems, and law enforcement, but also the sending countries in the form often of loss of its most skilled, ed-ucated, and ambitious persons.

The United States currently tends to receive immigrants mainly from Mexico, Central America, and the Caribbean but now from other countries as well. Britain receives immigrants mainly from its former colonies in the

---

[3]Immigration is discussed in Jack Millman, *The Other Americans* (New York: Viking, 1997); Roberto Suro, *How Latino Immigration Is Transforming America* (New York: Knopf, 1998); Daniel James, *Illegal Immigration: An Unfolding Crisis* (Washington, D.C.: Mexico-United States Institute, 1991); Barry R. Chiswick (ed.), *The Gateway: U.S. Immigration Issues and Policies* (Washington, D.C.: American Enterprise Institute for Public Policy Research, 1992).

Caribbean, Africa, and South Asia (India, Pakistan). Continental Europe receives immigrants from three main sources: across the Mediterranean from North Africa and sub-Saharan Africa, from Turkey and the Middle East, and now increasingly, since the Iron Curtain has been torn down, from Eastern Europe and Russia. Japan is much more restrictive in its immigration policy and has brought in few immigrant laborers. But remember the rule of migration from poorer to richer countries. That means that oil-rich Saudi Arabia and the Gulf emirates bring in laborers from other, poorer Arab countries; that Nicaraguans emigrate to wealthier Costa Rica; Bolivians and Paraguayans, to richer Argentina and Chile; Malays, to Singapore; Chinese, to Hong Kong; and so on. Such patterns of immigration are nearly universal.

There has, of course, always been immigration but in recent decades the pace has greatly accelerated. The main factors are faster and easier transportation, modern communications which tell the story of greater affluence in the developed countries and provide a magnet for people to emigrate, and reduced immigration/passport restrictions because of the lowering of barriers among common market countries. Increased immigration may also stem from one country's political or diplomatic strategies abroad or from conscious decisions to import labor, either in general or to do low-level work that citizens of the receiving country no longer are willing to do.

In the 1960s and early 1970s, for instance, a number of the European countries were booming ahead so rapidly that they developed severe labor shortages, especially in low-paid jobs. So they began to import Spanish and Portuguese workers to do physical labor—persons from countries that were still in the economic doldrums. But then the Spanish and Portuguese economies began to expand, reducing the incentive for their workers to emigrate. Still needing labor, however, the wealthier European nations—primarily West Germany but others as well—began to bring in workers from further afield: Turkey, the Middle East, North Africa. The flow of immigrant labor eventually numbered in the *millions*, so that nowadays, if you buy a Mercedes, BMW, or Volvo, the chances are quite good it will have been made mainly by immigrant labor.

At first, immigration was thought to be temporary or seasonal. The term used was *guest workers*, comparable to the earlier *bracero* program in the United States—that is, workers (male) who would leave their families behind, work and earn money in the receiving country on a temporary (seasonal) or short-term (two or three years) basis, and then return to their own countries. But over time these workers began to stay longer, to bring their wives and children along, to have children in the host countries (which thus often qualified them for citizenship), to reside permanently in the host country. By this time their children have also grown up in the host country, attend its schools, speak German or Swedish and maybe not the language of their parents, and often marry into host country families. This means they have become permanent residents and often citizens; they will not go back to their original countries; and often a host of racial, religious, and cultural conflicts arise—with which persons in the United States are not unfamiliar. As long as the host country economy is booming ahead, these problems are often minimized; but when the economy turns stagnant, the charge is often raised that the immigrants (now often full citizens) are taking host country jobs, don't fit, are "difficult," and so forth. And that is when right-wing, xenophobic, neo-Nazi parties and political movements spring up aimed at punishing the immigrant minorities, forcing them out, or, at a minimum, pushing for tougher immigration laws.

Another source of large-scale immigration has been political or diplomatic decisions made by the host country. The main criterion has been human rights violation or persecution in some other country; the most sympathetic countries responding to these abuses have again been the Scandinavian countries and Holland. Sweden, for example, which has long opened its arms wide to political refugees, has about twenty thousand Chileans—refugees from the dictatorship of Augusto Pinochet in the 1970s who have stayed in Sweden long after Pinochet has gone. It has about fifty thousand Iranians, refugees both from the shah's authoritarian regime and from the ayatullah's, as well as numerous exile communities from other dictatorial regimes.

The Swedish policy, as in the United States, was one of assimilation, the "melting pot," although Swedish immigration policy was far more generous. It gave the immigrants an apartment, education, training, money for up to a year, and eventually a job. It sought to create "Swedes" out of all these usually dark-haired, dark-eyed peoples. But increasingly, as in the United States, Sweden and other receiving countries found many of the immigrants didn't want or failed to assimilate; retained their own language, customs, and ethnic ways; and failed to conform to the Swedish/Scandinavian ethic of orderliness, cleanliness, and hard work. Increased culture clashes resulted and a widespread wringing of the hands over what to do about the "immigrant problem."

A variation on this problem of political immigrants is presented in Britain and Holland. Many numbers of the British Commonwealth either have British passports or lay claim to having British citizenship. Before modern transportation and communication, this was not a major issue, but in recent decades the flow of people into a more prosperous Britain has become a larger tide. And like their counterparts in Germany and Scandinavia, the immigrants have now often been in Britain for two or more generations, were born in Britain, went to school in Britain, and are full British citizens—but are often the victims of racial prejudice because of their darker skins. Similarly in Holland: because of its former colonial empire, Holland has thousands of Indonesians, Moluccans, Surinamese, Antiguans, and others living within its borders who are fully Dutch citizens but no longer sure they want to forsake their old ways and become "little Dutchmen." Once again, cultural, racial, and eventually political discord are the result. To varying degrees, the same kind of clashes over identity, race, ethnicity, citizenship, and assimilation are occurring in other countries.

It is, of course, easier to assimilate small numbers of immigrants than large ones. Among the developed countries the United States has both the largest numbers of and the most diverse ethnic immigrant communities: perhaps 15 to 20 percent of the population. But in France, Germany, and Britain the number of immigrants now numbers in the millions, perhaps 5 to 10 percent of the population. Handling or assimilating 5 to 10 percent is far easier than dealing with 15 to 20 percent; nevertheless, in *all* the receiving countries the level of racial, ethnic, and political tension over immigration issues is rising. Multiculturalism may be the goal; but in countries such as France or Holland, multiculturalism is present mainly when their racially diverse soccer teams take the field.

Immigration is thus another hot, current, comparative politics issue. And like drugs, pollution, and the environment, it is both a domestic and an international policy issue, a combination of international and domestic thus called "intermestic." Once again the now-familiar comparative politics questions are present: if immigration policy is the dependent variable, then what are the independent or explanatory factors behind that policy, and how do they vary from country to country? Is it economic factors (the need for immigrant workers), political or diplomatic initiatives (opening the doors to political refugees), a sense of social or cultural superiority, or downright racial prejudice? Could it be (as in some countries) a result of war and the displacement of peoples, of famine and starvation causing people to flee, or the desire for a better life for one's self and one's family? Or varying combinations of several or all of these? We do not provide the final answer here, only hints and suggestions; the comparative politics methodology, however, points toward more detailed and systematic ways to explore answers to this question.

Regionalism/Decentralization

Regionalism and decentralization have become the rallying cries for many peoples in many nations.[4] Here is the paradox: at one level, globalization is

---

[4]Regionalizaton/decentralization are discussed in Richard Sagar, *Local Control and Accountability* (Thousand Oaks, CA: Carwin, 1996); Joel F. Handler, *Down from Democracy* (Princeton, NJ: Princeton University Press, 1996); William D. Coleman and Geoffrey R. D. Underhill (eds.), *Regionalism and Global Economic Integration* (New York: Routledge, 1998); Raquel Fernandez, *Return to Regionalism* (Washington, D.C.: World Bank, 1997).

going forward and countries are integrating into ever larger trading blocs, but at another they are being divided into smaller units by ethnic, nationality, political, religious, cultural, economic, and geographic differences.

The causes of this trend toward regionalism and decentralization are several. One cause is the upsurge in ethnic nationalism, not just in historically unsettled countries such as Spain or Yugoslavia but also in previously unified countries such as France (autonomy movements in Normandy, Brittany), Britain (Scotland, Wales, Northern Ireland), and Canada (Quebec). Another cause is that of good government and the sense that putting government and policy making closer to the people at local or regional levels serves that purpose. A third cause is the end of the cold war: so long as the cold war was being waged, the big superpowers effectively policed, discouraged, or snuffed out divisive ethnic or nationality movements within their spheres of influence; but now that the cold war is over, they cannot do that effectively anymore and, hence, ethnic and nationality movements that were suppressed so long are again surfacing. A fourth cause is a sense of economic injustice on the part of certain regions: both the North of Italy and the Basque and Catalan regions in Spain contribute more in taxes than other areas to the national treasury or than they get back from the central government in public services, and they would like a redress of this imbalance.

The form that regionalism may take also varies greatly. Germany has the only federal system in Western Europe where, like the United States, power is constitutionally divided between the federal government and the states (*Länder*). In Britain and France—historically more centralized countries— the issue is how much autonomy to grant to distinct regions that want to preserve their own language and culture. In Spain the issue is a thousand-year conflict that has ebbed and flowed over the centuries between a central state in Madrid seeking to enhance its power, and historically separatist regions that are seeking to reestablish their traditional rights to self-government. In Russia and Eastern Europe the trends seem to be toward disruptive and often chaotic ethnic nationalism, while in Scandinavia the primary motive of decentralization may well be old-fashioned, "boring" (compared with these others) good government.

The politics of regionalism and decentralization are fascinating. Here we present only two brief illustrations. In Italy we have a nation divided into a very wealthy, dynamic north and a poor, underdeveloped, almost Third World south. The north is well integrated into Europe, a center of fashion, art, prosperity, and creativity; while the south is isolated, more "Mediterranean," wracked by poverty, and dominated by patronage and traditionalism. For decades, if not centuries, the wealthy north has been heavily subsidizing the poor south, seemingly without having made more than a minor dent in the area's poverty and traditionalism, and now many northerners have grown weary of the effort. The issue ebbs and flows, but many in the north (and even a separate political party) would cut the south off, let it go its separate ways, and declare an independent nation in the north. That has not happened yet and may even be inconceivable, but the fact such a splitting of the country is being discussed seriously forces students of comparative politics to consider it seriously, too.

Another interesting case is Portugal. There, regionalism is being pushed mainly by the government as well as the Communist Party. Portugal is a comparatively small country where regional government may not be needed and may only add a new layer of bureaucracy to an already overly bureaucratic government. That is precisely what the government wants: a new layer of public administration that it can fill with their own supporters and use for patronage obligations. The Communist Party has a different set of motives: while it is declining in vote support at the national level, it nevertheless still dominates local government, particularly in Portugal's south. The party knows that, under new EU rules, European community assistance money can be channeled directly to these new regional governments rather than funneled through the national ministries in Lisbon which are controlled by another party and not about to share much of their budget with communists. So the CP is betting that, with the creation of regional governments, it can control the south, receive funding directly from the EU, and thus accomplish programs at the local and regional levels that, with its declining share of the vote, it cannot hope to do at the national level.

These are fascinating issues. Often when political scientists focus on state, regional, or local government, other political scientists sigh that that approach must be terribly boring. But when issues of regionalism and decentralization get tied into issues of ethnic nationalism, regional autonomy, the actual or potential breakup of larger states (Yugoslavia, Czechoslovakia, the Soviet Union, Canada), or the fascinating political maneuvering as here described for Italy and Portugal, that becomes very exciting material for further research.

Legal Rights for Gays

The issue of homosexual rights remains controversial and unsettled in most developed countries, although the trend is toward greater toleration.[5] In this respect, Europe is close to the United States, though there are interesting differences and variations.

In most of Europe unwed couples who are living together, whether gay or heterosexual, have no or little protection under the law to ensure pensions, inheritances, or health care for their partner if they should become sick or

---

[5]The data and analysis in this section derive from *The Economist* (July 5, 1997), 52.

die. Whether it is taxes, retirement income, welfare, inheritance, life insurance, or housing, unwed partners are treated in law as people without family. But now France has enacted a law called a "contract of social union" that gives cohabitating couples of whatever sexual orientation the same social, fiscal, and inheritance rights as those enjoyed by wedded partners. Other countries have already or are in the process of enacting similar provisions.

These changes in law reflect, as in the United States, the changes that have taken place in social, cultural, and religious attitudes toward marriage, informal unions, and gays in recent years, especially among young people. In France, for example, in a population of nearly sixty million, over two million couples now live together out of wedlock, twice the number of fifteen years earlier. The figures show that 38 percent of French children are born outside of marriage, which gives France one of the highest illegitimacy rates in the world, ahead of Britain at 36 percent and just behind the Swedish and Danish figures. As regards homosexuals, the French have long been homophobic, but opinion polls now show two-thirds of the public willing to grant equal rights to gay as married couples, which helps explain the new social union legislation. The same poll shows that more than 50 percent of the French could "accept" a homosexual son or daughter.

The new laws and attitudes put France roughly in the middle of the European countries on the issue of gay rights. At present, there is still a wide range of attitudes as well as legal standing for gays in the European and other developed countries. Table 10.4 shows the age of consent for both heterosexual and homosexual persons and whether there is legal recognition for homosexual couples. At this time, legal rights for homosexual couples are recognized by all the Scandinavian countries. Spain, Holland, Belgium, and, recently, France have enacted or are in the process of drafting legislation that, with some national variations, grant similar rights. Elsewhere in Europe, homosexual couples have no legal standing.

Table 10.4 indicates that the age of consent also varies. Among European countries, the commonest age of consent for both heterosexual and homosexual sex is sixteen. But in Sweden, Denmark, and France it is fifteen. Significantly, quite a number of countries—Austria, Britain, Finland, Greece—have higher age requirements (eighteen) of consent for homosexual sex than for heterosexual sex. In Spain the age of consent for both homosexuals and heterosexuals is twelve.

It is clear that in Western Europe as well as the United States (less so in other areas), traditional moral, religious, and personal attitudes toward sex, marriage, and homosexuality are changing. And these changed attitudes are now being reflected in changed laws as well as practices. Our purpose here is not to make moral judgments about these changes but only to suggest that this is another intriguing, current, front-burner issue worthy of further study and about which comparative politics and the comparative perspective have interesting data to present.

Table 10.4   Legal Rights for Homosexual Couples in Europe and Age of Consent

	Legal Recognition	Age of Consent Heterosexual	Age of Consent Homosexual
Sweden	Yes	15	15
Denmark	Yes	15	15
France	Yes	15	15
Netherlands	Yes	16	16
Belgium	Yes	16	16
Spain	Yes	12	12
Finland	Yes	18	16
Poland	No	15	15
Russia	No	16	16
Portugal	No	16	16
Italy	No	16	16
Germany	No	16	16
Ireland	No	17	17
Turkey	No	18	18
Austria	No	14	18
Greece	No	15	18
Britain	No	16	18

Source: Council of Europe.

Environmental Issues and Pollution

The environment has also become a major, hot issue in recent years—and not just in the United States.[6] Once again, our purpose in these few pages is not to try to solve the issue but to suggest areas of inquiry and research and to show how comparative politics can shed light on the subject.

Environmental issues are a lot like other issues—hunger, overpopulation, immigration, drugs—that have emerged in recent years and that are a product both of globalization and of new, rising consciousness. First, these issues are at one and the same time both global and national issues. All of us understand that issues such as acid rain, pollution, global warming, and the environment generally are not just local or national issues but, since they cross frontiers and national borders and affect us all, international and global

---

[6]On environmental issues, see Sheldon Kamieniecki (ed.), *Environmental Politics in the International Arena* (Albany, NY: State University of New York Press, 1993); and Miranda A. Schreurs and Elizabeth C. Economy (eds.), *The Internationalization of Environmental Protection* (Cambridge, Eng.: Cambridge University Press, 1997).

issues. Nor can they be solved by one nation acting unilaterally; international cooperation is necessary. At the same time, because international organizations are weak, often ineffective, and lack enforcement mechanisms, national societies and national legislatures are usually the first arenas of political activity where effective action is taken on the issue. And the problem for those who see the issue in purely global terms is that these nations often have quite different interests and perspectives on the issue. That, to students of comparative politics, makes the issue more interesting and should not be cause necessarily for lamentation.

The sharpest split has been between developed and developing nations. The developed or industrialized nations are often the largest polluters, and the results of their earlier polluting industries, automobiles, and habits are all around. They are usually the first to ring the alarm on any further environmental degradation. The developing countries in contrast are just that: poor and underdeveloped. They often want the industries, even the polluting ones and the jobs and economic growth that go with them, that the developed nations are inclined to reject. They resent the industrialized nations, which have already made it to developed status and are rich and prosperous, telling them that they should not develop their resources (such as in the Brazilian Amazon) or put up factories and smokestacks for the sake of what are often vague, future, environmental goals. They see "sustainable development" as an euphemism for outsiders to regulate their development and keep them poor. They also insist that, since the industrialized nations are responsible for the vast majority of the world's pollution, they and not the developing countries should pay for cleaning it up. The dilemma, of course, is that, while everyone (or nearly so) is against damaging the environment, that stand may come at the cost of keeping the developing countries poor. And that is neither a realistic nor a politically or morally sustainable position.

There are also differences between and among the developed countries. Canada blames the United States for the acid rain that begins as airborne pollutants from American factories in the Midwest but mainly falls as rain on Canadian provinces. Japan tends to blame both China and South Korea for the pollution that the prevailing westerly winds blow over the Japanese islands. The United States blames Mexico for the pollution in the border area between the two countries and the sewage that drifts across the Gulf of Mexico or flows from Tijuana into San Diego Bay. Western Europe with its clean streets and (mainly) fresh air looks aghast at American wastefulness, grime, pollution, and the "throw-away" society that contributes to these conditions.

Environmental issues can be approached on three main levels: national, regional, and international. At the national level, there is much that individual societies can do to reduce harmful emissions, clean up the air and water, and improve the environment. Most of the Western European countries and Japan are far ahead of the United States in these respects; a good comparative politics project would be to investigate how, why, and in what specifics. A second approach is regional, and at this level—beyond national politics but below the global dimension—a great deal can be accomplished. For example, under the North American Free Trade Agreement (NAFTA) the United States and Mexico are cooperating on a wide range of activities to improve environmental standards and quality in the border region. Across the Mediterranean Sea, the nations of North Africa and those of Southern Europe are cooperating on fishing agreements, the discharge of pollutants, sewerage treatment plants, and industrial waste in an effort to save the Mediterranean.[7] Similarly in the north of Europe, the Scandinavian nations of Denmark, Finland, Norway, and Sweden have entered into agreements with the newly independent Baltic nations of Estonia, Latvia, and Lithuania, plus Poland and Germany, to try to improve the condition of the Baltic Sea. One could think of some fascinating comparative politics research projects involving not just the attitudes and policies of the different countries involved but also a comparison between groups of nations and their cooperation levels in the Mediterranean and Baltic projects.

At the global level, given the absence of either strong institutions or consensus, it is likely that less can be accomplished. Nevertheless, much can be done in terms of education about environmental issues and the raising of consciousness. Global conferences about the environment can also be useful, both in terms of generating publicity for the goals desired and in enacting resolutions that national governments are then called to act upon. But so far—and that is what makes the issue so interesting to students of comparative politics—most of the action on environmental issues has come at the national and, secondarily, the regional levels.

The environmental issue, like many of those raised here, is interesting not only for its own sake but also for the comparative politics issues it raises. For like these others, the environment brings up questions of political culture and national values, of economic needs and demands, of dependency and the relations between developed and developing nations, of conflict and cooperation at the regional and international levels, of laws and comparative institutions as well as social forces.

It should not be thought that the issues raised in this chapter—women in politics, drugs, immigration, gay rights, the environment—exhaust the list of new and interesting issues. There are many others—terrorism, land reform, water rights, tourism, trade, population, hunger, energy, and many more— that are also worth studying from a comparative perspective. All of these are fascinating, current, front-burner issues that are not only worth knowing

---

[7]Peter M. Haass, *Saving the Mediterranean* (New York: Columbia University Press, 1990).

more about but that are also filtered through national values, interest group competition, political party maneuvering, elections, and institutions. And these, of course, all vary from country to country and region to region. But that is what comparative politics is all about: trying to understand better the similarities as well as differences among countries, regions, and the public policies that they pursue. Comparative politics and the comparative method offer us the tools both to understand these issues better and, if we are actively engaged, to advance the policy issues that we care deeply about.

11

Conclusion

Comparative politics is one of the most exciting and innovative fields in political science—indeed, in all of the social sciences. For students of comparative politics, the whole world is our global laboratory—and that laboratory is constantly expanding, changing, and becoming more interesting. The new or developing nations added greatly to the number of political units that we could study; in Tables 1.1 and 1.2 we listed 210 separate political units. Now, however, with the disintegration and fragmentation of Yugoslavia, Czechoslovakia, the Soviet Union, and perhaps other existing political systems, the number of independent entities seems likely to increase still more. Supranational organizations such as the European Union or comparisons between the EU and NAFTA add further to our possibilities for exciting comparative study.

The subject areas available for students of comparative politics to delve into or to write research papers about are even more numerous than the political systems available for study. We can do individual country studies, studies of pairs or groups of countries, regional studies, or even global studies. We can study specific institutions in a single country or across countries: the presidency, the armed forces, legislatures, churches, court systems, peasant movements, labor unions, educational systems, interest groups, political parties, and a host of others. We can study political processes and functions comparatively: interest aggregation, political socialization, or political communications. We can study decision making in different political systems from a comparative perspective, or we can study public policy: agrarian reform, education policy, population policy, or industrial policy in the advanced nations. We can study gay rights, women in politics, comparative welfare policy, immigration policy, and a host of others.

Not only are there a great variety of countries and subject areas within them to sink our teeth into, but in recent decades comparative politics has been the field in political science in which the most innovative and interesting theoretical developments have occurred. Development theory, political culture studies, the study of corporatism, bureaucratic authoritarianism, dependency studies, the study of indigenous theories of change, organic statism, transitions to democracy, globalization, the new institutionalism, rational choice theory, and political economy studies have all been pioneered in the field of comparative politics. In addition, there are now mathematical models, sophisticated multivariate analyses, regression analyses, and computer-based studies that have opened up entirely new comparative politics research terrains.

The domain of comparative politics is really the entire globe—and virtually every political facet in it. Even the United States, viewed comparatively, is grist for the comparative politics mill. The problem for comparative politics is not finding sufficient subjects worthy of further study—we have an abundance of those—but narrowing our universe and our research projects down to manageable size, deciding what precisely we want to study, organizing our subject area or data, and learning how to analyze it.

Comparative Politics Methodology

What comparative politics does is examine systematically both the commonalities and the differences among political systems. It does that by approximating, to the degree possible, the conditions in a scientific laboratory. A good comparative politics study first formulates a hypothesis—let us say, that countries of lower socioeconomic development tend to have more military coups d'état than do advanced countries. To validate or disprove that hypothesis, it then designs a means or test to measure the numbers of coups in different countries at distinct levels of socioeconomic development. In designing the appropriate tests, it seeks to hold constant other factors that may be relevant: the religion of the country (countries) being tested, their geographic location, war or international intervention that might trigger coups, and so on. Then, based on the information generated, the study seeks to draw conclusions about the relationship between coups and levels of development.

This is a relatively formal and rigorous way of approaching comparative politics studies. To the extent such studies are possible, by all means let us carry them out in this way. The problem is that such rigorous methods are not always possible for the kinds of studies that we want to conduct or the most interesting subject areas that we want to investigate in comparative politics. Suppose we want to study comparatively the role of trade unions in Argentina and Brazil or political parties in France and Italy, or the processes of democratization in diverse countries, or the comparative politics of environmental policy. Can't we simply study these without having an elaborate, formal research methodology? Yes, we can—and should. Our ultimate purpose is to *understand* the similarities and differences between countries, and for that purpose a variety of means—library research, interviews, travel, and participant observation—may be used. In doing this research, however, we still need to be as rigorous, as systematic, as analytic as possible in our approach.

Let us take the hypothetical trade union study of Argentina and Brazil. Our goal is to find out why the unions are so different in the two countries. That itself is a form of a hypothesis, and it could be phrased as such. The next step is to ask, why are they different? Is it the different levels of socioeconomic development in the two countries? Is it the fact that one is a former Spanish colony and the other a former Portuguese colony? Is it the history of trade unionism in the two countries? Is it a reflection of action by the governments of the two states in helping shape the labor movement? Is it the nature and types of economic production and industrialization? Or perhaps several or *all* of these explanations in combination? Those possibilities provide alternative explanations or the bases for "tests" of the phenomenon to be studied.

Suppose that after doing our reading and study we are left with imprecise explanations or a vague "feel" that cannot be quantified or entered into a computer. In point of fact, the study of coups mentioned previously is easily quantifiable—just count the numbers of coups; in the study of trade union differences, however, we are interested in interpretive explanations that may not be quantifiable. Is that a reason to abandon or decide not to undertake the study? My own view is, no. We need to be eclectic in our research methodology and to gather data through a variety of means from a variety of sources. Some studies—the analysis of coups—lend themselves to rigor and quantification, and others, through careful analysis, can be made that way. But in *most* comparative politics studies we are left not with "hard" conclusions but with analysis and interpretation of a "softer" kind. That should not bother us overly. Comparative politics should strive for greater rigor, for precision, for testable hypotheses, for empirically based conclusions. But if we often fall short of that goal because the most interesting questions to be raised are not amenable to mathematical tests, then we should accept that as a fact of life and do the best we can with the data and materials we have. Recall that comparative politics is a science in the sense of being an "organized body of knowledge," but to be scientific it need not always imitate the experimental method of a natural science laboratory.

We need to be pragmatic in our approaches and not become slaves to a particular methodology. There is no reason to limit our field of inquiry or to ignore interesting research issues just because the topic to be explored is not amenable to quantification. Comparative politics is most often not like a chemistry or physics lab: Some things are quantifiable, but the most interesting issues often are not, or there are too many variables, or else the global human condition is too infinitely complex. We should not spend too much time lamenting those facts but should go about our comparative politics business, trying to be as rigorous and analytical as we can given the often imprecise materials we have to work with.

Comparative Politics: Particularistic or Universalistic?

Related to this issue, and one of the thorniest issues in the field, is whether the comparative politics concepts and categories that we use are universal or particular. Do our concepts apply to all nations and all places, or are they culture bound?[1] The answer is, some concepts probably do apply universally, but others need to be used very carefully. For example, democracy may be a universal concept, but its specific form and applicability often are not. Consider the act of voting. Most of us probably think of this as an act that is understood throughout the world in the same way, but it is not. *Our* usual understanding of voting is that it implies choice: voters choose among candidates. But in other countries or culture areas that also call themselves democracies, voting is often more a ratificatory or plebiscitary device than it is an act implying choice. Voters may be called on to give their support to a government by *ratifying* its continuance in office. The ratifying voting act is quite different from the choosing act. In some countries both forms of voting may be used. Thus, before we go too heavily into complex studies of voting behavior using mathematical formulas, we had better make sure we know exactly what voting means in the countries studied. Otherwise, we will be comparing apples and oranges.

The same or similar difficulties may be found in other areas of comparative politics. For example, in the United States we view coups d'état as illegal military

---

[1]Howard J. Wiarda, *Ethnocentrism in Foreign Policy: Can We Understand the Third World?* (Washington, D.C.: American Enterprise Institute for Public Policy Research, 1985); by the same author, *Non-Western Theories of Development* (Fort Worth, TX: Harcourt Brace, 1998).

usurpations of constitutional authority. But in many Third World countries the armed forces may have a legal, even constitutional, obligation to step into the political process if public order is being upset. Thus, we need to understand such coups in their own context rather than just through our own rose-colored glasses. Similarly, we have learned that human rights may mean different things in different societies or be accorded different priorities, and we need to take account of such differences in advancing a human rights policy. The same goes for other aspects of democracy: democracy may take Lockean forms (checks and balances) as in the United States and Britain or Rousseauian forms (organic, centralized, unified rule) as in France or Latin America, or some combination of these. Such comments are not meant to discourage comparison, and certainly not democracy, only to emphasize that we had better know precisely what we are talking about before we begin our studies.

Theory and Comparative Politics

The next question concerns where we should focus our studies. Should they be at the global level and at the level of what is referred to as "grand theory," or should they be at lower levels and at the level called "middle-range theory"? Grand theory usually refers to those kinds of studies in which large and even "ultimate" questions are raised and in which the universe of cases encompasses all the world's political systems. Topics in the grand theory tradition would include studies of the relations between development and democracy, socialism versus democracy, or democracy in developing countries.[2] For a considerable time scholars of comparative politics shied away from such topics because (1) they were usually thought to be too big to be manageable in a research sense, (2) they often involved large philosophical questions that seemed to be indeterminate and unanswerable, and (3) the regions studied (Africa and Latin America, let's say) were so different culturally and socially that it was difficult to imagine very many comparable features between them. But now, as we've seen in Chapters 6 through 8, we *know* that democracy is the preferred system of government on a global basis, other systems (authoritarianism and Marxism-Leninism) have been discredited, and certain things work in development and others don't. Hence, grand theory and global or universal studies are making a comeback, and there is clearly room for such studies in comparative political analyses. At the same time, while the grand *systems* debate is mainly over, there are many other issues at the level of grand theory and macropolitics that are worth studying: comparative industrialization, for example, and its social and political consequences.

---

[2] One of the best "global" studies is by Larry Diamond, Juan Linz, and Seymour Martin Lipset, *Democracy in Developing Countries* (4 vols.) (Boulder, CO: Rienner, 1988–1989).

Most comparative politics scholars, however, operate at the level of middle-range theory. Middle-range theory functions on two planes. First, it may focus on a single region, geographic area, or logically related group of countries—Latin America, Western Europe, sub-Saharan Africa, East Asia, the Middle East. Second, middle-range theory focuses not on the grand philosophical issues just mentioned but on more manageable, more discrete issues: comparative interest groups and political parties, the comparative study of legislatures, comparative housing policy, democratization in Eastern Europe, and the like. Such studies are easier to organize and carry out in a research sense because they usually involve a limited number of cases, the cases chosen are usually related in some logical way, and the issues raised are answerable systematically and more or less empirically, rather than involving large unknowns. Such middle-range questions, and the theories they generate, are at this stage still the preferred kinds of studies of most comparativists.

We need theory and models in comparative politics as a way to think about hypotheses, to order our data, and to ask the right questions. That also means, of course, that we remain open to new themes, new ideas, and new ways of thinking about these issues. The only question is, at what level should our theory be applied? At present, most of it is at the middle-range level: we have a large number of studies of Europe, Latin America, Africa, and Asia. But we have not had, since the 1960s and the fragmentation of the discipline, very many recent studies that cut across these geographic regions. Similarly, we now have a large number of studies of corporatism, of bureaucratic authoritarianism, and even of transitions to democracy in distinct areas. But we have few comparative studies of democratization in Southern Europe, Eastern Europe, Russia, East Asia, and Latin America, or of democratization as a global phenomenon. In other words, both in terms of the areas we study and the topics we research, we have a variety of "islands of theory" that focus on narrower, more manageable themes or areas. But we have relatively little at present in terms of an interlocking or integrative theory that ties all of these several islands of theory together or relates them to even larger global issues.[3]

Tasks for Comparative Politics

Comparative politics is a very exciting and innovative field these days. The field seems to have recovered from the malaise that afflicted it for a time in the 1970s following the decline of developmentalism as *the* unifying approach and the division of the field into competing ideological and methodological

---

[3]For a book containing chapters on each of these "islands of theory" as well as efforts to assess and integrate them, see Howard J. Wiarda (ed.), *New Directions in Comparative Politics*, rev. ed. (Boulder, CO: Westview, 1991).

paradigms. We should not be entirely surprised that such fragmentation occurred in the 1970s; after all, that was a decade when *all* institutions were under attack from various quarters, and comparative politics was no exception. But now the field is healthy and vigorous again—indeed, even healthier precisely because of the criticisms leveled and the new approaches offered. The new ideas and approaches gave comparative politics a diversity that it lacked before and opened our eyes to new ideas and ways of thinking. The cost of that, however, was less unity in the field and the proliferation of new approaches—itself, in my view, an exciting development.

Given this vigor and excitement, as well as the great variety of approaches, what should be the present and future tasks of scholars of comparative politics? We can identify five such tasks, proceeding from easier kinds of research projects to harder ones.

The first is to continue building up our case study material and our understanding of specific foreign countries. There are always new issues, new patterns, new relationships in all countries. These can be explored using the previous literature as a base point. Take a theme, a model, an idea, a group, or a policy; and then go explore it in a particular country. Such case studies are probably the easiest for the beginning student.

The second task is to do more comparative studies. These can involve two, three, or four countries. Again, latch onto a theme, reformulate it as a hypothesis, and then apply it in several countries. This is genuinely comparative analysis.

A third task reaches the level of what we earlier called middle-range theory. This might involve not just one or two countries, but a regional or culture area study (Africa, Latin America, Eastern Europe), or it might involve a specific theme or issue, such as trade unionism and national modernization, or the relations between armed forces interventions in politics and the levels of institutionalization in a society. This kind of project involves somewhat greater complexity, but it is still quite manageable. Other new subject matters in the field include comparative studies of leadership, of migration, of ethnicity, and of communications technology.

An extension of the third task is to take the research results from the project undertaken and use it to advance middle-range theory. We will call this task 4: theory expansion or innovation. What does our project or study tell us that is new about the hypothesis or idea or model with which we began? At the conclusion of our study, we must answer the "so what?" question. Does our study support the opening hypothesis, disprove it, or what? Middle-range theory is exciting, heady stuff.

The final task is grand theory and the larger, global comparisons, from which such theory often flows. This is harder to do, usually requires considerable research support, and probably should be done by comparative politics scholars with extensive experience in several areas of the field. The reasons for this include the complexity of the comparisons and variables to be studied, and the complex, high-level philosophical ideas involved. It is difficult, for example, to do comparisons among 200-odd countries of immense historical, cultural, social, economic, and political diversity. On the other hand, the decline and/or collapse of the Soviet Union and other Marxist-Leninist systems, and the seemingly universal march toward democracy, make such grand and global analysis useful. Another large theme is globalization and its cultural, social, economic, and political implications. The task is both to build bridges among the several large themes and islands of theory alluded to earlier (for example, connections between corporatism and development theory, or between dependency analysis and transitions to democracy, or between globalization and environmental policy) and to begin to erect once again an overarching, global theory for the field. The universal movement toward democracy, human rights, and more open or mixed market economies offers us hope that such a larger, or "grand," theory may again be possible.

On these bases comparative politics can be an exciting, innovative, pathbreaking field of inquiry. The author hopes that some of his enthusiasm for the field has been contagious.

Suggested Readings

Almond, Gabriel A., and G. Bingham Powell, Jr. *Comparative Politics: A Developmental Approach.* Boston: Little, Brown, various editions.

Almond, Gabriel A., and James S. Coleman, eds. *The Politics of the Developing Areas.* Princeton, NJ: Princeton University Press, 1960.

Almond, Gabriel A., and Sidney Verba, eds. *The Civic Culture Revisited.* Boston: Little, Brown, 1980.

Apter, David. *The Politics of Modernization.* Chicago: University of Chicago Press, 1965.

Arendt, Hannah. *The Origins of Totalitariansim.* New York: Harcourt Brace Jovanovich, 1951.

Baloyra, Enrique, ed. *Comparing New Democracies.* Boulder, CO: Westview, 1987.

Bauer, P. T. *Dissent on Development.* Cambridge, MA: Harvard University Press, 1976.

Bell, Daniel. *The Coming of Post-Industrial Society.* New York: Basic Books, 1973.

Berger, Suzanne, ed. *Organizing Interests in Western Europe.* New York: Cambridge University Press, 1981.

Black, C. E. *The Dynamics of Modernization: A Study in Comparative History.* New York: Harper & Row, 1968.

Boilard, Steve D. *Russia at the Twenty-First Century.* Fort Worth, TX: Harcourt Brace, 1998.

Braudel, Fernand. *A History of Civilization.* New York: Penguin, 1993.

Cantori, Louis J., and Andrew H. Ziegler, Jr., eds. *Comparative Politics in the Post-Behavioral Era.* Boulder, CO: Rienner, 1988.

Cardoso, Fernando Henrique, and Enzo Faletto. *Dependency and Development in Latin America.* Berkeley: University of California Press, 1979.

Collier, David, ed. *The New Authoritarianism in Latin America.* Princeton, NJ: Princeton University Press, 1979.

Coulter, Philip. *Social Mobilization and Liberal Democracy.* Lexington, MA: Lexington Books, 1975.

Dahl, Robert. *Polyarchy, Participation, Opposition.* New Haven, CT: Yale University Press, 1971.

Dealy, Glen. *The Public Man: An Interpretation of Latin American and other Catholic Countries.* Amherst: University of Massachusetts Press, 1977.

Deutsch, Karl. "Social Mobilization and Political Development." *American Political Science Review* 55 (September 1961): 493–514.

Diamond, Larry, Juan J. Linz, and Seymour Martin Lipset, eds. *Democracy in Devloping Countries.* Boulder, CO: Rienner, 1988–1989.

Dogan, Mattei, and Dominique Pelassy. *How to Compare Nations: Strategies in Comparative Politics.* Chatham, NJ: Chatham House, 1984.

Easton, David. "An Approach to the Study of Political Systems." *World Politics* 9 (April 1957): 383–400.

Eckstein, Harry, and David E. Apter, eds. *Comparative Politics: A Reader.* New York: Free Press, 1963.

Ehrmann, Henry W., ed. *Interest Groups on Four Continents.* Pittsburgh, PA: University of Pittsburgh Press, 1958.

Finer, Herman. *The Theory and Practice of Modern Government.* New York: Holt, 1949.

Frank, André Gunder. *Capitalism and Underdevelopment in Latin America.* Rev. ed. New York: Monthly Review Press, 1969.

Friedrich, Carl J. *Constitutional Government and Democracy.* Boston: Ginn, 1941.

Fukuyama, Francis. *The End of History and the Last Man.* New York: Macmillan, 1992.

Grew, Raymond, ed. *Crises of Political Development in Europe and the United States.* Princeton, NJ: Princeton University Press, 1978.

Harris, Nigel. *The End of the Third World: Newly Industrializing Countries and the Decline of an Ideology.* Harmondsworth, England: Penguin, 1986.

Hartz, Louis, et al. *The Founding of New Societies.* New York: Harcourt Brace, 1964.

Heidenheimer, Arnold J., et al. *Comparative Public Policy: Policies of Social Choice in Europe and America.* New York: St. Martin's, 1975.

Heisler, Martin O., ed. *Politics in Europe: Structures and Processes in Some Postindustrial Democracies.* New York: McKay, 1974.

Hibbs, Douglas A., Jr., and Heino Fassbender, eds. *Contemporary Political Economy.* Amsterdam: North-Holland, 1961.

Holt, Robert T., and John E. Turner, eds. *The Methodology of Comparative Research.* New York: Free Press, 1970.

Horowitz, Irving L. *Three Worlds of Development: The Theory and Practice of International Stratification.* 2d ed. New York: Oxford University Press, 1971.

Huntington, Samuel P. *Political Order in Changing Societies.* New Haven, CT: Yale University Press, 1968.

Huntington, Samuel P. *The Third Wave: Democratization in the Late Twentieth Century.* Norman: University of Oklahoma Press, 1991.

Huntington, Samuel P. *The Clash of Civilizations.* New York: Simon & Schuster, 1996.

Huntington, Samuel P., and Clement H. Moore, eds. *Authoritarian Politics in Modern Society: The Dynamics of Established One-Party Systems.* New York: Basic Books, 1970.

Huntington, Samuel P., and Joan M. Nelson. *No Easy Choice: Political Participation in Developing Countries.* Cambridge, MA: Harvard University Press, 1976.

Ilchman, Warren F., and Norman T. Uphoff. *The Political Economy of Change.* Berkeley: University of California Press, 1969.

Inglehart, Ronald. *Cultural Change in Advanced Industrial Societies.* Princeton, NJ: Princeton University Press, 1990.

Landes, David. *The Wealth and Poverty of Nations.* New York: Norton, 1998.

LaPalombara, Joseph, ed. *Bureaucracy and Political Development.* Princeton, NJ: Princeton University Press, 1963.

LaPalombara, Joseph, and Myron Weiner, eds. *Political Parties and Political Development.* Princeton, NJ: Princeton University Press, 1966.

Lerner, Daniel. *The Passing of Traditional Society.* New York: Free Press, 1958.

Lipset, S. M., "Some Social Requisites of Democracy: Economic Development and Political Legitimacy." *American Political Science Review* 53 (March 1959): 69–105.

Lowenstein, Karl. *Political Power and the Governmental Process.* Chicago: University of Chicago Press, 1957.

Macridis, Roy. *Modern Political Regimes: Patterns and Institutions.* Boston: Little, Brown, 1986.

Macridis, Roy. *The Study of Comparative Government.* New York: Random House, 1955.

Maniruzzaman, Talukder. *Military Withdrawal from Politics: A Comparative Study.* Cambridge, MA: Ballinger, 1987.

Marsh, James G., and Johan P. Olson. *Rediscovering Institutions.* New York: Free Press, 1989.

Mayer, Lawrence. *Comparative Political Inquiry.* Homewood, IL: Dorsey, 1972.

McCormick, John. *Comparative Politics in Transition.* Fort Worth, TX: Harcourt Brace, 1995.

McLennan, Barbara N. *Comparative Political Systems: Political Processes in Developed and Developing States.* North Scituate, MA: Duxbury Press, 1975.

Migdal, Joel. *Strong Societies and Weak States.* Princeton, NJ: Princeton University Press, 1986.

Millikan, Max F., and Donald L. Blackmer, eds. *Emerging Nations: Their Growth and United States Policy.* Boston: Little, Brown, 1967.

Moody, Peter. *Tradition and Modernization in China and Japan.* Fort Worth, TX: Harcourt Brace, 1995.

Moore, Barrington, Jr. *The Social Origins of Dictatorship and Democracy: Lord and Peasant in the Making of Modern World.* Boston: Beacon, 1966.

Moran, Theodore H. *Multinational Corporations and the Politics of Dependence.* Cambridge, MA.: Center for International Affairs, Harvard University, 1975.

O'Donnell, Guillermo, Phillippe C. Schmitter, and Laurence Whitehead, eds. *Transitions from Authoritarian Rule.* Baltimore: Johns Hopkins University Press, 1986.

Packenham, Robert. *Liberal America and the Third World: Political Development Ideas in Foreign Aid and Social Science.* Princeton, NJ: Princeton University Press, 1973.

Palmer, Monte. *Dilemmas of Political Development.* Itasca, IL: Peacock, 1988.

Pike, Fredrick B., and Thomas Stritch, eds. *The New Corporatism: Social-Political Structures in the Iberian World.* Notre Dame, IN: University of Notre Dame Press, 1974.

Powell, G. Bingham, Jr. *Contemporary Democracies: Participation, Stability, and Violence.* Cambridge, MA: Harvard University Press, 1982.

Przeworski, Adam, and Harry Teune. *Logic of Comparative Social Inquiry.* New York: Wiley, 1970.

Putnam, Robert. *Making Democracy Work: Civic Traditions in Modern Italy.* Princeton, NJ: Princeton University Press, 1993.

Pye, Lucian W. *Asian Power and Politics: The Cultural Dimensions of Authority.* Cambridge, MA: Harvard University Press, 1985.

Pye, Lucian W., ed. *Communications and Political Development* Princeton, NJ: Princeton University Press, 1963.

Pye, Lucian W., and Sidney Verba, eds. *Political Culture and Political Development.* Princeton, NJ: Princeton University Press, 1965.

Rostow, W. W. *The Stages of Economic Growth.* New York: Cambridge University Press, 1960.

Rudolph, Lloyd I., and Suzanne Rudolph. *The Modernity of Tradition.* Chicago: University of Chicago Press, 1967.

Rustow, Dankwart. *World of Nations: Problems of Political Modernization.* Washington, D.C.: Brookings Institution, 1967.

Rustow, Dankwart, and Kenneth F. Erickson, eds. *Comparative Political Dynamics.* New York: HarperCollins, 1990.

Said, Edward. *Orientalism*. New York: Pantheon, 1978.

Sargent, Lyman Tower. *Contemporary Political Ideologies*. Homewood, IL: Dorsey, 1981.

Schmitter, Philippe C., and Gerhard Lehmbruch, eds. *Trends toward Corporatist Intermediation*. Beverly Hills, CA: Sage, 1979.

Sigmund, Paul E., ed. *The Ideologies of the Developing Nations*. New York: Praeger, 1976.

Skocpol, Theda. *States and Social Revolutions: A Comparative Analysis of France, Russia and China*. New York: Cambridge University Press, 1979.

Somjee, A. H. *Parallels and Actuals of Political Development*. London: Macmillan, 1986.

Stepan, Alfred. *State and Society: Peru in Comparative Perspective*. Princeton, NJ: Princeton University Press, 1978.

Tiersky, Ronald. *France in the New Europe*. Fort Worth, TX: Harcourt Brace, 1994.

Tilly, Charles, ed. *The Formation of the National States in Western Europe*. Princeton, NJ: Princeton University Press, 1975.

Treverton, Gregory F., ed. *The Shape of the New Europe*. New York: Council on Foreign Relations, 1992.

Tsebelis, George. *Nested Games: Rational Choice in Comparative Politics*. Berkeley: University of California Press, 1990.

Veliz, Claudio. *The Centralist Tradition in Latin America*. Princeton, NJ: Princeton University Press, 1980.

Ward, Robert E., and Dankwart A. Rustow, eds. *Political Modernization in Japan and Turkey*. Princeton, NJ: Princeton University Press, 1964.

Weiner, Myron, ed. *Modernization: The Dynamics of Growth*. New York: Basic Books, 1966.

Wiarda, Howard J. *New Directions in Comparative Politics*. 2d ed. Boulder, CO: Westview, 1991.

Wiarda, Howard J. *Latin American Politics: A New World of Possibilities*. Fort Worth, TX: Harcourt Press, 1995.

Wiarda, Howard J. *Corporatism and Comparative Politics*. New York: Sharpe, 1996.

Wiarda, Howard J. *Non-Western Theories of Development*. Fort Worth, TX: Harcourt Brace, 1998.

Young, Crawford. *The Politics of Cultural Pluralism*. Madison: University of Wisconsin Press, 1976.

Index

Abu Dabi, 150
Acid rain, 209
Africa. *See also* North Africa; Sub-Saharan
    Africa
    authoritarianism in, 94–95
    immigrants from, 202
    political culture in, 75
    women in politics in, 195, 197, 198, 199
Agrarian reform model, 54
Albania
    economic conditions in, 158
    Marxist-Leninist ideology in, 125
    postcommunist transition in, 131
Algeria, 156
Alliance for Progress, 53, 143
Almond, Gabriel, 40, 50, 53, 55, 56, 63,
    66–68, 73–74, 79
American liberalism, 33, 35
American Political Science Association, 37
American Politics (Huntington), 74
American presidentialism, 36
Ancient civilizations, 25–30
Ancient Greeks, 25, 27–29
Ancient Romans, 25, 29–30
Angola
    democracy in, 107
    postcommunist transition in, 131
Aquinas, Saint Thomas, 30, 32
Aquino, Corazon, 107
Area studies, 8–9
Argentina
    economic growth in, 150, 152, 153
    immigration policy in, 202
    military regimes in, 87, 102
    trade unions in, 214
    transition to democracy in, 113
Aristotle, 27–29, 89
Ascription, 48
Asia. *See* also East Asia; South Asia;
    Southeast Asia
    authoritarianism in, 75
    democracy in, 107
    depressed areas in, 157
    economic development in, 45
    independence of countries in, 43, 141
    political culture in, 75

trading bloc forming in, 159
women in politics in, 195, 197,
    198, 199
Augustine, Saint, 30, 32
Australia, 195
Austria
    age of consent in, 207
    women in politics in, 195
Authoritarianism. *See also* Bureaucratic-
    authoritarianism
    as alternative to liberalism, 104
    decline of, 77
    explanation of, 101, 120, 121, 122
    possibility of return to, 116–117
    rise and fall of, 102–104, 109–110
    statist economies and, 152
    in Third World countries, 146
    totalitarianism vs., 121–124
    transition to democracy from, 100,
    110–112, 120–121, 165

Baathist form of socialism, 156
Balkans
    conflicts in, 192
    ethnic divisions in, 113, 137
    possible return to communism in,
    139–140
    postcommunist transitions in, 113, 131,
    136
Baltic Republics, 139
Bandung (Indonesia) conference of 1956,
    45, 141–142
Bangladesh, 157, 197
Barbados, 197
Barzini, Luigi, 66
Basic human needs, 163
Behavioral revolution, 39
Belgium, 174
    gay rights in, 207
Benedict, Ruth, 65
Bharain, 150
Bible, 26
Binder, Leonard, 53
Boas, Franz, 65
Bolivia
    authoritarianism in, 102
    as depressed area, 157
    immigrants from, 202
    transition to democracy in, 106
Bosnia-Herzogovina, 158
Botswana, 107

Brazil
  authoritarianism in, 102, 104
  economic growth in, 150, 152, 153
  environmental issues in, 209
  military regimes in, 87
  trade unions in, 214
  transition to democracy in, 107, 113
Bryce, Lord James, 36
Brzezinski, Zbigniew, 176
Buddhism, 64
Bulgaria
  economic conditions in, 158
  postcommunist transition in, 131, 139
  women in politics in, 195
Bureaucracy, 20, 182
Bureaucratic-authoritarianism (B-A).
    See also Authoritarianism
  explanation of, 87–89, 108
  rise of, 102, 103, 118, 119
Bureaucratization, 180–183
  at international and transnational
    levels, 183
Burma
  democratic stirrings in, 107
  economic growth in, 150
Bush, George, 200
Business, dominance of, 173–175
Bylorus, 131, 137, 139

Calvinism, 64
Cambodia, 76
Canada
  environmental issues in, 209
  as member of trading bloc, 159, 189
  regionalism in, 205
  women in politics in, 195
Capitalism, transition to, 91
*Capitalism and Underdevelopment in Latin
    America* (Frank), 81
Cardoso, Fernando Henrique, 81
Caribbean
  cost of labor in, 174
  immigrants from, 201, 202
  independence of nations in, 43, 141
Carter, Jimmy, 73, 109, 114, 127–128, 176
Castes, 58, 94
Catholicism
  history of, 31–32
  and lack of development, 64, 77–78
  political culture studies of, 64, 68–69
  in state–society relations, 92

  values in, 64
  and women in politics, 195, 197
Causation, 10
Central America, 201
Central Europe, 131. *See also* Europe;
    individual countries
Central Intelligence Agency (CIA), 45, 53
Charles River School, 143
Chile
  authoritarianism in, 87, 102
  economic growth in, 150, 152, 153
  immigrants in, 202
  refugees from, 203
  transition to democracy in, 107, 109, 113
  women in politics in, 197
China. *See* People's Republic of China
Chinese Revolution, 43, 45
Christianity, 30
Churchill, Winston, 117
Cicero, 29–30
Citizen participation model, 54
Civic culture, 66–69, 72
  defined, 67
The Civic Culture (Almond & Verba), 66–69,
    72, 73, 75
  as ethnocentric, 72
The Civic Culture Revisited (Almond &
    Verba), 73–74
Civil society, 108, 130
Civil war, 187
Clans, 58
The Clash of Civilizations (Huntington),
    76
Class conflict, 184
Climate, 33–34, 169
Cold War period. *See also* Post–Cold War
    period
  developmentalist studies and, 53, 59
  effects of, 38
  end of, 205
  features of, 44–45, 142
  foreign policy during, 46, 160–161
Coleman, James S., 50, 53
Colombia
  economic growth in, 150, 153
  nature of regime in, 102
Colonialism, 44
Columbus, Christopher, 30
Committee on Comparative Politics
    of the Social Science Research
    Council (CCP/SSRC), 63

scholars affiliated with, 59
studies of, 51, 52, 53
Common Market, 190
Commonwealth of Independent States (CIS)
  economic policy in, 134–137
  future of, 140
  political transition of, 137
Communalism, 94
Communication technology, 49, 72
Communism. *See also* Marxism-Leninism
  lack of belief in, 171
  transition from, 120–121
Communist Party, 127, 206
Communist states. *See also* Marxist-Leninist
    regimes; Postcommunist change
  crisis of political institutions in, 127
  cultural crisis in, 126–127
  disbelief regarding failure of, 124
  economic crisis in, 126
  ideological crisis in, 124–125
  impact of collapse of, 120, 139–140
  international pressures on, 127–128
  policy reforms in, 132–134
  social change in, 125–126
Comparative government, 37, 40
Comparative politics
  in ancient civilizations, 25–30
  approaches to studies in, 17–21, 40, 69, 218
  defined, 7–11
  drawing conclusions in studies of, 20
  explanation of, 1, 6, 7–8
  as a field, 118–119, 212–213, 217
  implications for future, 98–99, 167–168
  indigenous theories of change in, 93–95
  introduction to, 17
  issue of ungovernability in, 186–187
  methodology of, 12–15, 167, 213–215
  during Middle Ages, 30
  models and paradigms in, 15–17
  during Modern period, 30–36
  need for new definitions and categories, 166
  new issues in, 194, 210–211
  overview of, 25
  particularistic or universalistic nature of concepts in, 63, 215–216
  reasons to study, 11–12
  relationship to international politics, 191–193
  requirements for research in, 14–15

  as a science, 214–215
  tasks for, 217–218
  theory and, 216–217
  twentieth-century developments in, 36–41
  types of studies made by students of, 8–10
  in U.S. universities, 36–41
Computer skills, 184–185
Confucianism, 68
  beliefs in, 64, 74
  cultural factors in, 75, 149, 200
Constitutions, 111
Corporatism
  as alternative to liberalism, 104
  connotations of, 84
  degrees of, 179–180
  and democracy, 180
  emergence of, 84
  explanation and approaches to, 84–87, 91, 93
  institutions of, 180
  modern system of, 177–180
  relations involved in, 86
  rise of, 103
  shift away from, 103–104, 110
Corruption
  size of bureaucracy and, 182
  size of public sector and, 157
  in statist economies, 152
  in Third World countries, 144
Costa Rica, 102, 202
Counter reformation, 32
Countries
  basic indicators for world's, 1–6
  classifications of, 6–7
  comparative studies of, 7–8
  studies of individual, 8
  types of studies of, 8–10
Coups d'etats, 214, 215–216
Croatia, 158
Cuba
  Marxism-Leninism in, 76, 131
  regime in, 106, 445
Cultural anthropology, 65
Cultural crisis, 126–127
Cultural differences, 76
Cultural factors, 65, 76–77. *See also* Political culture
Culture
  defined, 67
  and development theory, 147

Culture (*continued*)
    patterns of beliefs and, 68
    in political culture approach, 71
Cyprus, 105
Czechoslovakia, 128, 137
Czech Republic, 137
    economic conditions in, 158
    postcommunist transition in, 131, 139

Decentralization, 182, 204–206
Decision making, 20
De Madariaga, Salvador, 66
Democracy
    civic community and, 77
    civic culture necessary for, 138
    correlation between development and, 7,
        10, 49, 102, 168–169
    definition of, 101
    degrees of, 101, 172
    in depressed areas, 156–157
    in developed countries, 168–170
    education and, 49, 169
    facets of, 215–216
    forms of, 136, 138
    institutions of, 180
    issues in transition to, 100, 110–112, 136,
        165
    movement toward, 95, 100–101, 107–110,
        120, 162
    patterns of success and, 166
    political culture of, 76
    political ideology and, 171–172
    political stability fostered by, 162
    prospects and implications for, 117–119
    returns to, 104–107, 146
    strengths of, 112, 113–114, 171–172
    varying views of, 102–104, 216
    weaknesses of, 112, 115–117
Democracy in America (Tocqueville), 36
Democratization
    comparative studies of, 217
    developmentalist theory and, 49, 55,
        61, 146
    in oil-exporting states, 150–151
    transitional issues, 110–112, 146
Denmark
    age of consent in, 207
    central planning in, 154
    environmental issues in, 210
    natural resources in, 170
    women in politics in, 195

Dependency and Development in Latin America
    (Faletto & Cardoso), 81–82
Dependency theory
    bureaucratic-authoritarianism and, 88
    contributions and limitations of, 83
    explanation of, 81–82, 161
    influences on, 80–81
    rise of, 103
    and world systems approach, 80–84
Depressed areas
    development in, 157–158
    not included in trading blocs, 160, 190
Deutsch, Karl, 48, 49
Developed countries, 7. *See also*
        First World; Industrial market
        economies
    demands on government in, 186–188
    environmental issues in, 209
    new trends in, 170–175
    patterns of success in, 168–170
    postmodern issues, 176–186
    women in politics in, 195, 198–199
Developing countries, 7. *See also*
        Third World
    environmental issues in, 209
    patterns of development in, 148, 151
    women in politics in, 195, 198–199
Developmentalist approach
    alternatives to, 98–99
    criticisms of, 52–55, 56–60, 79, 80, 87, 93
    early literature on, 47–52
    origins of, 35, 43–46, 161
    proliferation of studies in, 52–55
    reassessment of, 60–61, 118
Development economics, 142–145
Development theory
    dependency theory vs., 81
    fundamental presumption of, 102, 103
    mistakes of, 145–149
    neoclassical approach to, 161
Dictatorships. *See also* Totalitarianism
    in depressed countries, 157
    in low-income countries, 9
Domestic forces, 108–109
Dominican Republic
    authoritarianism in, 102, 122
    military intervention in, 80
    transition to democracy in, 107
Drug issues, 177, 199–201
    legalization and toleration of drugs, 200
Drug traffic, 116

Dubai, 150
Duvalier family, 106, 109
Duverger, Maurice, 97
East Asia. *See also* Newly Industrialized
    Countries (NICs); individual countries
    authoritarianism in, 100, 102
    patterns of development in, 148–150, 153
    transition to democracy in, 107, 129
Eastern Europe. *See also* Europe; individual
    countries
    collapse of Marxism-Leninism in, 76
    economic conditions in, 134–135
    ethnic discontent in, 125
    ethnic nationalism in, 205
    immigrants from, 202
    patterns of development in, 158
    political change in, 137–138
    political culture in, 138
    Reagan foreign policy and, 109
    social policy in, 132–134
    state of communist parties in, 127
    totalitarianism in, 123, 124
    transformation taking place in, 138,
        142, 165
    transition to democracy in 100, 107, 113,
        129, 139
East Germany, 158. *See also* Germany
Easton, David, 40, 50
Eckstein, Harry, 74
Economic development
    agenda for, 162
    based on political systems, 163
    in communist countries, 126, 134–137
    correlation between democracy and, 9,
        50, 102, 107–110, 162, 168–169
    measurement of, 55, 160–162
    social change following, 144, 146, 148
    state-led, 144
Economics
    Keynesian, 143
    Marxian, 34–35
Economists, 47–48
Ecuador
    authoritarianism in, 102
    transition to democracy in, 107
Education
    about environmental issues, 210
    democracy and, 49, 169
    in developed countries, 184–185
Egypt
    development in, 156

in nonaligned movement, 141
Eisenhower, Dwight D., 143
Eisenhower administration, 41
El Salvador
    authoritarianism in, 102
    civil war in, 187
    ethnic strife in, 187
    transition to democracy in, 107–109
Empire, 29
The End of History (Fukuyama), 77, 171
Englishmen, Frenchmen, Spaniards
    (De Madariaga), 66
Environmental issues, 183, 208–211
    levels of approach to, 209–210
Environmental policy, 134
Estonia, 210
Ethiopia
    ethnic strife in, 187
    postcommunist transition in, 131
Ethnic nationalism, 130, 205, 206
Ethnic strife
    in communist countries, 125
    in transition to democracy, 130
    ungovernability and, 187
Ethnocentrism
    defined, 11, 12
    in developmentalist approach, 57
    in political culture studies, 65, 72
Europe. *See also* Eastern Europe;
    Southern Europe; individual
    countries
    decentralization in, 205
    drug issues in, 200
    economic prosperity in, 128
    education in, 184
    environmental issues in, 209
    erasing national borders in, 189–190
    gay rights in, 206–207
    immigration in, 202
    new interdependencies in, 188
    political culture in, 65
    transition to democracy in, 100, 107
    women in politics in, 195
European Economic Community
    (EEC), 159. *See also* European
    Union (EU)
European Union (EU), 160, 189, 190,
    206, 212
    description of, 159
Exports, 149. *See also* Trading blocs
Faletto, Enzo, 81

Families, 58
Farmers, 174
Fascism
    collapse of, 171, 172
    corporatism's association with, 84
Federalism, 137
Federal Republic of Germany. *See* Germany;
    West Germany
Ferdinand of Aragon, 31
Finer, Herman, 97
Finland
    age of consent in, 207
    environmental issues in, 210
    women in politics in, 195, 197
First World. *See also* Developed countries
    dependency theory view of, 81–82
    description of, 142, 165
    designation of, 165
Foreign aid
    basis of, 70
    developmentalist approach to, 50, 54,
        160–161
    implications for U.S. programs of,
        152–164
    for Russia and Eastern Europe, 136
Foreign policy
    changes in communist countries and, 121
    during Cold War period, 45–46
    emphasis of democracy in, 109–110, 114
    understood through comparative
        politics, 12
Formal-legal approach, 38, 79, 99
France
    age of consent in, 207
    drug policy in, 200
    farmers in, 174
    gay rights in, 207
    immigration in, 204
    separatist movements in, 187, 205
    size of bureaucracy in, 182
    studied in U.S. universities, 36
    women in politics in, 196
Franco, Francisco, 104, 105, 122
Frank, André Gunder, 81
Friedrich, Carl, 97
Fukuyama, Francis, 77, 171, 176
Functionalist model, 50–51, 58

Galbraith, John Kenneth, 143
Gambia, 197
GATT compatibility, 189

General Agreement on Tariffs and Trade
    (GATT), 189
Genocides, 66
Geography, 169
Georgia, 131
German Democratic Republic. *See* East
    Germany; Germany
Germany. *See also* East Germany; West
    Germany
    decentralization in, 205
    drug policy in, 200
    environmental issues in, 210
    farmers in, 174
    future power for, 190
    immigration policy in, 203–204
    manufacturing in, 174
    political culture in, 67
    studies of, 37
    totalitarianism in Nazi, 37–38, 121, 122
    women in politics in, 196
Ghana, 197
Glass ceiling, 199
Global comparisons, 9–10
Global economy
    business' influence in, 175
    free market necessary in, 142
    future of, 188–190
Globalization
    business and, 175
    negative trends and, 201
    news and culture and, 19
    study of, 71, 219
    vs. regionalism and decentralization,
        204–205
Global trade. *See also* Trading blocs
    increase in, 160
    patterns of, 190
Gorbachev, Mikhail, 127, 129
Gordon, Lincoln, 143
Government
    post–World War I studies in, 37
    studies of formal-legal institutions of, 38,
        79
Governmental institutions, 19
Graft. *See* Corruption
Grand theory, 216, 218
Great Britain
    age of consent in, 207
    drug policy in, 200
    farmers in, 174
    illegitimacy rates in, 207

immigration in, 201
political culture in, 67
refugees in, 203
regionalism in, 205
separatist movements in, 187
size of bureaucracy in, 182
studied in U.S. universities, 36, 37
women in politics in, 196, 197
Greece
age of consent in, 207
ancient, 27–29
civil war in, 187
new role for military in, 115
transition to democracy in, 106, 129
Gross national product (GNP)
economic growth measured in, 160
U.S., 191–192
Guatemala, 197
authoritarianism in, 102
transition to democracy in, 107, 109
Guyana, 157

Hagen, Everett, 47, 143
Haiti
as depressed area, 157
transition to democracy in, 107, 118
women in politics in, 197
Harrison, Laurence, 77–78
Heilbroner, Robert, 47, 143
High-income countries, 7
High technology, 174, 184–185
Hinduism, 68
Hirschman, Albert, 143
Hobbes, Thomas, 32, 33
Holland
drug policy in, 200
farmers in, 174
gay rights in, 207
immigration policy in, 203–204
refugees in, 203
Homosexual rights, 206–208
Honduras
authoritarianism in, 102
transition to democracy in, 107
Hong Kong
economic growth in, 149, 155
immigrants in, 202
as member of Asian trading bloc,
159
women in politics in, 195
Houphouet-Boigny, Felix, 158

Human rights, 109, 127–128, 216
violation of, 203
Hungary
economic conditions in, 158
postcommunist transition in, 131, 139
state of communist regime in, 128
Huntington, Samuel P., 57, 74, 76
Hypothesis, 213

Iceland, 195
Ideology
crisis of, 124
end of, 171–172
Illegitimacy rates, 207
Immigrant labor, 202
Immigration, 38, 201–204
acceleration of, 202
assimilation and, 203, 204
patterns of, 202–203
refugees, 203
Import substitution
authoritarianism and, 88, 108
explanation of, 162
Independence movements, 43–44, 102, 141
India
authoritarianism in, 102
democracy in, 107
immigrants from, 202
independence of, 43, 141
patterns of development in, 154–155, 159
women in politics in, 197
Indigenous theories of change, 93–95
Indochina, 43
Indonesia
authoritarianism in, 102
economic growth in, 150
independence of, 43
as member of Asian trading block, 159
in nonaligned movement, 142
Industrialization, 58, 64
Industrial market economies
basics needed for, 134–135
bureaucratization in, 180–183
corporatism and corporatist structures in,
177–180
countries with, 168
demands on government in, 186–188
and developmental success, 158
explanation of, 168
farm and union groups in, 173–175
global political economy and, 188–190

Industrial market economies (*continued*)
  ideology and, 171–172
  political parties and, 172–173
  in post–Cold War era, 191–193
  postmodernity in, 176
  privatization vs., 136
  profile of, 168–170
  public policy change in, 183–186
  transition to, 165
Industrial Revolution, 35, 65
Inglehart, Ronald, 75–76
Interest aggregation, 19
Interest groups
  for comparative politics studies, 18
  decline of old and emergence of new,
    172–173
  ungovernability and, 187–188
International Monetary Fund (IMF), 153
International politics, 191–193
International relations, 12
Iran
  authoritarianism in, 122
  Islamic Revolution in, 49, 75, 94
  refugees from, 203
  war with Iraq, 192
Iraq
  development in, 156
  in Persian Gulf War, 192, 193
  war with Iran, 192
Iron triangle, 178
Isabella of Castile, 31
Islam, 64, 68
Islamic fundamentalism, 75, 76, 94
Islamic model of development, 94
Islamic world, authoritarianism in, 102, 107
Israel, 156, 168
The Italians (Barzini), 66
Italy
  cultural factors in development,
    76–77
  democracy in, 77, 104
  farmers in, 174
  political culture in, 66, 67, 76–77
  regionalism in, 205–206
  sixteenth-century, 31
  studies of, 37
  totalitarianism in, 37, 122
  women in politics in, 196
Ivory Coast
  democracy in, 107, 157–158
  economic growth in, 157–158

Japan
  corporatism in, 85, 179–180
  culture of, 95, 147
  drug issues in, 200
  economic growth in, 128, 149, 150, 174
  education in, 185
  environmental issues in, 209
  establishment of democracy in, 104
  farmers in, 174
  future power for, 190
  immigration policy in, 202
  as member of Asian trading bloc, 159, 189
  political culture in, 65
  women in politics in, 195, 196
Johnson, Lyndon, 53
Jordan, 156

Kennedy, John F., 41, 53, 60, 143
Kennedy, Robert F., 80
Kenya, 107
Keynesians, 143
Khomeini, Ayatollah, 49, 94
King, Martin Luther, Jr., 60, 80
Kosovo, 158
Kuwait
  development in, 150, 156
  Iraqi invasion of, 156

Labor
  cost of, 174
  immigrant, 174, 202
Labor strife, 111, 130
Labor unions
  corporatist institutions and, 175
  decline of, 173–175
  public sector, 181
  studying, 214
Landes, David S., 64–65
LaPalombara, Joseph, 53
Latin America. *See also* individual countries
  authoritarianism in, 102
  corporatism and, 85–86
  dependency theory applied to, 161
  depressed areas in, 157
  economic growth in, 135, 150
  independence of countries in, 44, 141
  military-authoritarianism in, 87, 102
  model of development for, 94, 151
  patterns of development in, 151–154
  political culture in, 74–75, 77–78
  pressure to privatize in, 135

roots of politics in, 64
state–society relations approach
  applied to, 92
transition to democracy in, 94, 100,
  106–107, 113, 129, 153
women in politics in, 195, 197, 198, 199
Latvia, 210
Lebanon, 187
Lee Kwan Yew, 107
Leites, Nathan, 65
Lerner, Daniel, 48, 49
Less developed countries (LDCs), 160
Leviathan (Hobbes), 32
Lewis, W. Arthur, 161
Liberal capitalism, 47
Liberalism
  distinguished from corporatism, 85
  Lockean view of, 32–33
  modern, 36
  as route to development, 104
Libya, 156
Life expectancies, 169, 184
Lifestyle issues, 176–177, 183–184, 194–211
Linz, Juan, 122
Lipset, Seymour M., 48, 49, 61, 63
Literacy rates, 169
Lithuania, 210
Lives of the Noble Grecians and Romans
  (Plutarch), 26
Locke, John, 32–33
Loewenstein, Karl, 38–39, 97
Lomé Agreement, 190
London School of Economics, 143, 154
Low-income countries, 6
Luxembourg, 170
Lycurgus, 26–27

Machiavelli, Niccolò, 31, 32, 89
Macridis, Roy, 39–40, 42, 50, 79, 97
Mahgreb. *See* North Africa
Malaysia
  democratic stirrings in, 107
  economic growth in, 150
  as member of Asian trading bloc, 159
Marcos, Ferdinand, 107, 109, 163
Market economy. *See* Industrial market
  economies
Marx, Karl, 34–35, 65, 89, 174
Marxism-Leninism. *See also* Communism;
  Socialism
  alternatives to, 45, 46, 54, 85

collapse of, 76
dependency theory and, 80–81
discrediting and disbelief in, 101, 117,
  124–125, 171
economics in, 34–35
end of, 77
political culture and, 63
political economy approach and, 89–91
revived, 73
state in, 92
Marxist-Leninist regimes. *See also*
  Communist states
  destabilizing effect of democracy on, 120
  economic problems of, 34–35, 134–137
  impact of collapse of, 138–139
  policy reforms in, 131, 132–138
  as ultimate form of historical
    rationality, 123
Mead, Margaret, 65
MERCOSUR (Southern Market), 159
Mexico
  cost of labor in, 174
  economic growth in, 150, 153
  environmental issues with, 209, 210
  immigrants from, 201
  importance to U.S., 188
  as member of trading bloc, 159
  political culture in, 67–68
  type of economy in, 152
  women in politics in, 197
Middle Ages, 29, 30
Middle class
  in communist countries, 125
  education and, 185
  in Third World, 146
Middle East. *See also* North Africa;
    individual countries
  authoritarianism in, 102
  classification of countries in, 7
  concept of democracy in, 100
  immigrant labor from, 202
  immigrants from, 202
  independence of countries in, 43, 141
  oil-exporting states of, 150–151, 156
  patterns of development in, 156–157
  political culture in, 75
  women in politics in, 195, 199
Middle-income countries, 6–7
Middle-range theory, 217, 218
Military
  in democratic transition, 110, 115

Military (*continued*)
  loss of power of, 108
  protection of middle class interests by, 146
  seizure of power by, 87, 103
Models, 15–17, 28
Modern Democracies (Bryce), 36
Modern era, 30–36
Moldavia, 158
Montesquieu, Baron de la Brède et de,
  33–34
Morris, Bruce, 47
Mozambique, 131
Multiculturalism, 204
Muslims, 76
Myrdal, Gunnar, 143

Namibia, 107
Nasser, Gamel Abdul, 141, 143
National borders, 189–190
National character studies, 65
National Defense Foreign Language
  (NDFL) program, 54
Nation-state, 30
Nazis, 66
Neoliberalism, 185–186
Neoscholasticism, 32
Netherlands
  drug policy in, 200
  women in politics in, 195, 196
New Deal, 143
New institutionalism, 80, 97–98
Newly Industrialized Countries (NICs)
  economic development in, 128, 148–150,
    153
  emergence of, 191–192
New Zealand, 195
Nicaragua
  democratization of, 10, 106
  as depressed area, 157
  immigrants from, 202
  postcommunist transition in, 131
Nigeria, 107
Nixon, Richard, 70, 73, 80
Nonaligned movement. *See also* Third World
  emergence of, 45
  features of, 142
Nonethnocentric theory of development, 94
Noriega, Manuel, 106, 192
North Africa. *See also* Africa; Middle East;
  individual countries
  authoritarianism in, 102

democracy in, 100, 107
environmental issues in, 210
immigrant labor from, 202
immigrants from, 202
independence of countries in, 141
North American Free Trade Association
  (NAFTA), 159–160, 210, 212
North Korea
  invasion of South Korea by, 45
  Marxism-Leninism in, 76, 125, 131
Norway
  environmental issues in, 210
  women in politics in, 195, 196, 197

O'Donnell, Guillermo, 88, 102, 108
Oil crises, 73, 108, 115
Oil-exporting nations. *See also* Middle East
  patterns of development in, 150–151,
    156–157
  rise of, 192
Old Testament, 26
Organicism, 103
Organic statism, 103–104
Organization of African Unity (OAU), 192
Organization of American States (OAS), 192
Organized labor. *See* Labor unions
Orientalism (Said), 75

Pakistan, 197
  authoritarianism in, 102
  democracy in, 107
  immigration from, 202
  independence of, 43, 141
Panama, 106
The Pan-American Dream (Harrison), 77–78
Paraguay, 106, 202
Parochial political culture, 67
Parsons, Talcott, 48–49, 50, 55, 56
Particularism, 48, 63
Peace Corps, 41, 53, 143
People's Republic of China
  economic growth in, 150
  emergence of, 43
  environmental issues in, 209
  immigrants from, 202
  in nonaligned movement, 142
  patterns of development in, 155–156, 159
  political culture in, 74
  state of Marxism-Leninism in, 76, 131
  transformation taking place in, 142
  transition to democracy in, 113

Persian Gulf War, 192, 193
Personal freedoms, 177
Peru
  authoritarianism in, 102
  transition to democracy in, 106
Philippines
  authoritarianism in, 102, 104
  economic growth in, 150
  as member of Asian trading bloc, 159
  transition to democracy in, 107, 113
Pinochet, Augusto, 106, 109, 203
Plato, 27–29
Plutarch, 26
Poland
  economic conditions in, 158, 174
  environmental issues in, 210
  postcommunist transition in, 131, 139
  state of communist regime in, 128
Polanyi, Karl, 47
Political action committees (PACs), 172
Political anthropology, 44
Political change, 63
Political communications, 19
Political culture. *See also* Political culture
    studies
  cautions on use of, 78
  in communist countries, 126–127
  for comparative politics studies, 18
  concept of, 62, 71
  of democracy, 138
  distinguishing the types of, 67
  explanation of, 67
  history of approaches to, 63–66
  issues in, 64
  and political development approach, 70
Political culture studies
  acceptance of, 65–66
  criticisms of the approach, 70–73
  decline of, 73
  development of, 63
  ethnocentrism in, 65
  increase in, 68–69, 73–78
  methods of research, 77–78
Political development, 43, 55. *See also*
    Developmentalist approach
  in communist states, 137–138
  functionalist plan of, 50–51, 58
  measuring, 55
  in oil-exporting states, 150–151
Political economy (PE) approach, 188–190
  emergence of, 44

explanation of, 91
influence of, 89–90
studies in, 91
Political history, 17–18
Political Order in Changing Societies
    (Huntington), 57
Political parties
  for comparative politics studies, 19
  decline of, 172–173, 177–178
Political scientists
  early development literature by, 50–52
  meaning of political development to, 55
Political socialization, 19, 51
Political society, 108
Political sociologists, 44, 55. *See also*
    Sociologists
Political stability, 162
Political systems
  ancient Greek classification of, 28–29
  change within, 21–23
  developmentalism and, 48
  systems model of, 21
Politics (Aristotle), 27
The Politics of the Developing Areas
    (Almond & Coleman), 50–51
Pollution, 177, 183, 208–211
Portugal
  authoritarianism in, 104
  civil strife in, 187
  immigrant labor in, 202
  interest group representation in, 178
  new role for military in, 115
  regionalism in, 206
  transition to democracy in, 100, 105, 112,
    129
  women in politics in, 195
Post–Cold War period
  international politics in, 191–193
  literature of, 76
  political culture studies in, 76
Postcommunist change
  patterns of, 128–132
  possibilities for, 138–140, 164
Postmodernity
  bureaucratization and state downsizing,
    180–183
  changing public policy, 183–186
  corporatism and corporatist structures,
    177–180
  issues of, 176–177
  "ungovernability" and, 186–188

Poverty
    advanced nations' views of, 183
    culture of, 169–170
    pockets of, 169
    relationship between government type
        and, 7, 169–170
Prebisch, Raúl, 143, 161
The Prince (Machiavelli), 31
Privatization, 136, 182
Protestantism, 64
    values in, 64
    and women in politics, 195, 197
Protestant Reformation, 31, 32, 35
Psychological orientation of peoples, 67
Public policy, 186
    studies of comparative, 20
    transformation in, 183–186
Public services, 185
Putnam, Robert, 76–77
Pye, Lucian, 53, 55, 71, 74

Rational choice theory, 80, 95–96
Reagan, Ronald, 109, 114, 128, 182
Refugees, 203. *See also* Immigration
Regionalism, trend toward, 204–206
Regional studies, 8, 9–10
Regional trade agreements, 160
Religion
    and comparative politics, 26
    decline of, 177
    economic development and, 64
    political culture studies of, 68–69
    politics and, 64
Religious values, 64
Renaissance, 31
Republic of China. *See* Taiwan
The Republic (Plato), 27
Research, 214
    political culture, 77–78
Research funding
    allowing for foreign travel, 46
    developmentalist approach to, 45, 59
    for study centers by CIA, 45, 54
Romania
    economic conditions in, 158
    postcommunist transition in, 131, 139
Rome, ancient, 25, 29–30
Roosevelt, Franklin D., 143
Rosenstein-Rodan, Paul, 143
Rostow, W.W., 47, 50, 53, 54, 63, 79, 143,
    161, 162–163, 176

Rousseau, Jean-Jacques, 34
Russia. *See also* Soviet Union
    collapse of Marxism-Leninism in, 76
    economic change in, 136
    ethnic nationalism in, 205
    immigrants from, 202
    political change in, 137–138
    size of bureaucracy in, 182
    transformation taking place in, 142
    transition to democracy in, 113, 129, 139,
        100, 107, 113, 139
    unique characteristics of, 130
    women in politics in, 195

Said, Edward, 75
Sakharov, Andrei, 126
Salazar, Antonio de Oliveira, 86, 104, 178
Saudi Arabia
    assistance programs of, 156
    immigrant labor in, 202
    patterns of development in, 150
Scandinavia
    decentralization in, 205
    drug policy in, 200
    environmental issues in, 210
    farmers in, 174
    gay rights in, 207
    immigration policy in, 203–204
    refugees in, 203
    women in politics in, 195, 196–197
Second World. *See also* Communist states
    description of, 142, 165
    designation of, 165
Separatist movements, 137–138, 187
    cultural differences and, 76
Serbia, 158
Service industry, 174
Service sector, 184
Sexual freedom, 177, 207
Sexual orientation, 177
Seychelles, 197
Singapore
    authoritarianism in, 102, 107
    economic growth in, 149
    immigrants in, 202
    as member of Asian trading bloc, 159
    women in politics in, 195
Slovakia
    formation of, 137
    postcommunist transition in, 131, 139
    women in politics in, 195

Slovenia, 139, 158
Smith, Adam, 89
Social change
    in communist states, 125–126
    in developed countries, 169–170
    following economic development, 144,
        146, 148
    in NICs, 149
    in oil-exporting states, 150
    and shift to democracy, 108
Social democrats, 143, 171
Socialism
    African, 158
    Baathist, 156
    during Cold War period, 45, 123
    control of politics under, 34–35
    failure of, 142, 161
    Third World leaders trained in, 143, 154
Social justice, 162
Social mobilization, 49, 103
Social modernization, 55, 57
Social Science Research Council (SSRC), 51.
        See also Committee on Comparative
        Politics of the Social Science Research
        Council (CCP/SSRC)
Sociobiology, 63
Socioeconomic background, 18
Sociologists, 48–50. *See also* Political
    sociologists
Somoza, Anastasio, 10
South Africa, 107, 197
South America, 157. *See also* individual
    countries
South Asia
    immigration from, 202
    trend toward democracy in, 107
Southeast Asia, 107, 113
Southern Europe. *See also* Europe;
        individual countries
    corporatism and, 85
    environmental issues in, 210
    pressure to privatize in, 136
    transition to democracy in, 100, 101, 105,
        113, 129–130, 139, 164–165
    women in politics in, 195
South Korea
    authoritarianism in, 102, 107
    economic growth in, 149
    environmental issues in, 209
    invasion of, 45
    as member of Asian trading bloc, 159

    toleration for opposition in, 107
    women in politics in, 195
Soviet Union. *See also* Russia
    collapse of, 137, 140, 186, 188, 191, 192,
        212
    Communist Party in, 127
    economic conditions in, 126, 136
    ethnic discontent in, 125
    international pressures on, 127–128
    political culture in, 138
    Reagan foreign policy and, 109, 128
    social conditions in, 132–134
    totalitarianism in, 38, 121, 123
Spain
    age of consent in, 207
    authoritarianism in, 104, 122
    civil strife in, 187
    civil war in, 187
    ethnic nationalism in, 205
    farmers in, 174
    gay rights in, 207
    immigrant labor in, 202
    new role for military in, 115
    regionalism in, 205
    separatist movements in, 187
    transition to democracy in, 106, 112, 129
    women in politics in, 196
Sparta, 26–27
The Spirit of the Laws (Montesquieu), 33
Sri Lanka, 197
The Stages of Economic Growth
        (Rostow), 176
State downsizing, 180–183
State–society relations approach, 91–93
State system, 19
The State (Wilson), 36
Statist economies
    authoritarianism and, 154
    drawbacks of, 152, 161
    explanation of, 151–152
Stereotyping, 65–66
Stroessner, Alfredo, 106, 109
Structure, in political culture approach, 71
Suárez, Francisco, 32
Subject political culture, 67
Sub-Saharan Africa. *See also* Africa
    authoritarianism in, 102, 107, 113
    democracy in, 100, 107
    depressed areas in, 156, 157
    immigrants from, 202
    independence of countries in, 102, 141

Suharto, General, 163
Sukarno, Achmed, 141, 143
Suriname, 157
Sweden
    age of consent in, 207
    environmental issues in, 210
    immigration policy in, 203
    refugees in, 203
    women in politics in, 195, 196
Switzerland
    drug policy in, 200
    farmers in, 174
    natural resources in, 170
    statist economy in, 152
Syria, 156
Systems theory, 21, 26, 40

Taiwan
    authoritarianism in, 1–7, 102
    economic growth in, 149
    as member of Asian trading bloc, 159
    toleration for opposition in, 107
    women in politics in, 195
Tanzania, 107, 197
Technological advances. *See also* High technology
    in air travel, 46
    in communications, 49, 72
    implications of, 175, 184–185
Tendency statements, 167
Thailand
    democratic stirrings in, 107
    economic growth in, 150
    as member of Asian trading bloc, 159
Thematic studies, 10
Third World
    dependency theory and, 81–82
    depressed areas of, 157
    designation of, 165
    development theory and, 44, 58–59,
        142–148, 160–162
    Eastern Europe as part of, 158
    emergence of, 141–142
    India as part of, 154–155
    influence of Westernism on, 95
    Latin America as part of, 151–154
    Middle East as part of, 156–157
    need for structural change in, 160–162
    new trading blocs in, 159–160, 190
    NICs as part of, 148–150
    oil-exporting states as part of, 150–151

postcommunist transition in, 131
urbanization in, 58
U.S. assistance for, 162–164
and world transformations, 164–166
Tobago, 197
Tocqueville, Alexis de, 36
Totalitarian communism, 120
Totalitarianism
    authoritarianism vs., 121–124
    during Cold War period, 38
    economic depression and, 157–158
    explanation of, 121–122
    Rousseau's political system as forerunner
        to, 34
    transition to democracy from, 110–111
    as useful model, 123
    World War II and introduction of
        phenomenon of, 37–38
Trade unions. *See* Labor unions
Trading blocs
    exclusion of depressed areas in, 159–160,
        190
    formation of, 159–160
    future for, 189
Traditional institutions, 58, 59, 94
Trans-Caucuses, 131
Travel, revolution in, 46
Trend analysis, 167
Tribes, 58, 94
Trinidad, 197
Trust (Fukuyama), 77
Tunisia, 156
Turkey, 202

Uganda, 197
Ukraine, 131, 137, 139
Underdevelopment Is a State of Mind
    (Harrison), 77–78
Ungovernability, 186–188
Unions. *See* Labor unions
Unitarism, 137
United Nations
    data available from, 9
    growth of organizations within, 183
    membership in, 141
    rising importance of, 192
United States
    bureaucratization in, 181
    corporatism in, 179
    decline of, 191–192
    dependency theory and, 83

drug issues in, 199–200
education in, 185
environmental issues in, 209, 210
farmers in, 174
funding of study centers by, 59
gay rights in, 206, 207
immigrant labor in, 203
immigration policy in, 201
interest groups in, 187–188
as member of trading bloc, 159
policy during Cold War period, 44–46
political culture in, 67
political parties in, 172
women in politics in, 195, 196
Universities
    comparative politics in, 36–41
    government-supported development
        programs in, 54
    study of international affairs in, 45
Urbanization, 58
Uruguay
    authoritarianism in, 102
    transition to democracy in, 107, 113
    women in politics in, 197
Utilitarians, 35

Venezuela
    economic growth in, 150, 152, 153
    nature of regime in, 102
Verba, Sidney, 53, 66–69, 73–74
Vietnam
    developmentalist approach in, 55–56, 60,
        76
    Marxism-Leninism in, 76, 131
Vietnam War, 73
    protests against, 55, 70, 81, 89
Voting, 215

Walesa, Lech, 129
Wallerstein, Immanuel, 82–83

Ward, Robert, 53
Watertgate affair, 70, 73, 80, 89
The Wealth and Poverty of Nations (Landes),
    64–65
Weber, Max, 35, 36, 39, 64, 65
Weiner, Myron, 53
Welfare states, 169
Western culture, 71–72, 77–78, 95, 125
Western Europe. See Europe
West Germany. See also Germany
    immigrant labor in, 202
    return to democracy in, 104
Wildavsky, Aaron, 74
Wilson, Woodrow, 36
Women in politics, 194–199
    at the cabinet level, 195–198
    cultural factors in, 198–199
    levels of economic development and, 197
    in ministerial posts, 195
    religious differences in, 197
Working class, 125–126
World Bank, 9, 182
World systems approach, 80–84
World War II
    emergence of democracy after, 104
    impact on study of comparative politics,
        37–38, 39

Yugoslavia
    ethnic and religious conflicts in, 76, 187,
        205, 212
    in nonaligned movement, 142
    political and economic conditions in, 158
    political issues in, 137, 158
    postcommunist transition in, 131

Zaire, 187
Zambia, 107